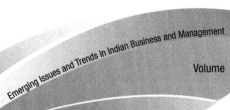

Emerging Issues and Trends in Indian Business and Management

Volume 1

INDIA'S TECHNOLOGY-LED DEVELOPMENT

Managing Transitions to a Digital Future

Emerging Issues and Trends in Indian Business and Management

Series Editors: Vipin Gupta *(California State University San Bernardino, USA)*
Samir Ranja Chatterjee *(Curtin University, Australia)*
Alka Maurya *(Amity University, India)*

Published

Vol. 1   *India's Technology-Led Development: Managing Transitions
to a Digital Future*
edited by Vipin Gupta, Samir Ranja Chatterjee and Alka Maurya

Emerging Issues and Trends in Indian Business and Management

Volume 1

INDIA'S TECHNOLOGY-LED DEVELOPMENT

Managing Transitions to a Digital Future

Editors

Vipin Gupta
California State University San Bernardino, USA

Samir Ranjan Chatterjee
Curtin University, Australia

Alka Maurya
Amity University, India

World Scientific

NEW JERSEY · LONDON · SINGAPORE · BEIJING · SHANGHAI · HONG KONG · TAIPEI · CHENNAI · TOKYO

Published by

World Scientific Publishing Co. Pte. Ltd.

5 Toh Tuck Link, Singapore 596224

USA office: 27 Warren Street, Suite 401-402, Hackensack, NJ 07601

UK office: 57 Shelton Street, Covent Garden, London WC2H 9HE

Library of Congress Cataloging-in-Publication Data

Names: Gupta, Vipin, 1968–   editor. | Chatterjee, S. R. (Samir Ranjan),
    1945–   editor. | Maurya, Alka, editor.
Title: India's technology-led development : managing transitions to a digital future /
    editors, Vipin Gupta, California State University, San Bernardino, USA,
    Samir Ranjan Chatterjee, Curtin University, Australia, Alka Maurya, Amity University, India.
Description: New Jersey : World Scientific, [2023] | Series: Emerging issues and trends in
    Indian business and management ; Vol. 1 | Includes bibliographical references and index.
Identifiers: LCCN 2022061338 | ISBN 9789811271779 (hardcover) |
    ISBN 9789811271786 (ebook) | ISBN 9789811271793 (ebook other)
Subjects: LCSH: Technological innovations--Economic aspects--India. |
    Information technology--Economic aspects--India. | Economic development--India.
Classification: LCC HC440.T4 I555 2023 | DDC 338.954--dc23/eng/20230104
LC record available at https://lccn.loc.gov/2022061338

British Library Cataloguing-in-Publication Data

A catalogue record for this book is available from the British Library.

For any available supplementary material, please visit
https://www.worldscientific.com/worldscibooks/10.1142/13292#t=suppl

Desk Editors: Soundararajan Raghuraman/Nicole Ong

Typeset by Stallion Press
Email: enquiries@stallionpress.com

Printed in Singapore

About the Editors

Vipin Gupta is a Professor, Author, TruthSeeker and Motivator at the Jack H. Brown College of Business and Public Administration, California State University San Bernardino, USA. He has a Ph.D. in managerial science and applied economics from the Wharton School of the University of Pennsylvania. He is a gold medalist from the Post-graduate Program of the Indian Institute of Management, Ahmedabad, India. Professor Gupta has authored more than 180 journal articles and book chapters and published 30 books, including the co-edited *Culture, Leadership, and Organizations: The GLOBE Study of 62 Societies*. Besides delivering lectures and keynotes, he has presented at international academic conferences in more than 60 nations. He has been on the governing board and organizing committee of several international conferences. As a 2015–2016 American Council of Education fellow, he visited 62 universities, colleges and higher education institutions in nine European nations, the USA and India. In his most recent project, he has self-published twelve self-authored books under the series "Vastly Integrated Processes Inside Mother Nature" in 2021 and 2022 (Vipingupta.net).

Alka Maurya is Professor of International Business at Amity International Business School, Amity University, India. She is a Computer Science Graduate and has received her Master's in International Business from Indian Institute of Foreign Trade, New Delhi, India, and PhD in International Business from Jiwaji University, Gwalior, India. She has over 27 years of experience in teaching, research and consulting. Before coming into academics she worked with various export promotion bodies

v

in India as well as on preparing strategies for promoting export from India. She has presented her research work in various national and international forums on various topics related to international business. She has published 10 books and several research papers/case studies in her area of specialization. She is also invited as speaker/resource person for various international conferences and seminars in the area of International Business. Teaching is her passion, and she is shaping the young minds to take up the challenges in this dynamic and competitive environment.

Samir Ranjan Chatterjee is an Emeritus Professor renowned for his role as university academic, research scholar and International trainer and consultant for more than five decades. Besides his home base at Curtin University in Australia, he has lived and worked for extended periods in India, China, USA, UK, France, former Yugoslavia, Japan, Singapore, Mongolia, Malaysia, Indonesia and Hong Kong. During 1994–1995, he lived in Mongolia for a year as the United Nations Adviser in the development of management education in the country, and worked there until 1999 as Director of large capacity-building programs funded by the United Nations Development Program. During 1999–2003, he was an international expert reviewer with the Asian Development Bank on a US\$ 250 million higher education sector reform project in Indonesia. From 2013–2015, he was the Project Adviser of a "Pro-Poor Capacity-Building" Program for Senior Public Sector Executives in Mongolia funded by the Australian Government. He has been a Fellow of the Australian Institute of Management and a Fellow of the Australian Society of CPAs. He has authored and co-authored 11 books, including a book on Indian Management published by Sage, 35 book chapters and about 200 scholarly journal publications and refereed international conference papers. He is on the editorial board of many international scholarly journals. He serves as the Doctoral thesis examiner of many Australian and Asian Universities. He was the President of the Society for Global Business and Economic Development (SGBED) and currently chairs the organization's Board of Trustees. Prof. Chatterjee was a National Shortlisted nominee for the "2017 Australian of the year" award.

Contents

Part I
The Civilizational Approach

https://doi.org/10.1142/9789811271786_0001

Chapter 1

India's Technology-Led Development: Emerging Issues and Trends

Vipin Gupta[*,§], **Samir Ranjan Chatterjee**[†,¶] and **Alka Maurya**[‡,‖]

California State University, San Bernardino, USA

†*Curtin University, Bentley, Perth, Australia*

‡*Amity University, Noida, India*

§*vipin.gupta@csusb.edu*

¶*Samir.Chatterjee@cbs.curtin.edu.au*

‖*amaurya@amity.edu*

Introduction

The recent disruptions caused by the pandemic have shaken the fundamental foundations of global business to their core, creating unprecedented challenges for management scholars and practitioners. In addition, over the past few decades, the general adoption of communication technologies and the evolving trends towards digitalization and Industry 4.0 have revolutionized the way work organizations are managed and led. Business model innovation and the developing importance of sustainability have also emerged as strategic platforms for all types of organizations. Technology-led managerial transformation has now become critical for 21st century business.

The irresistible shift of global business leadership from the West to the East demands new imagination and a reconfiguration of the managerial mindset. The evolving geographical power shifts coupled with the rise of technology-led corporations are fundamentally transforming managerial paradigms in India. One of the key sectors of the economy that needs a new technology-based turnaround approach is manufacturing. It is surprising that in spite of her widely discussed "demographic dividend", India has become increasingly dependent on the manufactured imports from other nations, particularly China. Having close to 600 million people between the ages of 20 to 30, skill development and talent management will revitalize a new wave of technology-led development.

As the contemporary strategy and international literature demonstrates, the industrial paradigm of reliance on the off-the-shelf globally tradable technology for corporate, national and international development has serious limitations. The new paradigms of digitization and robotics are offering opportunities to codify and automate the local ways of managing logistics, operations and services. How has, is, and should India tap these opportunities to develop global leadership in integrated method and machinery solutions?

By virtue of the size of its population, geographical inequities in development and pre-dominance of self-employed and micro, small and medium-sized enterprises, India faces unique challenges for the sustainability and growth of business and economics. In fact, the global pandemic of 2020 has shaken the fundamental foundations of business and economics in all nations. The undercurrents of the fourth industrial revolution have also been affecting each nation of the world in different ways. Technology-led development will continue to disrupt societies, companies, industries and jobs for the next century. Acquisition and deployment of technological knowledge capital will become the key imperative for organizations and societies.

In the past, the mantra for the growth of local firms was to globalize international supply chains by becoming their learning nodes, and by servicing integrated globalized learning to the global hubs. In the post-COVID world, as the global hubs give their own intellectually protected local voice to the values acquired historically from diverse local hubs, local firms in the emerging markets need fundamentally divergent models for sustaining their growth. At the corporate and national levels, India is increasingly focusing on the policies for giving voice to globalizing the local as the path forward for all businesses and economies. Local knowledge embedded within local businesses and economic networks, which have not been appropriated by the transnational networks of the MNCs for their private gains, offer unique opportunities for globalizing the local firms as well as the national networks that support them.

The technologies that are currently being hailed as enablers of the fourth industrial revolution are not limited to high-speed internet on fibre optics, cloud-based storage as it leverages access and mobility to gather and analyze large amounts of data. Such resources were never before accessible to all levels of economy. Real-time data collection and advancement in artificial intelligence (AI) technology including 3D printing have presented industries with opportunities never imagined before.

This book investigates four approaches in understanding the perspectives for integrating technology with holistic development:

- *A Civilizational Approach*: This integrates cultural, historical as well as geographical nuances in a way totally different from the Western positivistic models. This includes a transformation of the strategic mindset in dealing with the economic power shift from the West to the East.
- *A Stakeholder Approach*: This involves moving away from a mere participant or observer role and embracing the "Stakeholder" role. For example, the concept of the self-reliant India (*"Atmanirbhar Bharat"*) is one such mindset reorientation approach. It involves investigating "Can India fulfil its potential and become the second largest economy in the world by 2050 in terms of purchasing power resourcefulness?"
- *A Knowledge Partnership Approach*: This lays the foundations of India's technology-led development through education, training, research and talent management. Using the success of technology advantaged industry sectors like pharma, ICT and medical equipment to spread a countrywide "pebble in the pond" transformation.
- *A Strategic Development Approach*: This unlocks the economic growth and wealth creation potential by keying marketing and branding at the ecosystem level. Technical skills prepare one for only followership. Technological skills propel one into leadership through networking of the followers with diverse technical skills. Organizational skills make one an entrepreneur through proficient integration of diverse networks into an exchange system. Ecosystem skills guide one to be a manager of the diverse exchange systems for ascending worker social

benefit-cost ratio of exchange. Strategic development of the diverse workforce systems is key to ascending social benefit-cost ratio of technology-led development in any market.

Part 1. Civilizational Approach

India is an old and mature civilization that has become an emerging power at the global level over the recent decades. India's way of managing technology is grounded in its culture, history and geography.

Culturally, technologies are expected to meet multi-dimensional objectives of the **nation**, such as employment, equity, energy conservation and capital risk mitigation. Old and new technologies co-exist both within the same organizations as well as across different organizational forms. A premium is put on the capability of the workforce to manage legacy and administrative issues of integrating diverse generations of technologies.

Historically, India has pursued a philosophy of partnerships with both East and West with **local-to-local** connections. Different regions of India have had strong linkages with different parts of the world. For instance, Southern India has had strong cultural relations with Southeast Asia and South Africa dating thousands of years. Eastern India has had a rich and vibrant archaeologically substantiated history of relationships with Indo-China region of tens of thousands of years. Western India has more than a million years of archaeological history of migratory and trade linkages with Eastern Africa and Western Europe. Similarly, Northern India has had linkages with Europe since the earliest times in human archaeological history. Diverse techniques and technologies sourced and adapted from different sciences and nations from different time periods pre-exist in India. New-age technologies work together with these legacy systems throughout the value chain. The managerial challenge in organizational design and coordination is radically different from the earlier models. The new technology-led development can only succeed when it is accompanied by a new strategic platform of knowledge partnership, unlike its recent predecessors like ecosystems theory, network theory, contingency theory or transaction-cost theory, the most significant divergence lies in knowledge partnerships. As routine work and physically demanding work are increasingly being replaced by robotics, more space has opened up for creative and cognitively demanding jobs.

Geographically, India is uniquely characterized by the different cultural, economic and political spaces within and without the states. Although Hinduism is the dominant religion, the practices of Hinduism vary significantly across different states. The presiding deities in the different regions of India are different. A fiercely independent, perfected feminine form of divinity, Mother Durga, presides in the collectivistic East. An illuminating interdependent, masculine form of divinity, Shiva, along with his family, presides in the individualistic West. A perpetuating androgynous form of divinity, Mohini and her diverse masculine forms as Vishnu, presides in the South. A creative greeter form of divinity, Krishna and his diverse feminine forms as the manifesting devis, presides in the North. The origin and imperatives for these diversities can be traced to the diverse archaeological and historical experiences in the different parts of India and corporate-type initiatives of the ruling dynasties and guiding gurus of yesteryears for differentiating their regional identity guided by these experiences. Digital revolution in India has revolutionized the way people management is conceptualized and organizations are redesigned. Managerial culture is being reshaped by new structure, behaviour and processes within organizations. Stronger priority is needed on knowledge sharing teams, collaboration, improvement in information sharing capabilities, creativity and flexibility of workforce and similar other multilevel managerial changes.

Building on this Chapter 1 that offers a global perspective, Chapters 2–5 examine these national, local and corporate perspectives of technology-led development in India.

In Chapter 2 "Human Resource Management in Digital India", Minu Zachariah and Neetha Avaneesh take a cultural approach for understanding the national ethos of stakeholder orientation. They note, "The business entities of today are aware of the vital role played by technological interventions in value creation. HR technological interventions are no exceptions either. These interventions, are aligned to business goals and help businesses achieve their bottom lines. Nevertheless, some business owners are apprehensive about the way forward while adopting technology". With illustrations of the Indian organizations that have successfully implemented technological solutions for managing human resources, the authors conclude "emphasis is laid on business value creation for stakeholders due to HR technology adoption".

In Chapter 3, "Lean Leadership in India: Transforming the Transactional Challenges with Mature Followership", Alagiri Govindasamy, Usha

Ramanathan and Nadia Kougiannou enrich the cultural angle of the national transformational ethos with a historical approach to the local transactional ethos. The authors note that the Indian ethos has for ages advocated for "wholesomeness both among leaders and followers, togetherness in the workplace, a sustained decision-making system with approval of all parties concerned and larger societal impact from organizations than achievement of merely short-term commercial goals". Historically, due to the followership mindset introduced within India, people have been caged into their self-imposed limitations of dependence on power distance and leaders. Based on a review of 793 journal articles from around the world, the authors show how transformational leadership needs to be integrated with a lean approach for transactional efficiencies and decision-making proficiencies. The authors conclude with the "guiding principles to enhance the lean leader's decision-making process". They emphasize that the "lean leaders from India need to empathically appreciate Indian ethos to steadily transform their subordinate's faith in their self-inspired forward-thinking process to achieve higher-order corporate goals than typical transactional work".

In Chapter 4, "Blockchain Fragmented Clusters for Advancing HR Saliency: The Case of India", Rukma Ramachandran, Vimal Babu and Vijaya Prabhagar overlay the geographical perspective over the issues of culture and history, highlighting the issues of corporate ethos and centralized governance of a highly decentralized solution. The authors report how different states of India are moving ahead with the adoption of the nascent blockchain technology and some organizations have even implemented blockchain for human resource management functions. Based on an extensive review, they emphasize that "In India, blockchain is gaining traction, especially in the banking, insurance and payment card industries. In order to reap the benefits of Blockchain on a bigger scale, players in most of these industries are teaming together to form a consortium. On the other hand, some conglomerates have expressed an interest in using Blockchain to optimize business operations across their subsidiaries and business partners". There are also efforts to apply blockchain for connecting diverse data nodes from fragmented clusters through inclusion of rural and other remote areas of India. Thus, blockchain when repurposed with the cultural ethos of inclusion, diversity and empowerment has found strategic advocates and emerged rapidly in unexpected ways.

Part 2. Stakeholder Approach

India has a rich tradition of organizational and sectoral initiatives at the micro level complemented with the intersectoral and multiregional initiatives at the macro level. Multi-level initiatives move the members away from a mere participant or observer role into an active embracing of the "stakeholder" mindset. Such initiatives are at the core of the concept of self-reliant India (*"Atmanirbhar Bharat"*) — a mindset that is not about isolation, but agency that helps each member descend their dependence on the empowerment from a third party. It is about finding power, motivation and confidence within and activating that spirit within each member. Only then the unique gifts of each citizen in the society can be tapped for the developmental growth of each organization, region, nation and indeed the world. The Indian approach is unabashedly idealistic. It is governed by the ideals of leaving a better legacy for the children and transcending beyond the challenges faced by the parents in their lives.

Within organizations, Indian firms boast of a diverse workforce, comprising locals, migrants from different states, and people of diverse beliefs, ideologies, experiences, languages, cultures and orientations. India's policy has been focused on the globalization of inclusion while liberating the private sector. With increased digital literacy and resources, the people at the grassroots are increasingly investing more of their resources for purchasing goods and services offered by the foreign firms and the large private sector enterprises. Consequently, India has experienced one of the fastest rates of wealth and income polarization in the world over the past 30 years.

The organizations in India are situated in the local communities of practice. Historically, different communities of India specialized in different occupations and trades. Over time, members of these communities have migrated to different parts of the nation. Therefore, India is often called a nation of migrants, where each person has a story of how and when their family moved from somewhere to settle somewhere else. The knowledge base for the diverse techniques is situated as much at the national level as at the organizational level. There is a rich interaction cutting across organizational boundaries due to a culture of family collectivism. At the interorganizational hub level, the knowledge is pooled as a common resource for addressing the community challenges. People tend to maintain their friendships and contacts as they move across organizations.

The public sector plays a key role in technology development and localization of the technology transfer through many public sector research entities. The multinational sector supplements that with transfer of older technologies no longer competitive in their home markets. However, as the local firms have developed resources, many multinational firms have also adopted a stakeholder approach and set up research and technology testing infrastructure in India for gaining corporate control on the local *jugaad*. India has gained a unique place in the world for affordable frugal innovations that effectively substitute the expensive hardware. Further, Indian firms have also expanded their research alliances and bases internationally for adapting their approaches to the diverse global imperatives.

Chapters 5–8 investigate these globalization, nationalization, localization and corporatization dimensions of the technology-led development in India.

In Chapter 5, "Technology-Enabled Future of School Education: Policy Priorities and Economic Models for Rural India", Neelakshi Saini and Shanker Prakash set the foundations for the stakeholder approach by considering the policy priorities for the globalization of EdTech in school education in India and how they engage diverse stakeholders. The authors also illustrate economic models being put in practice in different parts of India. They highlight that urban India has progressively adopted technology in education, including online classes and study from home, led by the private sector. However, to help offset the rural resource and infrastructure constraints, public sector, including national and state governments and their agencies, have taken a lead in universalizing the information and communication technology in rural education. Additionally, non-government agencies are working with both private sector as well as public sector entities for making each rural child a digitally competent citizen.

In Chapter 6, "Public–Private Partnerships in EdTech for Transforming Rural India: How Start-Ups are Shaping the Post-COVID Landscape", Aparna Saluja notes how the nationalization of EdTech is seen in India as having the potential to help address standard of living deficits in rural India. By making transformation of values cost-effective and agile, technology offers a way for people in deficit conditions to leapfrog ahead. The only requirement is to make that technology accessible at the mass level backed by skill development and integrate technology for establishing strong infrastructure in the areas of education, healthcare, agriculture and rural industry. Through the public–private partnership model, the government of India has multiplied the inclusion in technology education and developed start-ups focused on technology innovation for rural people. She concludes, "Collaboration with government and non-government organizations and institutes aided the adoption of EdTech in rural India. The EdTech start-ups are building activities in both rural and underdeveloped metropolitan regions aimed at catering to the less privileged segments of the student population, particularly those enrolled in government and affordable private schools".

In Chapter 7, "Integrating Diverse Approaches of Informal Sector for Sustainable e-waste Management", Georg Jahnsen, Shweta Dua, Priyanka Porwal and Navita Mahajan examine the organizational challenges for the localization of technology for the sustainable e-waste management system. The first-step in creating a national-level system is to create awareness of the known issues and solutions. When every person as a local node within the e-waste management cycle becomes a stakeholder, the management of the e-waste becomes sustainable. A self-management approach can then flower on its own. The key is to rapidly broadbase the governance roles as a way to reduce the imposed governance costs and enhance self-governance benefits.

In the case examined by the authors, the e-waste management system campaign was "launched in 27 States and 3 Union Territories of India with involvement of all stakeholders as a part of the system". It was complemented with "various digitalized initiatives like developing information, electronics and communication framework, websites and mobile applications, conducting workshops, activities, training the trainers and campaigns across cinema halls, logos, mascots, posters, leaflets and banners". As a result, "the mass awareness program witnessed a huge success with coverage to more than 200 million viewers", with 300,000 stakeholders and 6,000 government officials participating in 600 workshops.

In Chapter 8, "Exploring the Growth of India's Foreign Direct Investment Equity Inflow amid COVID-19 Outbreak", Ifeanyi Mbukanma and Ravinder Rena offer an excellent insight into the corporatization of Indian technological endowments. Bucking the global trend, India continued to be attractive for the foreign direct investors at the peak of the pandemic. In a year where the nations around the world experienced dramatic falls in incoming foreign direct investments due to contracted economic activity amidst COVID-19, the investments into India dramatically rose and remained stable the year after. Historically, most international direct equity investments into India were manufacturing oriented. However, now, services and information, electronics and communication as well as the pharma sector account for the bulk of investments. While foreign direct investment has been found in the literature to boost the local technological base and productivity, many international firms are attracted by the technical strength of the Indian workforce. The Indian workforce brings significant efficiencies not only in the workforce costs but also in the network integration costs through reengineering of the software solutions. Additionally, diversity within India offers a cost-effective model for developing diverse service options and to scale those options worldwide.

Part 3. Knowledge Partnership Approach

India's technology-led development is grounded in education, training, research and talent management. The focus on human resource development opens doors for knowledge partnerships between the haves and have-nots, the informal sector and the formal sector, the local firms and the global firms, the rural enterprises and the urban enterprises. On the flip side, with the globalization of diversity, there are risks of hollowing-out the local knowledge bases. When an urban firm goes into the rural area, it trains the rural stakeholders in its standard operating procedures. From the perspective of the rural market, the value of the urban firm's standard operating procedures is significant — it is key to boosting the local value-added, productivity, and advancement. Many technology-advantaged industry sectors like pharma, ICT, and medical equipment have multiplied the trading benefits for leading a countrywide "pebble in the pond" transformation.

However, since there are numerous rural market options, the key for the viability of a rural network is the ability of each rural stakeholder node to bring unique local insights for advancing the urban firm's standard procedures. From an economics perspective, the firm's standard operating procedure has zero value in the urban market. Many firms have similar standards based on the tools their employees have mastered from various advanced and specialized education and training institutions. However, the same operating standards yield disproportionate returns in the rural market until similar institutions are developed in the rural market. The disproportionate returns comprise three elements:

- Zero returns but efficiency in operations due to the organizations having in place the formal sector-wide standards. Zero returns allow the firms to be competitive and grow through cost leadership strategy. Inclusion of the rural stakeholders is key to helping realize economic returns through savings in manpower costs.

- Proportionate returns with proficiency of operations due to the technological value-addition. The techniques and technologies that are normative in an urban market become formative in a rural market. They give form to innovations by attracting resourceful and talented workforce, networks and exchanges. The firms who invest in developing strategic awareness of these innovative linkages, and tactically develop approaches for creative engagement of local stakeholders using local solutions, generate proportionate returns. The proportionate returns include not only economic returns but also human returns. The imposed standard operating procedures turn the stakeholders who have been accultured to alternative approaches to become antagonists seeking to gain acceptance of the approaches they are accultured to. Thus, they help catalyzse a transformative growth that becomes a basis for cost-effective differentiation. The urban firms enjoy savings in manpower and method costs as they invest in machine and material costs. Logistics is typically more costly in the rural and remote areas because of the limited forms of connectivity and the variable quality of those forms. Machine costs are also typically higher due to the infrastructural deficits that require expensive electric generators, water transportation and storage system, and travel and out-of-station costs for the maintenance personnel.

- Disproportionate returns with the perfection of operations due to the ecological value-addition. As the rural stakeholders successfully advance their local approaches to the table, they become confident protagonists of creating new linkages to improve material and machine cost-effectiveness. Examples include considering the use of local materials and developing local skills for addressing maintenance and quality control issues. Further, over time, the cost of engaging global solutions falls as the firms integrate more of their operations digitally, use video conferencing and other novel technologies for remote servicing, and additional workforce in the urban areas develop proficiency for handling maintenance and logistics issues, thus alleviating the reliance on the constrained supply of the qualified maintenance staff. Additionally, technologies developed over time become human centred, allowing for easier local fixes through *jugaad* and other culturally informed approaches. It takes significant time for the local protagonists to realize compensation parity with the urban counterparts. The urban firms do not go around sharing information about the supernormal proficiency of their rural workforce. Some even make sure that their rural workforce remains loyal by creating a family-type culture, celebrating personal and family events.

As the international firms have entered India and developed rural linkages, they have been able to appropriate these disproportionate returns to gain absolute supremacy across different sectors. The integration of global resources with the local cultural insights has allowed them to become favourites of the rich and famous. The demonstration-effect on the urban middle class and on the rural lower class has been notable. Consequently, the firms investing in India have enjoyed disproportionate growth, even as the rural markets have experienced growing volatilities and disproportionate entropy. Rise in polarization serves as an excellent excuse for the marketing of corporate social responsibility and sustainability initiatives. Operating in a market that is stable carries negative points in ecological and social sustainability index. But if you are operating in a bottom-of-the-pyramid market, that is a huge motivating tool for the employees and stakeholders.

As the urban and the global firms become attuned to the local cultural knowledge bases, the local regions experience growing volatility in their national value with the automation of those cultural solutions. The urban and global firms are more inclined to automate the cultural knowledge traded from the local rural networks because that knowledge is alien to their standard operating procedures. It is more costly to train their core workforce about the value of that unique knowledge, given that their core workforce is conditioned to using the universal, common knowledge. The mindset of the core workforce is essentially fixed and closed, with a not-invented-here syndrome. The predominant way for a firm to accrue psychological value from the traded cultural knowledge is to fast track its automation priorities. Such fast-tracking ascends the workforce value-added in the urban and global markets, adding to the social value of the core workforce while subtracting the social value from the peripheral networks.

As global machines are used as robots to substitute the local human work, the cultural knowledge within the local networks stops developing further. They reinforce the focus of the local workforce on inner development and openness to discard and freely offer material know-how for the universal development. Thus, throughout India, we see the following sequence of technology-led development over time:

- First, organization of all the diversity that existed historically into first digital codes and then programming them into software (knowledge repositories) and then constructing hardware that cost-effectively replicates the software, thus rendering both initial frontline coders of knowledge and middle programmers of know-how virtually irrelevant. Leading to huge polarization of wealth at the top among the founders, who run the organizations like a substitutable machine.
- Second, community spread of the codification planning, software programming and hardware performing culture, in a way that puts those planning codification in privilege positions, those programming develop aspirations to the privilege of managing the burgeoning programmer groups, and those performing depress their aspirations and remain unorganized and keep on using *jugaad* through deep archival exploration of their archaeological base in their communities, with everybody entirely oblivious how they are playing into the invisible hand for hollowing out the common base they have — having already diffused the diverse base to the international community
- Third, national policy endorsement of the priorities on first codification planning, then on software programming, and finally on hardware performing, as a way to offer employment, responding to the burgeoning and shifting international demand, as India keeps on getting hollowed out.
- Fourth, multinational disinvestment from India (example Ford) apparently writing off billions in losses, putting India to shame, and taking all the *jugaad* at no cost for recycling and marketing to India at premium values, laden with positive human rights, gender empowerment and environment sustainability themes.

Chapters 9–12 highlight the four-step tug-of-war between the local and the global: globalizing, nationalizing, localizing and corporatizing.

First, Globalizing: the process begins with the global globalizing the nationally evolving technology at the local level.

Second, Nationalizing: the local responds with a negotiated trading of national technology with a growing aspiration for participating as a responsible citizen.

Third, Localizing: with rising citizenship power, the local becomes a key node of innovation in the global organization, enjoying disproportionate growth.

Fourth, Corporatizing: with rising prosperity of the local, the global increasingly resists local innovations and local engagement seeking at par growth in its prosperity — notwithstanding significant standards of living disparities between the local and the global. The local is discredited for its low social, human and ecological value-added, because its networks are disproportionately urban and global. The global is credited for its high social, human and ecological value-added, because its networks have gained to include proportionate growth of the local and the rural. Consequently, the economic, national and psychological value of the local and the rural begins diminishing, while that of the global and the urban reaches the pinnacle.

In Chapter 9, "Indian Fintech Companies: Scope and Challenges", Seema Garg, Pranav Tewari and Navita Mahajan examine the top-down globalization of financial technology solutions in India in the context of the COVID-19 pandemic. The authors conclude, "Financial technology allows the digitization of transactions, which makes them safer for the end user. Fintech is enabling cheaper operational costs and a more user-friendly graphical user interface for the financial technology services in India. It is changing the attitudes and behaviours of persons in the Indian financial sector".

In fact, the government of India has made financial inclusion and digital payment system top priorities. To discourage cash hoarding, the government demonetized all large currency notes, equivalent to about US$10 and US$20 in late 2010s. The government has also opened banking accounts of low-income citizens for direct transfer of subsidy and other government incentives. Such developments have removed the bureaucracy involved in processing these payments and the significant transaction costs of the middlemen skimming off large commissions. During the pandemic, digital India initiative became a channel for rapid growth of the formal sector that has well-developed mobile and web presence and payment systems. There has been unprecedented wealth polarization as a disproportionate share of the incomes earned locally was channelled to the formal and the global sector, accruing disproportionate returns on the investments by the wealthy entities. Those wealthy entities had limited interest in proportionate purchasing of the local goods and services. With their natural instincts, the urban wealthy invested in the luxuries offered by the global wealthy. With supernatural inspiration, the global wealthy invested in the space station luxuries seeking to assure that the future generation of their children are assured resources and longevity of life, when the life on Earth becomes unliveable due to the rapid entropy in social, human, ecological, economic, national and psychological values.

In Chapter 10, "Innovative and Technology-Led Strategies Adopted by Start-ups in India during the COVID-19 Pandemic", Kumar Mukul, Vanka Padmaja, Jayadatta Shreepad, Yashaswini Murthy and Megha Balasubramanyam investigate the bottom-up nationalizing of the technology solutions led by the Indian start-up entrepreneurs in the context of the pandemic. The authors note, "with limited customer base, restricted revenue, changing investment patterns, dynamic business model expectations during the crisis period, the start-ups had to rethink their business strategies and leaders had to set new pathways for their ventures". The success of different start-ups varied as a function of their adoption of the national best practices. These best practices included "investing in R&D, technological upgradations, continuous quality improvements, networking, social media presence and continuously seeking noble and "innovative ways" to operate and connect with their stakeholders". By embracing social media, the start-ups negotiated space for bringing their innovative ways to the forefront. These start-ups not only survived, but also grew, seeing the opportunity in the challenges brought forth by the pandemic. In this way, these start-ups have become valuable case studies for all firms, especially the legacy firms that found these start-ups valuable partners for helping address the pandemic-exacerbated bottlenecks in their value chains.

In Chapter 11, "Digital India and the Future of Work Enabled by COVID: Employees as Qubits Self-Managing the Work Transformation", Apoorva Goel studies the localization of employees as a technology solution. Apoorva Goel notes how in the aftermath of the pandemic, cognitive technology is creating a new class of digital labour. The organizations are expediting the procedures and decreasing the operational expenses through automation. Based on the current trends, she notes that as the machines are taking over the redundant work, they are "leaving time for the professionals to focus on areas where human judgement is required".

Indeed, the COVID-19 pandemic has become a classic case of the massive transformation of the organizations from in-person networks to remote work networks. If one considers any pre-pandemic research, nobody would have ever predicted the speed and efficiency of organizations in making such a massive transformation. In fact, the only way such a transformation is feasible is when the stakeholders are willing to take on self-managing responsibilities for mastering the science of working remotely and art of managing such work efficiency, leaving aside all their apprehensions. The pandemic made the future of work that was once seen as best fitting fiction novels a reality of the present in no time. Moreover, this reality was as inclusive, diverse and equitable as was possible, given the pre-existing disparities in the access to macro infrastructure, meso structures and micro resources.

In Chapter 12, "COVID-led Adoption of Video Resumes for Deep Archival Candidate Screening in India", Apoorva Goel, Ankita Modi and Richa Awasthy analyze the corporatizing of the candidate screening process in the aftermath of COVID-19. The authors report findings of two empirical studies: an interview study and a survey study. The interview study highlighted that the recruiters face significant challenges in the cost, time and quality of hiring from diverse places in India. Therefore, video resumes have grown in popularity. The survey study, based on a geographically diverse pool of candidates, revealed that the candidates had a generally unfavourable view of the video resumes. Some feared that it puts a focus on the weaknesses in their communication skills and impedes their ability to show their natural gifts. Others reported anxiety about the video resumes being shared broadly or misused without any strict privacy norms. For instance, "Women are usually more cautious in sharing photos and videos on social platforms due to the reason that their content may be misused or tampered with".

Overall, the study highlights that the technology-led development has a potential to accentuate the pre-existing as well as non-existing gaps in equity, diversity and inclusion on diverse parameters. The programmed solutions may lead to the exclusion of those who created the programming solutions in the first place. Consequently, the performing with the programmed solutions could strengthen the privilege for certain groups. And after programming, the programmed solutions could disempower those who were most devoted to the technical and programming skills.

Part 4. Strategic Development Approach

Traditionally, the focus in India has been on gaining excellence in technical skills. The general belief is that if one has technical excellence, Mother Nature will naturally bring that excellence to the attention of others and make one's life meaningful. Over time, such a belief has made people very proactive in showcasing all their strengths at every moment of their life like there is no tomorrow. Organizations around the world consider people of India excellent followership assets in the context of the knowledge-based technology-led development initiatives. India has become a flourishing market for the followership theories from the West as well as East. Everybody wishes the people of India to know that their followership is valued, so that the people of India value their leadership.

Since there is significant worldwide competition in search of the best followership assets in India, the value of leadership has rapidly fallen to zero. The firms are willing to invest in India only if they are assured of excellent followership by the managing agents and network brokers. Marketing and branding have become increasingly popular for the firms seeking to salvage the leadership benefits of attracting followership. Such branding accentuates the power distance and attracts all the stakeholders towards the celebrity organizations whose names are at the top of the minds in various communities. Cost-effective trading of local solutions is the key to technological growth. Technological skills for the proficient networking of the followers of diverse technical skills by virtue of reputation are essential for the organizational leadership. Organizational skills make one an entrepreneur through a proficient integration of the diverse networks into an exchange system. Ecosystem skills guide one to be manager of the diverse exchange systems for ascending the worker social benefit-cost ratio of exchange. Strategic development of the diverse workforce systems is key to ascending the social benefit-cost ratio of the technology-led development.

India is a unique paradigm in herself for the selfless international development, by promoting technology leadership globally and technology followership locally, as a slow, painful, but assured process for multilateral technology entrepreneurship. The India paradigm has four dimensions:

- First, organization of all members of the diverse communities who are ashamed of India lacking leadership for fulfilling their aspirations as Non-resident Indians (NRIs), rising to leadership roles driving technologies globally.
- Second, community recognition of the contributions of the NRIs, and granting them dual citizenship without voting rights, as a way to get them to invest back into India and help India gain leadership as well.

- Third, national recognition of NRIs by inviting them to roles in research and development in educational institutions, as corporate mentors and board leaders, and government policy mentors
- Fourth, international recognition of NRIs, by empowering the NRIs to take on foolish efforts, such as dismantle Hinduism, that are blatantly discriminatory at institutions that immediately silence anybody if one were to speak of dismantling any religion, other than Hinduism, by calling out their hypocrisy in the name of academic freedom and discourse that has failed to even recognize that the knowledge trading and other aspects now institutionalized as the best practices of MNCs are the appropriation of the intellectual properties of the emerging markets. A case in point: *India Today* featured a student who shared how she was told by her professor that once yoga was appropriated by the West, it was stripped of Hindutva, so that it could be accultured to the Western way and fed back at premium costs to the world.

Chapters 13–16 highlight the four dimensions of how technology-led development becomes the path of technology-led entropy without a strategic awareness of the sensible way to manage such development through the principle of reciprocity and equitable exchange. When an organization is given a free pass to appropriate the intellectual properties of its employees for increasing returns, thus indirectly making the communities bereft, who invested in inculcating creativity within these employees as children, the ownership of these properties, the individuals and the communities become dependent on the organizations. The organization is a normative solution. It works well as long as everyone is willing to accept the same solution: The shared becoming. The shared becoming is the principle of salvation, situated deeply in the Western belief system.

However, when the individuals and the communities are not willing to accept the normative growth rate, they risk being excluded from the organization. As long as the followers are willing to remain followers and accept lower incomes and power, they are valued stakeholders and knowledge partners for the leaders leading the organizations and deciding the organizational membership boundaries. However, when the followers seek parity with the leaders, they do violate the norms of shared becoming. And, then they cease to be ideal citizens. It becomes perfectly just and justifiable to exclude them from the organization for the sake of the organization's survival.

India's technology-led development is now at that stage of development. Is India willing to accept devoted followership? If not, then the writing is on the wall, it is just invisible as of now. Japan and China were valuable partners for the international community so long as they offered low-cost meccas. Once they ceased to become the low-cost meccas and started organizing the knowledge bases from around the world, they became a threat to the international community.

There is an urgent need for an awareness of these realities within India, so that India can play a proactive role in managing and organizing its own intellectual properties deep-rooted across different communities. When India has no need to go around the world seeking to organize alien knowledge-bases, India will not be a threat to any nation's technology-led development. By focusing on realizing at-par development of the "BOP" (Base of the pyramid) within India using metrics of the top of the pyramid from India itself, India will stop the race of seeking to catch up with other nations. By not engaging in the game of competition, India will descend the pressure of the survival of the fittest. By becoming fit internally, she can ensure each child's survival without the need to be fitter than fit.

The first step in this process is to stop relying on the theories imported from the international community. India has no need to try to be fittest in the world, just because the world-famous theories say so. Seeking to be fittest is not part of the Indian ethos. Indian ethos transcends the notions of relativity that pervade modern science. The focus of the Indian ethos is on the present. The present is the absolute. The past is relative to the present, because we make the present the metric for evaluating the proportionate contributions of the diverse past moments towards the present. The future we create is beyond absolute. We are the creators of that civilizational future. That future is our children. Our children are the stars of the creation, they are the units of technological growth. Having a fundamental clarity about the essence of the wisdom of India is key to transcending the followership mindset that is aggravating the challenges of the technology-led development.

Against this backdrop, in Chapter 13, "Cyber branding in India", Veeramangala Sali and Bommagowni Anitha examine the ease with which cyber branding is allowing global and urban firms to destroy traditional marketing loyalties and relationships. Using several examples from across sectors in India, the authors conclude, the Internet "has enormous potential in comparison to traditional mass media. The ease with which

consumers transition from awareness to action on the Internet is a significant distinction and a source of contention for e-marketers". Thus, **technology has become the "globalizer" of technological growth.**
In Chapter 14, "A Typology of Digital Marketing Channels with a Special Reference to India", Uttam Kaur and Aarti Dangwal find that "while the customers [in India as well as worldwide] have a positive use of digital channels across the choice process", they equally value the use of different channels. The digital channels pressure the customers into sacrificing the value of the different channels for the sake of immediate gratification. Thus, customers, across the different channels like B2B, B2C, C2C and C2B, become vulnerable to significant fraud and losses. **Thus, the organization of different channels has become the "nationalizer" of the technological costs.**

In Chapter 15, "Role of Artificial Intelligence in Ajanta Caves and Hampi", Veenus Jain and Pallavi Mohanan examine the leading role of technologies in helping to discover the pre-existing developments that are not visible and are not co-existing within our minds. They underscore the potential of the normative technology to "lead ways to constructing macro perspective on humanities" taking the case of collecting, preserving and accessing efforts of cultural heritage worldwide. They add, "Cultural Heritage is a pivotal part of our humanity and comprehensive understanding of these unique heritages aids in developing a holistic understanding of our future". India has joined hands with the international community in using the state-of-the-art Artificial Intelligence "to preserve, access and experience the historic sites of Hampi and Ajanta Caves". **Thus, the ecosystem of co-existing developments that led to the unsustainability of the technologies in the past has become the "localizer" of the technological exchange, seeking to harvest what has been lost.**

In a nutshell, this chapter highlights that the preservation of our ancestral heritage through its proactive and strategic exploitation for our personal and universal conscious well-being is in our hands. If we do not take that seriously, then civilization may have to wait thousands of years for the technology to develop for going back in time to figure the opportunity costs of our inertia. Further, while technological exchange sustains international collaboration, lack of technological exchange invites international invasions that make the technology-led development unsustainable.

In Chapter 16, "Digital Mission for India to achieve SDG 9 for building resilient infrastructure, sustainable industrialization and fostering innovation: A study of Navratna Companies in India", Navita Mahajan,

Meghna Mehta, and Seema Garg put the issue in the context of the United Nations Sustainable Development Goal # 9. The authors observe, "SDG 9 focuses on improving the overall lives of citizens of a country by improving present infrastructural facilities and fostering the growth and introduction of new, advanced and sustainable technologies. For this goal to be achieved, it is the responsibility of the governments all over the world to work towards making their nations technologically advanced and bold enough to foster innovative projects". They investigate "how the Digital India initiative by the Government of India mission has impacted the industries operating in India and how the incorporation of technologies has affected the overall productivity of Indian enterprise".

The Navratna companies are the giant public sector enterprises in the manufacturing sector. Since the launch of the Digital India mission in 2015, the Navratna firms have helped significantly improve online infrastructure and the accessibility of the Internet among citizens. However, there remains potential to do much more. These firms have been constrained by the bureaucratic systems of manpower, materials, machines and methods. To overcome these challenges, the government is seeking to privatize these enterprises to broadbase their impact.

As a concluding chapter, it shows the promise of an organized approach focused on pan-India development. Such an approach allows nations to cost-effectively leverage their limited resources for realizing significant mass effects that are otherwise difficult to achieve. However, as the organization limits its focus to the specific organizing techniques, the sustainability of the growth in those mass-effects is threatened. **In other words, the government as the incorporator incorporating the national costs as the opportunity for national benefits has limited reproductive, guider benefits.** One must supplement such government-organized corporatization with the citizen-managed corporatization over time. Each child must become an incorporator, instead of living with a superficial agency as an agent of the incorporating principal.

Conclusion

Taken together, the four approaches to technology-led development highlighted by the contributors to this edited book underline four key distinctive elements of the Indian approach.

First, Principle of Personalization. The Indian approach puts less value on the technology than on the development of the technical skills to sustain the technological growth through the followership initiatives. This makes the Indian workforce highly attractive for those seeking to codify these technical skills and diffuse the codified abstracts as their private intellectual property rights.

Second, Principle of Socialization: The Indian approach puts less value on the development of the technical skills than on the sharing of such development for the universal social benefit through the leadership initiatives. This makes the Indian networks highly attractive for those seeking to catch-up and capitalize on the community of practice know-how.

Third, Principle of Institutionalization: The Indian approach puts less value on sharing the development for the universal social benefit than on the development of the exchange of know-how on how to act entrepreneurially in universalizing the pre-existing techniques for personal social benefit. Selfless exchange for the universal benefit is the key to Indian ethos of *Vasudhaiva Kutumbhakam*: the doctrine of the emanation of the present world as an infinite family from the one who matters by virtue of selfless exchange. This makes the Indian exchange highly attractive for those seeking to substitute Indian partners and ride on the self-reliant wagon (*Atmanirbhar Gaari*).

Fourth, Principle of Secularization. The Indian approach puts an absolute value on the development of each and every person, regardless of the identity of that person. One who gives the gift of one's absolute consciousness (*Paramatma*) to everyone is worshipped as an absolute guru (*Param Guru*). An absolute guru is accorded an absolute status, above that of any deity or God. An absolute guru is the living guru who is alive and becomes immortal by giving the gift of absolute consciousness to everyone for managing their followership, leadership and entrepreneurship.

A strategic awareness of these four approaches is the path for knowing the limitations of becoming everyone's absolute consciousness. When anyone personifies your identity and knowing, the uniqueness of that person as a child is lost. Even though on the surface each child is a copy of the parents, in reality, each child is born with unique gifts. There is a critical need for each child to cultivate and develop their true and essential nature for knowing their potential. Each child has a potential to be a primordial greeter: one who gives the gift to each person, the technique and the technologies, for being who they are, breathing their uniqueness, and leveraging the universality of the uniqueness for making contributions par excellence.

A contribution that empowers each person to be a primordial greeter as well. When each person enjoys a conscious well-being, it becomes possible to transcend the limits of the universal conscious well-being (Chatterjee, 2020; Chuang & Graham, 2018; Dutta *et al.*, 2020; Gupta *et al.*, 2022; Gupta, 2021a–h, 2022a-d; Karuppiah *et al.*, 2022; Wu *et al.*, 2022).

References

Chatterjee, S. (2020). Exploring managerial work in the era of Industry 4.0: Reflections on theory and practice. Paper presented at "The 4IR: Challenges and Opportunities for the Future of Work" Conference, Indian Institute of Technology, New Delhi, India, January 17–20.

Chuang, S. & Graham, C. (2018). Embracing the sobering reality of technological influences on jobs, employment and human resource development. *European Journal of Training and Development, 42*(7/8), 400–416.

Dutta, G., Kumar, R., & Sindhwani, R. (2020). Digital transformation priorities of India's discrete manufacturing SME's — A conceptual study in perspective of Industry 4.0. *Competitiveness Review: An International Business Journal, 30*(3), 289–314.

Gupta, A., Singh, R., & Gupta, S. (2022). Developing human resources for the digitization of logistics operations: Readiness index framework. *International Journal of Manpower, 43*(2), 355–379.

Gupta, V. (2021a). What is divine energy: Power of managing the science of everything. Independently Published: Amazon.

Gupta, V. (2021b). What is present reality: Power of managing the limit of science. Independently Published: Amazon.

Gupta, V. (2021c). Is present reality: The superscience of the transcendental value. Independently Published: Amazon.

Gupta, V. (2021d). Is divine energy: The secret of the limitless immanent value. Independently Published: Amazon.

Gupta, V. (2021e). What is consciousness: The factor creating the law of limitation. Independently Published: Amazon.

Gupta, V. (2021f). What is para-consciousness: The potential beyond what we know. Independently Published: Amazon.

Gupta, V. (2021g). What is self-awareness: Looking beyond the law of attraction. Independently Published: Amazon.

Gupta, V. (2021h). What is human factor: The key to a joyful life. Independently Published: Amazon.

Gupta, V. (2022a). What is trading factor: Mathematics beyond Einstein. Independently Published: Amazon.

Gupta, V. (2022b). What is cultural factor: Biology beyond Darwin. Independently Published: Amazon.

Gupta, V. (2022c). What is exchange factor: Physics beyond Newton. Independently Published: Amazon.

Gupta, V. (2022d). What is technological growth. Chemistry beyond Boyle. Independently Published: Amazon.

Karuppiah, K., Sankaranarayanan, B., & Ali, S. (2022). Evaluation of key factors for Industry 4.0 technologies adoption in small and medium enterprises (SME's): An emerging economy context. *Journal of Asia Business Studies*. Doi: 10.1108/JABS-05-2021-0202.

Wu, W., Liang, Z., & Zhang, Q. (2022). Technological capabilities, technology management and economic performance: The complementary roles of corporate governance and institutional environment. *Journal of Knowledge Management*, *26*(9), 2416–2439.

https://doi.org/10.1142/9789811271786_0002

Chapter 2

Human Resource Management in Digital India

Minu Zachariah[*,‡] and Neetha Mary Avanesh[†,§]

*Department of Management Studies and Research Centre,
B.M.S. College of Engineering, Bangalore, India*

*†School of Business and Management,
Christ (Deemed to be) University, Bangalore, India*

‡minu_zach.mba@bmsce.ac.in

§neetha.mary@christuniversity.in

Abstract

The business entities of today are aware of the vital role played by techno-logical interventions in value creation. HR technological interventions are no exceptions either. These interventions are aligned to business goals and help businesses achieve their bottom lines. Nevertheless, some business owners are apprehensive about the way forward while adopting technology. This chapter focuses on the various technologies that aid HR functions, its implementation framework keeping in perspective the key apprehensions, considerations and competency requirements. The chapter highlights few Indian organizations that have adopted it. The findings show that emphasis is laid on business value creation for stakeholders due to HR technology adoption.

Introduction

In today's digital era, HR digital transformation is inevitable regardless of the fact that the enterprises accept it or not. Technology has brought in a paradigm shift in the role of HR from being involved in various transactions to being more creative and innovative in workforce strategizing roles, adding value to business (Salamzadeh *et al.*, 2019). The pandemic further accelerated the HR digital transformations in most of the organizations and there has been continuous progress, making HR a technology-driven profession (Agast, 2020). The problem with some of the organizations is that they struggle to catch up with the technology due to lack of agility and fail to use the technology to its full potential. While still others are either not informed, updated or aware of the tools that aid HR in reducing time spent on administrative tasks. An HR system survey conducted by CedarCrestone in 2010 showed that organizations successfully adopting sophisticated HR technology tools outperform those that do not. This chapter, therefore, revisits various HR technological solutions that help organizations to stay competitive and relevant in an increasingly digital world while upholding human touch.

Status of HR Technology in India

The human resources industry in India has been adopting technology-powered solutions for talent acquisition, onboarding, performance management, etc., relatively early (Yadav, 2020). However, adoption of HR technology has seen a huge surge in recent years creating a rising trend in investments by start-ups with focus on HR solutions. The investment in HR solutions in 2018 was $55 million and rose to $116 million within a year showing the importance given to HR technology by companies. The highest level of adoption of HR technologies is in IT and Communication sector followed by manufacturing, engineering and banking. Highest amount of automation was present in HR operations giving HR managers time to focus on employee-centric initiatives. Overall, companies are interested in investing in HR technology for better efficiency and reduced costs across the board (Zimyo, 2020). According to the *Economic Times*, 70 percent of multinational companies in India have automated half of their HR functions, 20 percent of the companies have invested in some form of technology in 2020 (Sahaye, 2020). Yet, there is a long way to go to unleash the potential in this sector.

Knowledge of HR Technology Implementation, the Need of the Hour

The aim of this study is to provide information to HR Managers and academicians on how to integrate technology with Human Resource Management to run a business successfully on the basis of secondary data available.

Considerations for HR Technology Implementation

HR technology adoption is a key decision to be taken by any organization as it involves transformational change. It has to be carried out in a planned manner to minimize resistance and gain strategic advantages. Figure 1 illustrates how HR technology creates strategic value for business. Figure 2 illustrates the elements to be considered while implementing HR strategy.

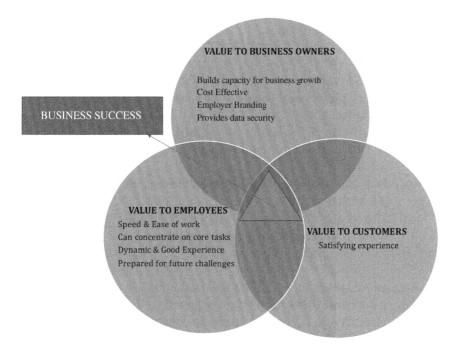

Figure 1.   Value Creation for Business Using HR Technology

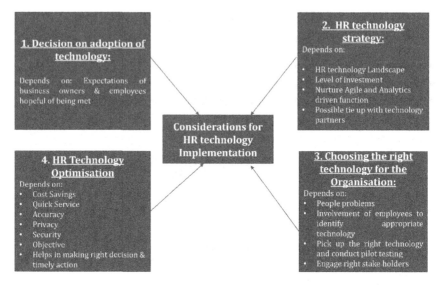

Figure 2.   Elements Considered for HR Technology Implementation

(i) Basis on which decision to adopt HR technology is made

(ii) HR technology strategy

(iii) Choosing the right HR technology for the organization

HR leaders should choose the right technology fit as follows:

(a) The selection of the technology should depend on the people-related problems at hand currently that could be solved with the aid of technology.

(b) Involve employees in identifying the HR technology requirement as they come across problems on a day-to-day basis and find solution.

(c) Pick the technology that best suits the organization and conduct pilot testing.

(d) The organization has to engage the right stakeholders to implement this HR technology initiative.

(iv) HR technology optimization.

Addressing potential upskilling and reskilling needs of employees throughout their career life keeps them prepared to succeed in the evolving work place. It also keeps the workforce engaged and ready for future challenges (Malik, 2019).

Framework to Facilitate HR Technology Implementation in an Organization

Figure 3 illustrates a framework for HR technology implementation.

(i) *Develop a team to transform technology*: The digital teams should start with good leaders — typically Chief level executives with vision — who can influence and have the ability to work with others as required to build the right transformation culture (Gareiss, 2021).

(ii) *Culture facilitating digital technology*: Digital culture in an organization can be developed by focusing on articulating the required changes in the organization, activating leadership skills for engaging people in adapting to digital change, aligning the organization to the new embedded culture (Subin, 2020).

(iii) *Leadership skills required to involve employees for digital transformation*: The leader should be sensitive to cultural differences, cater to individual needs if required, has to know various dimensions of the business for which he has to be a jack-of-all-trades and uphold integrity to mobilize the support (Birbal, 2021).

(iv) *Infrastructure*: The HR leaders who are forward-looking would definitely harness the digital resources by gaining insights to redefine obsolete models and implement technologies such as analytics, digital labour and AI to bridge the gap between human and digital resources (KPMG Research, 2019).

Figure 3.   Framework for HR Technology Implementation

The HR Functions that can be Integrated with Technology for Improved Performance

(i) *Talent acquisition*: Many organizations take assistance of customized Applicant Tracking Systems (ATS) to ensure that they are able to reach out to the right candidates at the right time (Garcia, 2021). Organizations also make use of Candidate Relationship Management, which allows recruiters to maintain a pool of prospective candidates. The Employee Referral Software also facilitates the HR managers to source potential candidates from the recommendations of its current employees. The Employee Assessment Software helps an organization decide whether a candidate is suited for an open position. Further, the role played by many technology and social media companies in talent acquisition cannot be negated. The application of AI recruiting tools is gaining prominence.

(ii) *Training and development*: The present pandemic forced organizations to adopt interactive online platforms to achieve their continuous learning objectives. Many employers have been making use of Learning Management Software (LMS) to customize training programs, track employees learning process and assess their performance. LMS is known to provide advanced digital user interfaces for online training courses for both on-site and remote workers. It facilitates selection of customized training material and enhanced third-party content from other providers as well. Further, the growth of Employee Self-Service Tools has resulted in saving a lot of time and effort for both the employee as well as the manager as the team need not approach their superior with constant clarifications on the workflow. This results in higher administrative task efficiency, better transparency, real-time updating of work and enhanced team morale.

(iii) *Employee engagement*: Employee engagement platforms and apps play a vital role in ensuring that the employees are well-connected and enthusiastic about their work. The mobile apps with social media offer interactive platforms which enable posting, commenting and sharing information. The gamification techniques that are gaining prominence have taken employee learning to a different level. Other engagement strategies include sophisticated employee recognition programs, app-based enterprise-wide contest platforms and software to coordinate volunteer civic projects.

(iv) *Performance management*: The use of real-time performance management tools would offer employees and HR personnel more visibility into the team's performance (Tech Magic, 2019). The real-time performance tracking tools enhance the learning and development experience of the employees and help in keeping track of their accomplishments in real time.

(v) *Compensation management*: Software packages have been developed to determine the most lucrative pay rates in order to attract and retain the best talents in the industry. The usage of time and attendance software to track the time spent by the employee at work, which would in turn be used for wage and salary computation, has also gained prominence.

(vi) *Employee wellness and wellbeing*: Initiatives to combat stress and promote employee wellness have been gaining more prominence in the recent past. Video conferencing solutions such as Skype, Google Meet, Zoom and Microsoft Teams have been highly effective in sharing wellness-focused webinars and other fitness focused presentations to off-site employees (Rasool *et al.*, 2021).

(vii) *Data security*: The use of Trusted Global Network for HR Data, which enables data access for eligible parties, and the Identity Access Management, which ensures data storage security, is gaining prominence across industries.

(viii) *Employee retention*: People analytics tools help in identifying the employees' preferred learning style, their engagement levels, facilitate accurate mapping of their skill sets and so on.

(ix) *Succession planning*: Organizations use succession planning software to identify critical jobs, available skill sets, potential vacancies and so on.

Illustrative Organizations that have Embraced HR Technology in One Form or the Other

(a) Tata Consultancy Services, an Indian multinational IT services and consultancy firm, has developed its own customized analytics services, namely, TCS Workforce Analytics. It makes use of AI-driven assessment tools and analytics to offer data analytics solutions on talent experience, compliance, productivity and employee wellbeing.

(b) Infosys Technologies, the Indian IT services and consultancy major, constantly strives to provide seamless employee experience through AI and automation technologies. It uses its own applicant tracking system that enables electronic handling of recruitment. It has an employee referral program termed as ConnectInfy.

(c) HCL Technologies has been trying to improve the attrition rate through its technology makeover. It has been trying to retain its staff by reducing employee discomfort by employing artificial intelligence, machine learning tools and gamification techniques (*HRK News Bureau*, 2022).

(d) BYJU'S, one of the leading multinational EdTech platforms offering personalized student programs, has aligned with dotin Inc., a SaaS company to improve its recruitment and retention strategies. BYJU's leverages on dotin's AI-based technology to determine optimal candidate alignment and core candidate motivations to facilitate employee retention (Press Release, 2021).

(e) Tata iQ, a six-year-old startup created by the Tata Group, engaged in big data and analytics, utilizes graph technology in its hiring process. With the aid of graph network, they are able to tap and map unknown relations using AI, thereby finding the right fit for the organization at a faster pace (Pushkarna, 2021).

(f) Tech Mahindra, an Indian multinational information technology services and consulting company, has been employing next-gen technologies like Artificial Intelligence, Machine Learning to address real-time HR issues by delivering innovative solutions and services. They had introduced K2, the first HR humanoid in their Hyderabad and Noida campuses. K2 leverages on Artificial Intelligence technology, addresses general and specific HR-related employee queries as well as handles personnel requests like providing payslip, tax forms and so on. Tech Mahindra had also implemented a Facial Recognition System to register the attendance of employees, which has drastically reduced the time spent by an employee in updating the timesheet (Information Technology, 2019).

References

Agast, R. (2020). Paradigm shift in HR Technology, a key to drive the future of work. *People Matters*. https://www.peoplematters.in/blog/hr-technology/paradigm-shift-in-hr-technology-a-key-to-drive-the-future-of-work-27748.

Birbal. (2021, December 30). Leadership skills that could transform a workplace. https://www.cronj.com/birbal/leadership-skills.

CedarCrestone 2009–2010 HR Systems Survey. 12th Annual Edition.

Garcia, D. (2021, September 23). 10 Most important types of HR technology in 2021. *ScoutLogic*. https://www.scoutlogicscreening.com/blog/important-types-of-hr-technology.

Gareiss, R. (2021, February 8). Building a digital transformation team: 8 essential roles. *Techtarget Network.* https://www.techtarget.com/searchcio/tip/Building-a-digital-transformation-team-8-essential-roles.

HRK News Bureau. (2022, January 20). HCL to improve employee lifecycle through 'Hire to Retire'. https://www.hrkatha.com/news/hcl-to-improve-employee-lifecycle-through-hire-to-retire/.

Information Technology. (2019, June 24). Tech Mahindra introduces K2, Artificially Intelligent human resource Humanoid. https://www.mahindra.com/news-room/press-release/tech-mahindra-introduces-k2-artificially-intelligent-human-resource-humanoid.

KPMG Research Report. (2018). The future of HR 2019: In the Know or in the No. https://assets.kpmg/content/dam/kpmg/tw/pdf/2018/11/KPMG-Future-of-HR-survey-report-2019.pdf.

Malik, A. (2019, October 8). Optimize HR Tech to meet employee needs, now and in the future. *HCM Technology Report.* https://www.hcmtechnologyreport.com/optimize-hr-tech-meet-employee-needs/.

Press Release (2021, August 26). dotin Onboarded by BYJU'S for AI software hiring needs. https://www.hrkatha.com/industry-news/dotin-onboarded-by-byjus-for-ai-software-hiring-needs/.

Pushkarna, A. (2021, September 10). How Tata iQ utils graph technology to hire the right talent. https://www.hrkatha.com/features/how-tata-iq-utilises-graph-technology-to-hire-the-right-talent/.

Rasool, S. F., Wang, M., Tang, M., Saeed, A., & Iqbal, J. (2021). How toxic workplace environment effects the employee engagement: The mediating role of organizational support and employee wellbeing. *International Journal of Environmental Research and Public Health, 18*(5), 2294.

Sahaye, V. S. (2020, March 12). How AI is now being used to hire instead of replacing people. *Economic Times.* https://cio.economictimes.indiatimes.com/news/next-gen-technologies/how-ai-is-now-being-used-to-hire-instead-of-replacing-people/74586694.

Salamzadeh, A., Tajpour, M., & Hosseini, E. (2019). Corporate entrepreneurship in University of Tehran: Does human resources management matter? *International Journal of Knowledge-based Development, 10*(3), 276–292.

Subin. (2020, February). Importance of transformation HR: Technology-driven model. *Gillion.* https://www.cronj.com/blog/transformation-hr.

Tech Magic. (2019, November 19). Top 10 human resource technology trends. https://medium.com/@TechMagic/top-10-human-resource-technology-trends-eb6671f7d4b5.

Yadav, N. (2020, March 13). The expanding role of technology in India's HR industry. *India Briefing.* https://www.india-briefing.com/news/expanding-role-tech-india-hr-19780.html/.

Chapter 3

Lean Leadership in India: Transforming the Transactional Challenges with Mature Followership

Alagiri Govindasamy[*], **Usha Ramanathan**[†]
and Nadia Kougiannou[‡]

*Nottingham Business School, Nottingham Trent University,
Nottingham, UK*

[*]*alagiri.govindasamy2018@my.ntu.ac.uk*

[†]*usha.ramanathan@ntu.ac.uk*

[‡]*nadia.kougiannou@ntu.ac.uk*

Abstract

Lean is an accepted management philosophy in the Indian Industry deeply rooted in many industry segments since its initial adoption by the TVS group in 1985 (Prashar, 2014). Lean leadership is a specific set of leadership attributes to realize the lean outcome by leaders' self-transformation and promote meaningful followership among their subordinates to meet common corporate objectives. This assumes significance for a traditional country like India, surviving with a vibrant ethos, rich cultural heritage and unique socio-economic patterns for more than two and a half millennia. Indian people are living by their cultural ethos.

The Indian ethos advocates wholesomeness both among leaders and followers, togetherness in the workplace, a sustained decision-making system with approval of all parties concerned and larger societal impact from organizations than achievement of merely short-term commercial goals.

The gap is found from the literature questions on how lean leaders from India can motive their followers to break their limitations and how both leaders and followers get benefited from the Indian ethos. This review explores 793 journal articles from prominent databases.

This study provides guiding principles to enhance the lean leader's decision-making process.

Introduction

Organizations are consistently looking for a proven management framework to become more agile and the lean system is one such promising management system (Elnadi *et al.*, 2013). The lean system warrants an organization-wide improvement strategy with approval from all employees irrespective of hierarchical levels to ensure a higher degree of quality adherence, elimination of no added value activities and reduction of cost elements based on facts (Lodgaard *et al.*, 2016). The lean drastically differs from other management frameworks on account that the leaders from all hierarchical levels need to have a solid understating of the lean concepts and diligently follow the daily lean practices (Emiliani & Emiliani, 2013). Mere preaching and giving directions to followers will not work in the lean system as the leaders are supposed to live with lean thinking daily (Emiliani & Emiliani, 2013).

Indian companies are steadfastly adopting Lean since 1985 across various industries (Prashar, 2014), and superior performances have been reported by several Indian companies to the tune of 83.14%

reduction in lead time, 12.62% reduction in processing time, 89.47% reduction in work-in-process and 30% manpower requirement reduction (Vinodh & Joy, 2012; Vinodh *et al.*, 2015).

Indian ethos

Indian ethos is the time-tested and living construct that has survived for more than two and a half millennia and contains the essence of the deeper Indian mindset, various civilizational impacts and the effect of multiple religions (Sharma, 2003). The Indian ethos is the most versatile construct, silently absorbing various perspectives and frameworks over the flow of history and the soul to enlighten more than a billion people across the world (Sharma, 2003). This ethos is intact and alive even today, despite various onslaughts like commercial exploitation, forced conversions and colonization tactics by foreign powers over a long time (Sharma, 2003). The time-tested Indian ethos transforms the leadership attitude by consolidating contemporary ethics and motivating leaders to see the larger picture like taking care of their followers' unspoken needs, ready to sacrifice their interests for the benefit of their subordinates, while still focusing on discipline-orientation to protect organizational interests (Sinha, 1995). The Indian ethos foundation comes from noble concepts like humanity, compassion for others, looking out for others' interests more than self-interest and social justice (Mathur, 2019). The family orientation concept of the Indian ethos promotes some unique qualities among leaders like fairness, easy accessibility, elimination of mental barriers and development of individualized consideration for each follower. Simultaneously, they need to provide enough space and authority to their followers to take independent decisions (Sinha, 1995).

Lean leadership

Leadership is a decisive factor in the achievement of desired outcomes from any successful lean implementation (Burawat, 2019). The lean leaders have to lead from the forefront, consolidate all hierarchical energies into a single voice, demonstrate strong commitment despite many challenges in their way and not dilute their leadership vigour in favour of other organizational priorities (Laureani & Antony, 2017). Camuffo & Gerli (2018) advocated the idea that appropriate management behaviours and traits are required at different stages of the lean project and efficient leadership is an enabling factor towards changing the stagnant socio-cultural environment in an organization into an empowered and trust-based working environment.

Followership process

Followers play an important role in completing the purpose of leadership and one cannot talk about the leadership without followers' active participation in the leadership process. Riggio (2014) explained that leadership cannot be mandated by either a leader or follower, instead, both stakeholders must assume equal responsibilities to complete the leadership process rather than taking their extreme positions (Favara, 2009).

Leadership style is a highly focused research field, and many leadership styles are proposed by influential researchers. The smart lean leaders use transactional leadership style to get the basic work done from the followers and use transformational leadership style to push their followers out of their comfort zones to think about bigger corporate objectives (Alefari *et al.*, 2017). There is a call from the academicians to explore the intricate role of these two leadership styles on lean leaders' actions (Laohavichien *et al.*, 2011) and how few lean leaders successfully embrace transactional and transformational leadership styles on their journey towards lean excellence (Liu *et al.*, 2003).

The Indian industry is at a crossroads to make a meaningful contribution to the global economy with a sustained leadership framework and to leverage Indian heritage aspects to motivate both leaders and followers at this critical juncture. This necessitates two research questions, Research Question 1 **(RQ1)**: "How Indian ethos promotes a sustained lean leadership by leveraging matured followership process?" Research Question 2 **(RQ2)**: What is the optimum combination of transactional and transformational leadership styles to enhance the followership phenomenon in the lean leadership process in India?

Research Method

Selection of studies

The researcher has followed the systematic literature review methodology proposed by Moher *et al.* (2009). Two prominent databases namely Scopus and Web of Science are considered for this review work. To cover the latest additions from the management field, the last 10 years' duration were factored in this study. Refer to Figure 1 to review the search strings used to identify the relevant peer-reviewed journal articles for this study.

Data analysis framework

The adopted systematic review methodology for this review study comes with four distinct phases, (1) Identification, (2) Screening, (3) Eligibility and (4) Inclusion. This framework has a list of 27 checkpoints to be followed during the systematic review with proper filtering criteria to avoid

Database	Search string	Duration	Number of documents	Relevant subjects	Only articles	Only journals	English language	Useful based on abstract reading	Useful journals after critical review
Scopus	Lean AND Leadership	10 years	634	440	232	221	213	32	30
	Lean AND Transformational	10 years	64	42	20	20	19	10	0
	Lean AND Transactional	10 years	45	38	15	14	14	2	0
Web of science	Lean AND Leadership	10 years	44	44	31	31	31	20	2
	Lean AND Transformational	10 years	5	5	4	4	4	4	0
	Lean AND Transactional	10 years	1	1	1	1	1	0	0

Figure 1.   The Selection Mechanism to Identify the Relevant Journals

unrelated literature elements and to make a comprehensive and impactful review document (Moher *et al.*, 2009). In the identification phase, we searched the leadership style journal articles related to the lean system from Scopus and Web of Science databases. In the screening phase, the duplicate records were removed, and the abstract section was seriously reviewed to ascertain the applicability of the literature elements. In the eligibility phase, each journal article got reviewed in full length to evaluate the applicability of the peer-reviewed journal articles to make an informed decision. In the Inclusion phase, the author focused on critical aspects of the academic position from each peer-reviewed journal for this review chapter.

Results

The manufacturing and SME sectors are leading industry segments (refer to Figure 2) to embrace both these leadership styles. The automotive industry and other industry segments are quite inclined to adopt these leadership styles.

Brazil and Sweden led the number of journal articles featuring transactional and transformational leadership styles, and other countries that are active in this research paradigm are Thailand, India, Malaysia, Netherlands and Hungary (refer to Figure 3).

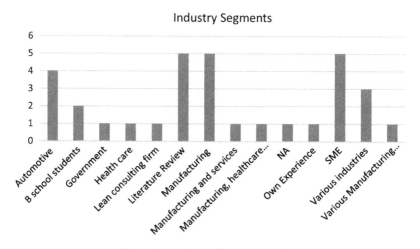

Figure 2.   Industry Segment Analysis

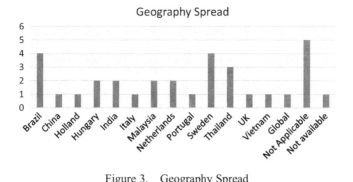

Figure 3.   Geography Spread

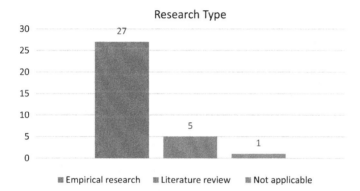

Figure 4.   Research Type

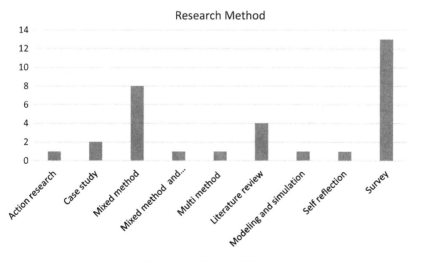

Figure 5.   Research Type

Table 1.   List of International Journals

Journal Name	Number of Articles
International Journal of Mechanical and Production Engineering Research and Development	1
Asia Pacific Business Review	1
European Management Journal	1
International Journal for Quality Research	1
International Journal of Operations & Production Management	2
International Journal of Quality & Reliability Management	1
International Journal of Supply Chain Management	2
Journal of Manufacturing Technology Management	3
Leadership & Organization Development Journal	2
Management and Production Engineering Review	2
Management Decision	2
Nordic Journal of Working Life Studies	1
Operations Management Research	1
Production Planning & Control	1
Research Journal of Business Management	1
Total Quality Management & Business Excellence	4
Quality Innovation Prosperity	1
The TQM Journal	1
Research Journal of Business Management	1
Leadership & Organization Development Journal	1
Production Planning & Control	1
International Journal of Lean Six Sigma	1

Empirical research is the major source for the selected list of journals and is followed by systematic literature review works (refer to Figure 4). One researcher explained his own experience in his journal article.

Figure 5 explains the major role played by the survey research method followed by a mixed-method research method to generate the necessary primary data for these leadership research studies.

Table 1 displays the spread of various leading international journals considered for this review study.

Analysis and Discussion

Lean leadership and the importance of the Indian Ethos

India has a diversity of religious beliefs, value systems and faiths (Chatterjee, 2009). The Indian ethos has a very long flow of history and is rooted in religious and spiritual aspects (Chatterjee, 2009). The Indian civilization achieved its highest maturity as it originated and absorbed various religions including Hinduism, Buddhism, Islam and Christianity, and cultivated harmony and brotherhood throughout history (Mahbubani, 2008). Apart from spirituality, the Indian contribution to global leadership excellence is a significant factor as the world's first management book, *Arthashastra*, was written by Kautilya in three millennium BC (Chatterjee, 2009). Nobel Laureate Amartya Sen proclaimed that the Indian heritage and ethos promote a well-balanced leadership process with spiritual, moral, analytical, harmonious, just, liberal and rational principles to promote a democratic and cohesive working environment (Sen, 2005). This necessitates that global companies that start their businesses in India need to appreciate and adopt long-standing Indian ethos in the workplace context to become successful in India (Chatterjee, 2009). The Indian tradition promotes the transformation of the inner world among leaders and followers, a subjective process against the objective measures promoted by the classical managerial system (Chatterjee, 2009). One of the hallmark features of the Indian workforce is duality, a set of behavioural patterns at the personal level and contrasting behavioural patterns expected by the modern workplace, and this creates a paradoxical position for the Indian workforce (Sinha & Kanungo, 1997).

Sustenance is one of the focus areas for many organizations in today's competitive marketplace and any new leadership framework based on long-standing Indian ethos will develop a more relevant leadership framework not only for India but for the entire world (Chatterjee, 2009). The emergence of new managerial excellence from Indian tradition will offer a compelling value proposition for companies across the globe (Chatterjee, 2007). The current crisis in an organization revolves around its materialistic and objectivist orientations like revenue and profit as organizations are largely ignoring the humanistic aspects today (Sharma, 1996). The identification and successful integration of time-tested wisdom, principles, values and ethical standards that compose the Indian ethos may guide a better way for organizational functioning

(Chatterjee, 2007). The Indian ethos says that wisdom should come from the top and management needs to propagate the positive vibration throughout the hierarchical structure (Chakraborty, 1996). The emerging consciousness on bringing traditional ethos to the business world has been echoed in recent times, emphasizing that today leaders are realizing that their main job is to promote the basic human spirit rather than merely focusing on materialistic aspects like top line and bottom line (Ray & Rinzler, 1993). Indian ethos stresses two aspects, from leaders and followers, Sradha, respect to superiors and Sneha, affectionate bonding with all stakeholders and happily accepting the opportunity to help others (Chatterjee, 2007). This phenomenon is reciprocated by one of India's successful businessmen Mr. Narayana Murthy, Founder of Infosys, who espouses that family values and thinking beyond one's own interests are hallmark features of the Indian workplace (Chatterjee, 2007).

The Indian ethos offers a precious set of behaviours that are conductive and applicable to the modern organizational leadership team, one is relationship-oriented behaviour, the other is decision-oriented behaviour to meet targets, and lastly value-based thinking process (Uhl-Bien *et al.*, 2014). There are three behaviour clusters noticed from the Indian ethos, namely the Sattva mindset of promoting value-based approach towards their followers, the Rajasik mindset of overpowering competition by unveiling superior outcome and the Tamasik mindset, which is the least preferable one as this mindset is one of profit orientation among the leadership team (Uhl-Bien *et al.*, 2014).

The ideology of spirituality in action from Indian ethos is a much-needed construct to modern organizations. This mandates a person to approach daily activities with a spiritual mode, encourages both leaders and followers to invest their best efforts without any expected results in mind, and believes in keeping good faith in whatever is done in the organizational context (Sharma, 2003). The time-tested spiritual value will ensure the leaders and followers end up always taking the right action even when no one is noticing, as this is the highest purification expected from oneself (Chakraborty, 2002). The Indian culture believes in offering equal opportunities to everyone, assuring welfare to all, and achieving inner happiness from everyone (Mathur, 2019). India's cultural tradition supports an organization's focus on wealth, but this is not the sole focus of their survival; rather, they need to look after the sustainable way of running their business as per prevailing wisdom in India (Mathur, 2019).

Lean leadership and the importance of leadership styles

The leadership style adopted by the lean leader sets clear objectives for followers (Jung, 2001) and the leader must play a crucial role to mentor the employees during lean transformation (Losonci *et al.*, 2011). Various leadership styles were discussed in the extant literature. Table 2 explains salient features from these leadership styles.

Table 3 explains that the contingent reward dimension is more supportive to the lean system than management by exception construct from transactional style.

We notice that all four internal dimensions from transformational styles are supportive to lean, but the higher utilization from idealized influence construct can be realized when the organization reaches a higher degree of lean maturity, not at the initial lean implementation phase (refer to Table 4).

Table 2.   Various Leadership Styles

Leadership Style	Author	Salient Features
Empowering	Liu *et al.* (2003)	Delegate enough authority to the followers by the leaders' confidence in them
Directive	Liu *et al.* (2003)	Go for unilateral decisions without consulting subordinates and instilling fear in subordinates' minds
Transactional	Bass (1997)	To set the minimum expectations to the followers and punish them if they do not meet the standards
Transformational	Toledo *et al.* (2019) and Poksinska *et al.* (2013)	Motivate the followers to adopt innovative ways to meet organizational objectives
Servant leadership	Toledo *et al.* (2019) and Poksinska *et al.* (2013)	Focus on the subordinates and fulfilling individualistic aspirations among them
Team leadership	Sahyaja *et al.* (2018)	Promote continuous improvement culture among the entire workforce by encouraging mutually acceptable principles

Table 3.   The Role of Transactional Leadership Style on the Lean System

Leadership Style	Internal Construct	Impact on the Lean System
Transactional	Contingent reward	To achieve the minimum standards to sustain the lean benefits — *Ideal one for the lean system*
	Active management by exception	The subordinates are under the fear that their leaders are proactively watching for deviations — *Not an ideal one for the lean system*
	Passive management by exception	The subordinates will get punishment from their leaders for the mistakes that happened — *Not an ideal one for the lean system*

Table 4.   The Impact of Transactional Leadership Style on the Lean System

Leadership Style	Internal Construct	Impact on the Lean System
Transformational	Individualized consideration	Identify the hidden potential from the subordinates and allow them to prove it — *Ideal one for a lean system*
	Attributed idealized influence	To motivate the subordinates by demonstrating great self-confidence and personality traits — *Not an ideal one for a lean system at the initial stage. May be applicable once some lean maturity is embedded in place*
	Behavioural idealized influence	Demonstrate integrity and ethical aspects to the followers — *Not an ideal one for a lean system at the initial stage. May be applicable once some lean maturity is embedded in place*
	Inspirational motivation	Inspire the subordinates to look for a better world — *Ideal one for a lean system*
	Intellectual stimulation	Provoke the subordinates to take continuous improvement activities on their own — *Ideal one for a lean system*

Further Discussions

We postulate the following two propositions based on the rich insights gained from this study to address research questions.

Proposition 1 — The role of Indian ethos to promote a sustained lean leadership by leveraging matured followership process

The proposed model described in Figure 6 explains three major components to offer a comprehensive lean leadership framework based on Indian heritage values and motivates the leaders to promote followership among their subordinates. The researcher addresses research question one (RQ1) from this proposition: "How Indian ethos promotes a sustained lean leadership by leveraging matured followership process?"

The first component, Indian ethos, is the foundation for this framework as leaders must embrace basic values like positive contribution to

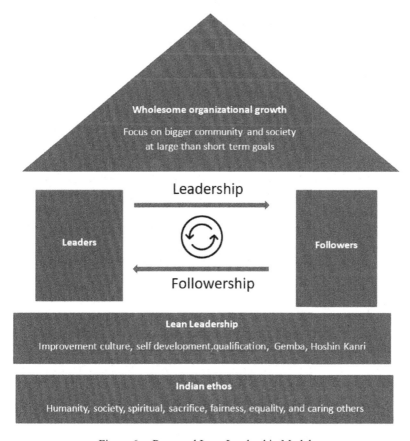

Figure 6.   Proposed Lean Leadership Model

community and society at large by their decision-making process; maintain spiritual cohesion from the workplace context by exhibiting higher-order thinking and care about their subordinates and other stakeholders. Fairness in dealing with various stakeholders, providing equal opportunity to all without any discrimination, and sacrificing one's own self-interest for the sake of others' well-being are some notable traits from the Indian ethos and any leader who follows these proven principles will find themselves running an organization based on a sustainable basis with mutual respect.

The second component, Lean leadership, is a set of unique behavioural aspects seen in successful lean leaders who are destined to collaborate with their followers to achieve sustained organizational goals. There are few lean leadership definitions noticed from the literature, the framework from Dombrowski & Mielke (2013) is a comprehensive one with five attributes. As per this model, the improvement thinking process is a vital element as leaders give chances to their followers to make mistakes and mould their subordinates to seek perfection in anything and everything. The development of followers is a major aim for lean leaders as they must identify unique strengths from each follower and give the necessary training program to transform passive listeners into proactive followers. The leaders must transform themselves to explore new avenues, practice lean practices daily and act as torchbearers to motivate their followers to live with lean principles. Both leaders and followers must aim for incremental learning from their workplace by getting their hands dirty. The knowledge acquisition process does not limit itself to formal classroom education. The *Gemba* or actual workplace is the prime area for both stakeholders as the customers are making payments to the organization only for the value-added activities from this area and not for any non-added value activities like leader's office. The leaders must spend a good amount of time in the *Gemba*, and all their tactical and strategic decisions should be based on the facts from the *Gemba*. The followers' suggestions must be incorporated in any decision-making process. The *Hoshin Kanri* or policy deployment is the art of aligning everyone from the organization to meet customer requirements and both tactical and strategic policy considerations must be implemented systemically.

The third component, Leadership, perhaps is the actual execution process with two stakeholders, Leaders and Followers. It is already accepted that there is no leadership process without meaningful followers in place. The leaders must ensure daily task completion and take care of their followers as their coach and mentor. The transactional leadership style constructs "Contingent reward" as supportive to leaders since they can ensure bias-free recognition in case followers are executing tasks as per guidelines or warn them in case of any deviations. The transactional leadership style will help the leaders with a unique set of capabilities to ensure basic work done from their subordinates.

Followership is an integral component of the leadership process as the leaders are transforming their subordinates into proactive, result-oriented and collaborative followers. The followership does not meet its goals without active participation from followers, as per this theory, the followers are supposed to be demanding, demonstrating risk-taking aptitude, and demanding their rightful place from their leaders. Followers can assume a leading role in the leadership process like expressing what they expect from their leaders, any course corrections required from leaders' behavioural patterns, and setting the rules of the game for their leaders. This kind of transformation among subordinates is not possible unless the followers assume a bigger role in the leadership process, so the leaders must offload their typical command and control system to empower their subordinates. Some notable followership behaviours are, respect, own freedom, own thinking pattern, idea generation, being self-driven, less dependent, striving for change, loyal to the organization, assuming accountability for one's own actions, planning to scale up to leadership roles, collaborative nature, and team orientation (Hurwitz & Hurwitz, 2009).

Proposition 2 — The ideal mix of transactional and transformational leadership styles

We address the second research question (RQ2) from this proposition: What is the optimum combination of transactional and transformational leadership styles to enhance the followership phenomenon in the lean leadership process from India?

The proposed model is described in Figure 7, to construct the optimum mix of transactional and transformational leadership styles as per the Indian ethos and to enhance the followership phenomenon in the lean leadership process. This proposed model will help the lean leaders to navigate through the delicate followership process, mould the lean leader's approach to adopting an ideal mix of transactional and transformational leadership styles and potential constraints, and offer necessary guidance

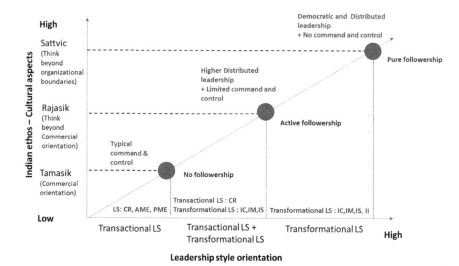

Figure 7.   Indian Ethos, Followership and Leadership Style Matrix

to achieve lean excellence. This model will remind the organization to focus on and promote an optimum mix of transactional and transformational leadership styles in conjunction with the desired level of Indian ethos to be followed as well as to promote followership from their organization.

One can refer to the abbreviations from Table 5 to correlate Figure 7 to understand the proposed lean leadership model.

There are three major components of this model.

(i) *Tamasik culture*: This Indian behavioural orientation results in a typical command and control in place with the lean leaders in the driver's seat and all subordinates need to follow their leaders' instructions without question. The leaders use two constructs from this leadership style, contingent reward to support or punish their followers based on task completion, and management by exception to instil a constant fear in their followers' minds in case of any deviation. The leaders do not think about growth and development plan for their subordinates. In this autocratic environment, the followers are passive, powerless and there is less chance to practice meaningful followership. There is no followership phenomenon found in this

Table 5. Abbreviations from Transactional and Transformational Leadership Styles

Transactional Style		Transformational Style	
Contingent reward	CR	Individualized consideration	IC
Active management by exception	AME	Attributed idealized influence	AII
Passive management by exception	PME	Behavioural idealized influence	BII
		Inspirational motivation	IM
		Intellectual stimulation	IS

kind of leader-centered environment. There is a good chance that any organization following this short-sighted strategy may result in lean implementation failure.

(ii) *Rajasik culture*: This Indian behavioural orientation from lean leaders results in believing their followers and slowly the leaders are empowering their subordinates with enough authority to take improvement actions on their own. The followers understand the sense of urgency to meet long-term corporate objectives in collaboration with their leaders and they exhibit their innate leadership in undertaking improvement activities on their own without waiting for their leader's approval. The leaders use contingent reward construct from transactional leadership style to keep their subordinates performing minimum expected work and they do not think about management by exception as this construct creates negative vibration among followers. Three major internal dimensions of transformational leadership style are individual consideration, inspirational motivation, and intellectual stimulation to empower their followers and make their followers adopt meaningful leadership processes. The leaders spend enough time to identify each follower's unique hidden potential, identify relevant training programs and give enough opportunities to each subordinate. The leaders diligently follow daily lean practices, spend a good amount of time with employees from the workplace and start inspiring their followers as role models. The followers start capitalizing on their intellectual strengths and start thinking beyond their current capacity, challenging the status quo, and becoming self-starters to take new initiatives. In this democratic environment, the subordinates are active followers, determined to be part of the larger organizational movement and they start being an integrated part of the leadership process. The followership starts blossoming in this trust-based environment. The lean movement originated from this kind of collaborative environment can sustain both short and long-term challenges and become a success story.

(iii) *Sattvic culture*: This Indian behavioural orientation from lean leaders results in a mutually collaborative environment where the followers are fully empowered to initiate improvement actions on their own, properly trained, and get the freedom to experiment with new ideas without any fear of possible mistakes. The followers are truly an integral part of the leadership process, collaborating with their leaders, starting to enjoy their freedom in the workplace, and assuming accountability for their actions. The leaders do not use transactional leadership style in this context as both leader and followers start looking for larger organizational goals rather than one-off task completion. The leaders start leveraging all four internal constructs from transformational leadership style like individualized consideration, inspirational motivation, intellectual stimulation, and idealized influence to empower their followers and give enough opportunity to their followers to become leaders. The true followership phenomenon is noticed in this cohesive environment where the follower's ability to take higher responsibility becomes the way of life, they start thinking beyond their interests, and unveil superior collaborative characteristics. The pure followership phenomenon is witnessed in this collaborative environment. Large change management programs like Lean initiatives will be successful in this collaborative environment and become a role model initiative for other companies to follow.

We conclude that demonstrating the optimum mix of transactional and transformational leadership styles as per the chosen Indian ethos enhances the tactical and strategic outcomes from the lean leaders. This is in line with Bass & Bernard (1985) and Bass & Steidlemeier's (1999) argument that successful lean leaders practice both leadership styles, but they display appropriate leadership styles as per the prevailing cultural context.

Conclusion

This review chapter proposes a lean leadership framework with three main components: 1. Collaboration with the prevailing ethos and cultural orientation of India and applying a few vital elements of the Indian ethos into organizational settings 2. Educating the leaders to promote mature followership among their subordinates by leveraging various internal constructs from the transformational leadership style. 3. Leaders must ensure that their followers should finish non-negotiable tasks on a daily basis to stay alive in the marketplace by adopting a transactional leadership style. This chapter attempts to explore the applicability of Indian tradition from two aspects, a moral perspective and a sustainability perspective that provides self-actualization opportunities to leaders and transforms the followers across organizational hierarchy to realize large change management programs like Lean. The Indian ethos offers a unique combination of subjective spiritual aspects for the lean leaders along with objective managerial outcomes, thus the lean leaders can run their organizations in a more ethical, spiritual and sustained way.

The application of the proposed theoretical framework will cover vital issues from both leaders and followers that are commonly experienced in the process of lean system implementation. This review study proved that the transformational leadership style is the right fit for lean initiatives as the leaders can transform themselves to embrace Indian heritage values, cultivate higher-order ownership among both followers and stakeholders, who enjoy a mutually trusted working environment. The study provides a calibrated lean leadership approach for firms to travel with precious Indian ethos and identify appropriate internal constructs from transactional and transformational leadership styles that are aligned with the company strategy. This study encourages organizations to start nurturing the ideal mix of both transactional and transformational leadership styles in their pursuit to achieve lean success and to instigate them to deviate from long-held reliance on lean tools to realize lean success.

There should be more studies to conceptualize optimum leadership theories that align with vibrant Indian ethos and to promote main Indian heritage aspects like community and human development orientation among leaders than mere short-term objective goals. This is one way we can avoid the erosion of time-tested and blossomed Indian ethos, keep it more relevant to modern organization context and transform leaders to support broader societal objectives. This review study is the maiden step taken in this constructive direction and offers a comprehensive framework with the guidance of Indian ethos. One cannot neglect the relevance of contemporary learning from the Indian ethos and there is a sense of urgency to find out a wholesome model to question the profit maximization goals from modern corporates and nurture the broader sense among leaders to run their organization with a focus on society at large than short-term profits. The final takeaway is that both leaders and followers should challenge the boundary of their innocence and start collaborating in a more meaningful way to run the organization such that it is beneficial to the society at large and defying the narrow and objective expectations from the modern organizations.

Limitations

One of the limitations is that this review study approached the relevance of transactional and transformational leadership styles of lean leaders from all hierarchical layers from an organization and was not limited to senior management or middle management or lower management. More insights can be explored from research studies that focus on specific management hierarchies like senior management. The adaptability and usefulness of the proposed lean leadership framework needs to be further evaluated by subsequent research studies. The composition of leadership styles must accommodate the lean maturity stage at a given point in time, hence detailed research studies are required to ascertain the degree of transactional and transformational leadership styles at each stage of the lean implementation. Most of the extant literature targeted the companies with successful lean implementation records to gather their lean leader's perception and it is imperative to go for a subsequent research study to focus on companies with failed lean attempts to create a balanced and comprehensive platform to offer unbiased findings.

Future Research Areas

The leadership style is heavily influenced by the leaders' basic value systems and behavioural aspects, hence future research studies are required to explore this intricate relationship between basic value system and behavioural expectations, and how they shape leadership style outcomes concerning lean implementations. Lean implementation needs careful planning and execution strategy at each maturity level from an organization and there is a need for subsequent research studies to find out the ideal mix of transactional and transformational leadership styles targeted at each maturity phase of lean implementation. The dynamic role of organizational culture on the lean leader's leadership style outcome needs to be examined by further research studies. Each managerial layer from an organization carries its priorities and challenges and any focused research to explain how transactional and transformational leadership styles enable each managerial layer will help the organizations. Each country has its unique national and cultural dimensions, and one of the cultural dimensions is called Power Distance, which results in the noticeable distance between leaders and their subordinates. This power distance dimension makes lean leaders' journey a challenging one as it motivates the followers to become submissive to their leader's directions, hence future research studies are needed to investigate the link between effective leadership styles and power distance as a national cultural dimension.

References

Alefari, M., Salonitis, K., & Xu, Y. (2017). The role of leadership in implementing lean manufacturing. *Procedia CIRP, 63*, 756–761. Doi: 10.1016/j.procir.2017.03.169.

Bass, B. M. & Bernard, M. B. (1985). *Leadership and Performance Beyond Expectations.* NY: Free Press.

Bass, B. M. & Steidlmeier, P. (1999). Ethics, character, and authentic transformational leadership behavior. *The Leadership Quarterly, 10*(2), 181–217. Doi: 10.1016/S1048-9843(99)00016-8.

Bass, B. (1997). Does the transactional-transformational leadership paradigm transcend organizational and national boundaries? *American Psychologist, 52*(2), 130–139. Doi: 10.1037/0003-066X.52.2.130.

Burawat, P. (2019). The relationships among transformational leadership, sustainable leadership, lean manufacturing and sustainability performance in Thai SMEs manufacturing industry. *International Journal of Quality & Reliability Management, 36*(6), 1014–1036. Doi: 10.1108/IJQRM-09-2017-0178.

Camuffo, A. & Gerli, F. (2018). Modeling management behaviors in lean production environments. *International Journal of Operations & Production Management, 38*(2), 403–423. Doi: 10.1108/IJOPM-12-2015-0760.

Chakraborty, S. (1996). *Ethics in Management: Vedantic Perspectives*. New Delhi: Oxford University Press.

Chakraborty, S. K. (2002). Ahimsa (non-violence) in the Indian ethos. *Journal of Human Values, 8*(1), 17–25.

Chatterjee, S. R. (2007). Human resource management in India: 'where from' and 'where to'? *Research and Practice in Human Resource Management, 15*, 92–103.

Chatterjee, S. R. (2009). Managerial ethos of the Indian tradition: Relevance of a wisdom model. *Journal of Indian Business Research, 1*, 136–162.

Dombrowski, U. & Mielke, T. (2013). Lean leadership — Fundamental principles and their application. *Procedia CIRP, 7*, 569–574. Doi: 10.1016/j.procir. 2013.06.034.

Elnadi, M., Shehab, E., & Peppard, J. (2013). Challenges of lean thinking application in product-service system. *ICMR2013*, 461–466.

Emiliani, M. L. & Emiliani, M. (2013). Music as a framework to better understand lean leadership. *Leadership & Organization Development Journal, 34*(5), 407–426. Doi: 10.1108/LODJ-11-0088.

Favara Jr., L. F. (2009). Putting followership on the map: Examining followership styles and their relationship with job satisfaction and job performance. *Journal of Business & Leadership: Research, Practice, and Teaching, 5*(2), 68–77.

Hurwitz, M. & Hurwitz, S. (2009). The romance of the follower: Part 1. *Industrial and Commercial Training, 41*(2), 80–86.

Jung, D. I. (2001). Transformational and transactional leadership and their effects on creativity in groups. *Creativity Research Journal, 13*(2), 185–195. Doi: 10.1207/S15326934CRJ1302_6.

Laohavichien, T., Fredendall, L. D., & Cantrell, R. S. (2011). Leadership and quality management practices in Thailand. *International Journal of Operations & Production Management, 31*(10), 1048–1070. Doi: 10.1108/01443571111172426.

Laureani, A. & Antony, J. (2017). Leadership characteristics for lean six sigma. *Total Quality Management & Business Excellence, 28*(3-4), 405–426. Doi: 10.1080/14783363.2015.1090291.

Liu, W., Lepak, D. P., Takeuchi, R., & Sims, H. P. (2003). Matching leadership styles with employment modes: Strategic human resource management perspective. *Human Resource Management Review, 13*(1), 127–152. Doi: 10.1016/S1053-4822(02)00102-X.

Lodgaard, E., Ingvaldsen, J. A., Gamme, I., & Aschehoug, S. (2016). Barriers to lean implementation: Perceptions of top managers, middle managers and workers. *Procedia CIRP, 57*, 595–600. Doi: 10.1016/j.procir.2016.11.103.

Losonci, D., Demeter, K., & Jenei, I. (2011). Factors influencing employee perceptions in lean transformations. *International Journal of Production Economics, 131*(1), 30–43. Doi: 10.1016/j.ijpe.2010.12.022.

Mahbubani, K. (2008). *The New Asian Hemisphere: The Irresistible Shift of Global Power to the East.* New York, NY: Public Affairs.

Mathur, B. P. (2019). Rethinking development: India's cultural ethos as foundation. *Indian Journal of Public Administration, 65*(1), 29–44.

Moher, D., Liberati, A., Tetzlaff, J., & Altman, D. G. (2009). Preferred reporting items for systematic reviews and meta-analyses: The PRISMA statement. *Annals of Internal Medicine, 151*(4), 264–269. Doi: 10.1136/bmj. b2535.

Poksinska, B., Swartling, D., & Drotz, E. (2013). The daily work of lean leaders — lessons from manufacturing and healthcare. *Total Quality Management & Business Excellence, 24*(7-8), 886–898. Doi: 10.1080/ 14783363.2013.791098.

Prashar, A. (2014). Redesigning an assembly line through Lean-Kaizen: An Indian case. *The TQM Journal, 26*(5), 475–498.

Sahyaja, C. H., Rajeshkumar, G., & Sekhararao, K. S. (2018). Role of lean manufacturing leadership on technology transfer in India: A facet of manufacturing industries with reference to Guntur District, Andhra Pradesh. *International Journal of Mechanical and Production Engineering Research and Development, 8*(3), 257–566.

Sen, A. (2005). *The Argumentative Indian: Writings on Indian History, Culture and Identity.* London: Penguin.

Sharma, S. (1996). *Management in New Age: Western Windows and Eastern Doors.* New Delhi: New Age International Publishers.

Sharma, S. (2003). Towards corporate VEDA: Indian ethos and corporate development. *1. Journal of Human Values, 9*(2), 163–172.

Sinha, J. B. P. (1995). *The Cultural Context of Leadership and Power.* New Delhi: Sage.

Sinha, J. B. P. & Kanungo, R. (1997). Context sensitivity and balancing in organizational behaviour. *International Journal of Psychology, 32*, 93–105.

Toledo, J. C., Dominguez Gonzalez, R. V., Lizarelli, F. L., & Pelegrino, R. A. (2019). Lean production system development through leadership practices. *Management Decision, 57*(5), 1184–1203. Doi: 10.1108/MD-08-2017-0748.

Uhl-Bien, M., Riggio, R. E., Lowe, K. B., & Carsten, M. K. (2014). Followership theory: A review and research agenda. *The Leadership Quarterly, 25*(1), 83–104.

Vinodh, S. & Joy, D. (2012). Structural equation modelling of lean manufacturing practices. *International Journal of Production Research, 50*(6), 1598–1607.

Vinodh, S., Selvaraj, T., Kumar, S., & Chintha Vimal, K. E. K. (2015). Development of value stream map for an Indian automotive components manufacturing organization. *Journal of Engineering, Design and Technology, 13*(3), 380–399.

https://doi.org/10.1142/9789811271786_0004

Chapter 4

Blockchain Fragmented Clusters for Advancing HR Saliency: The Case of India

Rukma Ramachandran*, Vimal Babu† and Vijaya Prabhagar Murugesan‡

*Paari School of Business,
SRM University, Amaravati, India*

*rukuma_r@srmap.edu.in

†vimalsairam@gmail.com

‡vijayaprabhagar.m@srmap.edu.in

Abstract

The study aims to review and evaluate the literature on Blockchain Technology (BT) and Human Resource Management (HRM) in businesses. The 6 W-Framework developed by Callahan (2014) is employed for the development of a conceptual framework on BT and HRM. The framework-based clustering of reviews from Indian cases allows researchers to address HRM saliency through the applications of BT. Further, it mitigates the challenges for potential recruiters and HR managers at the workplace. This study focuses on the major HR saliency, i.e. regulation, staffing and development, and change management.

The evolution of this study as a domain-based literature review offers diversified implications for modern organizations in India. Implementation of ledger technology in managerial functions will reduce the time, money and effort required by potential recruiters and HR professionals, advancing HR saliency. Furthermore, the management gains the opportunity to enjoy the tax-free source of the hiring system in Indian organizations.

Introduction

Blockchain technology (BT) is in its infancy period, even though researchers have been developing the concept of blockchain in various contexts (Chatterjee & Chatterjee, 2017). Blockchain began with a demonstration of diffusion of innovation features, particularly in financial services. Later on, the phase got evolved into an adaptable ecosystem that led towards decentralized application. Finally, Directed Acyclic Graph (DAG) gave the third-generation platform for blockchain and transcended the implementation challenges (Jani, 2019).

In India, BT has not yet been accepted widely, especially in the field of management. No firms in India use BT for HR functions (Mishra & Venkatesan, 2021), even though the reports show that it has been implemented in a few sectors. A report says, "56% of Indian businesses are moving towards blockchain technology…" (Malhotra, 2022). The union budget discussion 2021–2022 says, in India, the Finance Bill 2022 is regulating cryptocurrency and digital innovation for the growth in the country. The Cryptocurrency Bill 2021 is also an attempt to validate and legalize the operations of BT in Indian organizations (ASSOCHAM, 2017). Any transaction that happens through a crypto asset cannot be set off or deducted from profits, and losses cannot be carried forward to subsequent years. The bill laid a provision for TDS of 1% on the transfer of crypto assets (Malhotra & Puhan, 2022). In view of this, the Centre of Excellence (COE) for BT was launched for skill and knowledge acquisition. This is focused on interoperability of the BT ecosystem through global coordination. The COE for BT lays the key features of BT as a distributed ledger, with near real-time updates, chronological and time-stamped, cryptographically sealed, programmable, and enforceable contracts (NIC, 2022). States such as Andhra Pradesh, Telangana, Karnataka, West Bengal, Maharashtra, Tamil Nadu, Gujarat, Rajasthan, Uttar Pradesh, Kerala,

Madhya Pradesh, Goa, Delhi and Assam have already adopted technological development via BT (Jani, 2019). From the above studies and reports, it is evident that BT has a future in the finance sector in India, but the current study focuses on the progress of BT in other fields like management, particularly HRM.

The role of BT in HRM is the focus of this study. The current study is conducted after utilizing databases like google scholar, and Australia Business Dean Council (ABDC)-listed journals. Articles were retrieved, including certain peer-reviewed articles on BT. The search was done for keywords "application of blockchain", "adoption of blockchain", "HR saliency", "HR issues and decision-making", "challenges in blockchain", "introduction to blockchain", "blockchain in India" and "regulation in blockchain". The study also concentrates on the literature on the application, benefits and limitations of blockchain, particularly the cases from Indian organizations. This chapter has sections chronologically categorized into BT characteristics, applications of BT in India, diffusion of innovation theory, discussion, limitation and future research, and conclusion.

Review of Literature

In India, BT is gaining traction, especially in the banking, insurance and payment card industries. In order to reap the benefits of BT on a bigger scale, players in most of these industries are teaming together to form a consortium. On the other hand, some conglomerates have expressed an interest in using blockchains to optimize business operations across their subsidiaries and business partners.

In the sectors of trade finance, cross-border payments, bill discounting, supply chain financing, loyalty, and digital identification, many Indian companies have experimented with BT (ASSOCHAM, 2017). Early adopters of BT in India include some Indian banks, conglomerates and stock exchanges. Some of the common and successful literature reviews based on the application of BT in Indian industries are shown in Table 1. The post-adoption of BT is also mentioned in the table. As per the table, in India, blockchains are used for finance, land titling (document management) and crop insurance.

Out of 79 references collected from the implementation of BT in the Indian context, seven published journals were selected. This selection of articles was done on a random basis after excluding other than Indian cases from the total articles, non-published journals and other secondary

Table 1.　Application of BT in India

Application of BT	Challenges before BT Application	After Application of BT	References
Financial Inclusion	Lack of geographical access, high cost, inappropriate product and services, and financial illiteracy	Access through global transactions and mobile applications, lower transaction cost and faster settlement, providing financial history and guarantee transaction	(Schuetz & Venkatesh, 2020)
Land Titling	17 steps in the land registration process and issues such as multiple agencies and their ill-coordination, old and outdated records management, inadequate usage of IT systems, outdated and costly methods of survey, and fraud and corruption	7 simple registration process through blockchain and smart contract execution	(Thakur *et al.*, 2020)
Crop insurance	Challenges like identification of frauds, time-consuming and costly insurance providers, delay in identifying the perpetrator, and lack of transparency in authenticity	Execution of smart contracts via BT smoothening the initialization, registration process, issue and claiming of policy	(Jha *et al.*, 2021)

Banking functions	Traditional banking business models	Improvised banking functions such as digital currency, trade finance, BT in capital markets, supply chain financing, monitoring consortium account, and know your customer (KYC).	(Gupta & Gupta, 2018)
Logistics and Supply Chain Management	Supply chains are challenging due to the complexities in attaining objectives	BT promotes the potentiality of supply chan sustainability, and its role in supporting supply chain agility, trust, protection of Intellectual Property and perishable supply chain.	(Rejeb *et al.*, 2021)
Government	Lack of inefficiency in government departments, transparency, traceability and accountability of public records.	Implementation of BT in areas such a cryptocurrency, e-voting, shared economy, smart contracts, financial and health services, tourism, logistics, and water sustainability	(Verma & Sheel, 2022)
Healthcare	Lack of provision of equitable and efficient delivery of healthcare	Lifetime data of all medical records and proper health programs can be targeted when required	(Dhagarra *et al.*, 2019)

sources. From these, references other than published journal articles and reports were ignored. Articles ranging from 2016–2021 were considered for the study. Different forms of applications were grouped into categories that are listed in the table.

As per Table 1, BT in India is applied in the sectors such as financial inclusion, land titling, crop insurance, banking, healthcare, logistics and supply chain management as well as governmental processes. Financial inclusion, banking and insurance sectors have utilized BT in services such as trade finance, security, secure record-keeping, asset verification, cross-border payment, KYC, digital currency, monitoring consortium, capital markets and supply chain financing. Land titling, registration and other government and legal aids have applied BT in smoothening and simplifying the lengthy procedures by making them simple, with timely approvals. The application of BT in healthcare can lead to proper medical records maintenance and equitable and efficient healthcare delivery.

Research Methodology

The authors collected data that belong to BT and its applications. The Callahan (2014) model is used for research (Callahan, 2014). Stuart Haber and W Scott Stornetta are mathematicians who invented BT in 1991. Relevance and popularity were gained when Satoshi Nakamoto introduced bitcoins in 2008. Literature ranging from 2011 to 2022 has been critically reviewed. The data are collected from secondary sources, including journals, reports, web pages, conference proceedings, and e-books. The Google Scholar database was used to collect scholarly journals. Personal networks such as LinkedIn were utilized to learn more about this technology. In addition to these, the authors searched through relevant journals. Despite blockchains being invented in 1991, their relevance and popularity have been recognized since 2008. Since 2008, several research publications have been introduced in the field of BT. However, the users are still not aware of its applications, working and benefits. The users are facing adaptation challenges. The current study covers the aforesaid gaps.

Discussion

Even though BT has not penetrated the field of management, particularly in India, reports show that in some HR functions such as employee verification and candidate recruitment a few organizations have used it (Jani, 2019). The application of blockchains in the Indian context has already been discussed above. This section discusses HR saliency with HR decision-making operations when a mediating variable, blockchain, is included. This section discusses the theoretical framework of the relation between HR saliency, the decision-making process and HR outcomes, along with an intermediating variable known as the blockchain. Based on the above readings, a conceptual framework with numerous propositions is suggested to maximize the benefits of the blockchain system for decision-making, notably in HRM, as shown in Figure 1. The propositions are categorized under the concepts from pieces of literature on blockchain technology and HRM.

Conceptual framework

Regulation

Disputes are the essence of human behaviour. The behaviour, attitude and responses of individuals differ from other another. And therefore, disputes tend to occur in every business organization (Moffitt, 2005). So, it is likely that the HR managers' role in dispute resolution becomes keen. HR managers and line and operation staff, HR executives, employee representatives, trained mediators, union members, and other HR-related professionals also take turns to participate in the performance above (Saundry & Wibberley, 2014). Few other studies show (Brennan & Rajan, 2020; Khatri & Budhwar, 2002; Moffitt, 2005; Schuler & Jackson, 2001; Taylor, 2011) that dispute resolution is a key HR issue in every organization. Evidence is also available that adopts various models and thematic analyzes for dispute resolution (Bendersky, 2003; PON STAFF, n.d.; Saundry & Wibberley, 2014). Hence, we assume that:

Proposition 1a: Dispute resolution significantly contributes to HR saliency.

One of the reasons for the need for labour regulation is to manage the trustworthiness and validation of workers such as migrants. The verification of employees' backgrounds is mandatory such that the updation of their resumes is also ensured (Caballero *et al.*, 2004). To handle migrant workers, the major issues that arise are recruitment, trafficking and deployment (Christ & Helliar, 2021). In support of their employment, proper saliency should be maintained to enhance discipline in the organizational work environment (Doepke & Zilibotti, 2005). And this can be attained with proper labour regulation. Hence, we assume that:

Proposition 1b: Labour regulation significantly contributes to HR saliency.

Top management develops strategies and policies to achieve corporate goals and objectives (Pratik, n.d.; Taylor, 2011). The HR department will also develop subsidiary policies and plans for the company's personnel. Framing of these practices plays an important role. When the quality of the data available is low, such a decision-making process becomes more complicated. As a result, HR experts will find it more challenging to develop organizational policy and strategy (Casino *et al.*, 2019). Hence, we assume that:

Proposition 1c: Policy and strategy regulation significantly contribute to HR saliency.

Staffing and development

The most expensive HR process to date is recruitment and selection. Managers have a lot on their plates when it comes to recruitment (Bejtkovský *et al.*, 2018; Christ & Helliar, 2021). Being a salient function, the issue arises when there is no other option. Recruitment and selection are critical for the organization because the correct individual must be assigned to the proper job to achieve the intended results (Herschberg *et al.*, 2018). Hence, we assume that:

Proposition 2a: Recruitment and selection are positively related to HR saliency.

It can be difficult to determine the appropriate compensation for employees at times. Compensation becomes salient in managing employees (Aral *et al.*, 2012). Employees might be positively motivated by the remuneration and advantages provided by the company. Employees are financially motivated by compensation and benefits. As a result, HR experts must determine the appropriate monetary package for employees. Hence, we assume that:

Proposition 2b: Compensation and benefits are positively related to HR saliency.

Employees must be trained after the company has hired them. During the beginning stages, training and induction are provided. Giving training and induction becomes part of every organization's standard operating procedure. Trainers usually have a training module for this purpose (Jain *et al.*, 2021; Sun & Pan, 2008; Tsvetkova, 2017). It is salient to update these training modules. Because as the business's technology environment changes, so will the business's operations. Individual differences in learning capacity are also a significant factor in the shift in training modules (Prager *et al.*, 2021). Employees should be provided with training and development not only at the start of their job but also throughout their time with the company. Leadership development and executive development also enhance smooth performance in the organization to achieve the goals effectively and efficiently (Bian *et al.*, 2018). Hence, we assume that:

Proposition 2d: Training and development are positively related to HR saliency.

Workplace competency can be attained in any business's work environment. The competitive edge would boost the organization's production (McCartney *et al.*, 2020). Therefore, HR professionals must deal with the development of workplace capability. Hence, we assume that:

Proposition 2e: Workforce competency is positively related to HR saliency.

Change management

In an organization, management change or change management is nothing more than planning for a specific change in policy, legislation, software, culture or practice (Hanson, 2010). The normal culture for managing any change in management is to unfreeze, change and refreeze. This entails unfreezing present practices, modifying or transforming them into new ones, and then refreezing or fixing the new procedures in place for the organization's current and future activities.

In the fast-changing technical world, managers must be able to keep up with the latest technologies or risk losing the race (Marsal-Llacuna, 2018; Sivasankaran & Suganya, 2021). It's also true that keeping up with the latest technology takes a lot of time, money and effort. As a result, software compliance becomes a problem for the entire company. Hence, we assume that:

Proposition 3a: Software compliance positively influences the HR saliency.

Policy and strategy can alter an organization's routine procedures and practices (Mishra & Venkatesan, 2021). Time is also required for this adjustment to permeate the business's daily activities. Organizational culture is another term for this shift (John-Pierre Maeli, 2016). Because it includes the integration of facts from across the business, changing corporate culture is a challenging undertaking. Hence, we assume that:

Proposition 3b: Organizational culture influences the HR saliency.

Blockchain in HRM

BT has the potential to be disruptive (Bunduchi *et al.*, 2021). Curriculum vitae verification, database preparation for hiring employees, data for money approach, digital integration, service record maintenance, payroll management, workflow management and personnel administration are all examples of blockchain uses in HR (Fachrunnisa & Hussain, 2020; Koncheva *et al.*, 2019). In India, BT has been used in HR for employee verification and candidate recruitment only (Jani, 2019). The current study lays down a roadmap for the Indian organizations to adapt BT in managerial functions, particularly HR functions. If all of these operations can be contained within just a few blocks of a virtual network, this technology will undoubtedly be disruptive. There is a matter of contention over its applications and adoption (Chen *et al.*, 2021; Lowry, 2006; Alamelu *et al.*, 2017). BT offers *transparency* throughout the network by making the nodes share the records, thereby making it an open-source and data-transparent architecture. *Credibility* and *inclusion* are ensured by the privacy and security offered by BT through an encrypted server.

The current research focuses on how BT can help with data management and decision-making. Hence, we assume that:

Proposition 4: BT in HRM has a significantly positive mediating role between HR saliency and HR decision-making, in terms of transparency, credibility and inclusion.

HR decision-making and HR outcomes

One of the most crucial functions of management in a company is decision-making. Decisions are the lifeblood of management since they have such a significant impact on all of the organization's actions and outcomes (Lowry, 2006). Decision-making is done by measuring and predicting the profit and loss outcomes from the decisions (Abubakar *et al.*, 2019). To respond to the data accessible in the business environment, a decision-making process is required. Out of these alternatives, one best course of action is selected. Without alternatives, no decision-making is possible (Walger *et al.*, 2016). Even though these alternatives are enlisted to achieve organizational goals, one that ensures maximum benefit with minimum effort is selected. The responsibility relies on the part of in taking decision. The point of making a decision is to achieve effectiveness and efficiency in performance and, thereby, the goals of the organization (Sharma *et al.*, 2014). Therefore, the process of decision-making is considered a sensitive step of action that should be taken to reach desired outcomes.

The decision-making process is, directly and indirectly, related to cost and time. Some dependent variables of cost and time affect the process of decision-making. These variables are the order of decision-making, availability of time and cost in decision-making, and actual utilization of time and cost elements (Kim *et al.*, 2020). All these variables are integrated and give positive results using BT. Hence, we assume that:

Proposition 5a: HR decision-making is positively related to time and cost.

Many crucial decisions based on new facts are involved in digital transformation (Bejtkovský *et al.*, 2018), including rethinking old manufacturing and production processes, verifying new processes, and evaluating technologies (Laydon, 2019). It can feel like you're managing multiple objects at the same time. The obvious factors include choosing the optimal course of action while assessing and mitigating risks (Korpela *et al.*, 2017; Zhang *et al.*, 2019). The human resource is just as important in a transitioning organization since many people are likely to react with fear and suspicion. Hence, we assume that:

Proposition 5b: HR decision-making is positively related to digitalization and decentralization.

Effectiveness and efficiency are two phrases that have a lot to do with a business. Every firm must achieve its predetermined goals and objectives while focusing on its ability to continuously maintain its survival and profitability (Jain *et al.*, 2021). The effectiveness and efficiency of this process are quite important. On the one hand, a firm can greatly improve its level based on these two criteria; on the other hand, it might suffer losses if the results are not related to effectiveness and efficiency. As a result, a company's effectiveness and efficiency must be maintained at all times. Hence, we assume that:

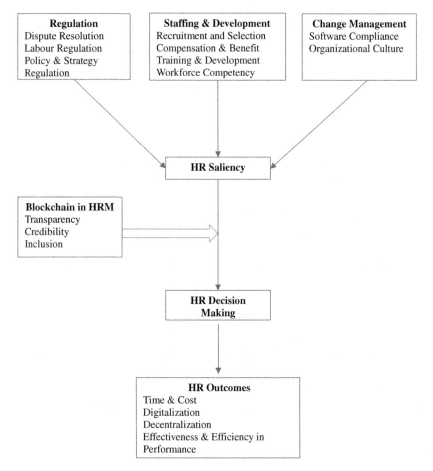

Figure 1.   The Proposed Conceptual Model

Proposition 5c: HR decision-making is positively related to effectiveness and efficiency in performance.

Limitations and Future Scope

Penetration of BT in the India organization might prove disruptive. Hence, the future scope of the study can be taken for the utilization of BT in other fields of management. Studies can be taken to include BT in interdisciplinary studies of HR such as HR analytics. The current study laid a qualitative platform only. There lies much future scope in studying the implementing and testing of the conceptual model in the HR department for any top-level management of an organization. However, in India, BT has not penetrated HRM functions, and hence it has become a limitation for gathering suitable reviews in this field of study. Future researchers can work on the empirical study in the field of BT for HR saliency. Implementation and execution of blockchains in managerial functions such as HRM, marketing, supply chain management, and logistics, can become areas for future scope of research. Review papers on the adoption of block-chains in the Indian context can also serve the purpose of future research.

Conclusion

A holistic approach towards the adoption of BT in India is highlighted in this study. The emergence of blockchains in the legal framework of the Indian economy has smoothened the penetration of BT into certain sectors like insurance, finance, banking, governance and healthcare. Blockchain was a novel approach for analyzing and solving complex decision-making challenges in any firm. The growth of BT in India is not as fast as the pace of the development of this technology globally. Only a handful of start-ups have emerged in India with the potential to change the Indian working ecosystem. The recent study sources the guidelines for implementing blockchain innovation in the field of HRM via smart contracts and block-chains. The existence and development of regulation, validation and legalization of BT in India will be a milestone for the upcoming sectors with the role of mediating blockchains. When clusters are fragmented by language, geography, culture and legacies, blockchain still has the potential to integrate into the Indian context.

References

Abubakar, A. M., Elrehail, H., Alatailat, M. A., & Elçi, A. (2019). Knowledge management, decision-making style and organizational performance. *Journal of Innovation & Knowledge, 4*(2), 104–114. Doi: 10.1016/j.jik.2017.07.003.

Alamelu, R., Nalini, R., Cresenta Shakila Motha, L., Amudha, R., & Bowiya, S. (2017). Adoption factors impacting human resource analytics among employees. *International Journal of Economic Research, 14*(6), 417–423.

Alharby, M., Aldweesh, A., & Van Moorsel, A. (2018, November). Blockchain-based smart contracts: A systematic mapping study of academic research (2018). In *2018 International Conference on Cloud Computing, Big Data and Blockchain (ICCBB)*, pp. 1–6. IEEE: Fuzhou, China.

Alharby, M. & van Moorsel, A. (2017). *Blockchain-based Smart Contracts: A Systematic Mapping Study*. Doi: 10.5121/csit.2017.71011.

Ali, O., Ally, M., Clutterbuck, & Dwivedi, Y. (2020). The state of play of blockchain technology in the financial services sector: A systematic literature review. *International Journal of Information Management, 54*, 102199. Doi: 10.1016/j.ijinfomgt.2020.102199.

Allam, Z. (2018). On smart contracts and organizational performance: A review of smart contracts through the blockchain technology. *Review of Economic and Business Studies, 11*(2), 137–156. Doi: 10.1515/rebs-2018-0079.

Aral, S., Brynjolfsson, E., & Wu, L. (2012). Three-way complementarities: Performance pay, human resource analytics, and information technology. *Management Science, 58*(5), 913–931. Doi: 10.1287/mnsc.1110.1460.

ASSOCHAM. (2017). *Blockchain Technology in India Opportunities and Challenges*. 2nd Global Summit, Bengaluru, India.

Bejtkovský, J., Rózsa, Z., & Mulyaningsih, H. D. (2018). A phenomenon of digitalization and E-recruitment in business environment. *Polish Journal of Management Studies, 18*(1), 58–68. Doi: 10.17512/pjms.2018.18.1.05.

Bendersky, C. (2003). Organizational dispute resolution systems: A complementarities model. *Academy of Management Review, 28*(4), 643–656. Doi: 10.5465/amr.2003.10899444.

Bernal Bernabe, J., Canovas, J. L., Hernandez-Ramos, J. L., Torres Moreno, R., & Skarmeta, A. (2019). Privacy-preserving solutions for blockchain: Review and challenges. *IEEE Access, 7*, 164908–164940. Doi: 10.1109/ACCESS.2019.2950872.

Bhaskar, P., Tiwari, C. K., & Joshi, A. (2021). Blockchain in education management: Present and future applications. *Interactive Technology and Smart Education, 18*(1), 1–17. Doi: 10.1108/ITSE-07-2020-0102.

Bian, Y., Mu, W., Leon Zhao, J., & Leon, J. (2018). Association for information systems AIS Electronic Library (AISeL) online leadership for open source project success: Evidence from the GitHub blockchain projects recommended citation. https://aisel.aisnet.org/pacis2018/189.

Böhme, R., Christin, N., Edelman, B., & Moore, T. (2015). Bitcoin: Economics, technology, and governance. *Journal of Economic Perspectives*, *29*(2), 213–238. Doi: 10.1257/jep.29.2.213.

Bonsón, E. & Bednárová, M. (2019). Blockchain and its implications for accounting and auditing. *Meditari Accountancy Research*, *27*(5), 725–740. Doi: 10.1108/MEDAR-11-2018-0406.

Brennan, M. P. & Rajan, N. (2020). HR issues: Sexual harassment, workplace diversity, cultural sensitivity, privileging, credentialing, denying privileges, difficult conversations. In *Manual of Practice Management for Ambulatory Surgery Centers*, pp. 239–252. Springer Nature, Switzerland AG. Doi: 10.1007/978-3-030-19171-9_16.

Bunduchi, R., Tursunbayeva, A., & Pagliari, C. (2021). Legitimizing disruptive technology: The case of blockchain in the human resources sector. In *Transforming Human Resource Functions With Automation*, IGI Global, pp. 1–19.

Caballero, R., Cowan, K., Engel, E. M. R. A., & Micco, A. (2004). Effective labor regulation and microeconomic flexibility, *Working Paper 10744, National Bureau of Economic Research*, Cambridge, MT. Doi: 10.3386/w10744.

Callahan, J. L. (2014). Writing literature reviews. *Human Resource Development Review*, *13*(3), 271–275. Doi: 10.1177/1534484314536705.

Casino, F., Dasaklis, T. K., & Patsakis, C. (2019). A systematic literature review of blockchain-based applications: Current status, classification and open issues. *Telematics and Informatics*, *36*, 55–81. Doi: 10.1016/j.tele.2018.11.006.

Chatterjee, R. & Chatterjee, R. (2017). An overview of the emerging technology: Blockchain. *2017 3rd International Conference on Computational Intelligence and Networks (CINE)*, pp. 126–127. Doi: 10.1109/CINE.2017.33.

Chen, S., Liu, X., Yan, J., Hu, G., & Shi, Y. (2021). Processes, benefits, and challenges for adoption of blockchain technologies in food supply chains: A thematic analysis. *Information Systems and E-Business Management*, *19*(3), 909–935. Doi: 10.1007/s10257-020-00467-3.

Chillakuri, B. & Attili, V. S. P. (2021). Role of blockchain in HR's response to new-normal. *International Journal of Organizational Analysis*, ahead-of-print(ahead-of-print). Doi: 10.1108/IJOA-08-2020-2363.

Cho, S. & Lee, S. (2019). Survey on the application of blockchain to IoT. *2019 International Conference on Electronics, Information, and Communication (ICEIC)*, pp. 1–2. Doi: 10.23919/ELINFOCOM.2019.8706369.

Christ, K. L. & Helliar, C. V. (2021). Blockchain technology and modern slavery: Reducing deceptive recruitment in migrant worker populations. *Journal of Business Research*, *131*, 112–120. Doi: 10.1016/j.jbusres.2021.03.065.

Christidis, K. & Devetsikiotis, M. (2016). Blockchains and smart contracts for the Internet of Things. In *IEEE Access*, Vol. 4, pp. 2292–2303. Institute of Electrical and Electronics Engineers Inc. Doi: 10.1109/ACCESS. 2016.2566339.

Dhagarra, D., Goswami, M., Sarma, P. R. S., & Choudhury, A. (2019). Big Data and blockchain supported conceptual model for enhanced healthcare coverage. *Business Process Management Journal*. BPMJ-06-2018-0164. Doi: 10.1108/BPMJ-06-2018-0164.

Dobrovnik, M., Herold, D., Fürst, E., & Kummer, S. (2018). Blockchain for and in logistics: What to adopt and where to start. *Logistics*, *2*(3), 18. Doi: 10.3390/logistics2030018.

Doepke, M. & Zilibotti, F. (2005). The macroeconomics of child labor regulation. *American Economic Review*, *95*(5), 1492–1524. Doi: 10.1257/000282805775014425.

Dolata, M., Kilic, M., & Schwabe, G. (2019, January). When a computer speaks institutional talk: Exploring challenges and potentials of virtual assistants in face-to-face advisory services. Hawaii International Conference on System Sciences (HICSS), Hawaii.

Fachrunnisa, O. & Hussain, F. K. (2020). Blockchain-based human resource management practices for mitigating skills and competencies gap in workforce. *International Journal of Engineering Business Management*, *12*, 184797902096640. Doi: 10.1177/1847979020966400.

Filimonau, V. & Naumova, E. (2020). The blockchain technology and the scope of its application in hospitality operations. *International Journal of Hospitality Management*, *87*, 102383. Doi: 10.1016/j.ijhm.2019.102383.

Francisco, K. & Swanson, D. (2018). The supply chain has no clothes: Technology adoption of blockchain for supply chain transparency. *Logistics*, *2*(1), 2. Doi: 10.3390/logistics2010002.

Gligor, D. M., Pillai, K. G., & Golgeci, I. (2021). Theorizing the dark side of business-to-business relationships in the era of AI, Big Data, and blockchain. *Journal of Business Research*, *133*, 79–88. Doi: 10.1016/j.jbusres.2021.04.043.

Gupta, A. & Gupta, S. (2018). Blockchain technology: Application in Indian banking sector. *Delhi Business Review*, *19*(2), 75–84. https://www.delhibusinessreview.org/V19n2/dbr_V19n2g.pdf.

Hanson, S. (2010). 10_14_13_Change_management_and_organizational_ effectiveness. *Cornell HR Review*.

Hanson, S. (2013). Change management and organizational effectiveness for the HR professional, Cornell HR Review. https://hdl.handle.net/1813/72938.

Hegadekatti, K. (2018). Blockchain and human resources management. *SSRN Electronic Journal*. Doi: 10.2139/ssrn.3232203.

Herschberg, C., Benschop, Y., & van den Brink, M. (2018). Precarious postdocs: A comparative study on recruitment and selection of early-career researchers. *Scandinavian Journal of Management, 34*(4), 303–310. Doi: 10.1016/j.scaman.2018.10.001.

Holub, M. & Johnson, J. (2018). Bitcoin research across disciplines. *Information Society, 34*(2), 114–126. Doi: 10.1080/01972243.2017.1414094.

Hughes, L., Dwivedi, Y. K., Misra, S. K., Rana, N. P., Raghavan, V., & Akella, V. (2019). Blockchain research, practice and policy: Applications, benefits, limitations, emerging research themes and research agenda. *International Journal of Information Management, 49*, 114–129. Doi: 10.1016/j.ijinfomgt. 2019.02.005.

Iansiti M. & Lakhani, K. R. (2017). The truth about blockchain. *Harvard Business Review, 95*(1), 118–127.

Jain, G., Sharma, N., & Shrivastava, A. (2021). Enhancing training effectiveness for organizations through blockchain-enabled training effectiveness measurement (BETEM). *Journal of Organizational Change Management, 34*(2), 439–461. Doi: 10.1108/JOCM-10-2020-0303.

Jani, S. (2019). *The Emergence of Blockchain Technology & Its Adoption in India*, Institute of Electrical and Electronics Engineers (IEEE), Doi: 10.13140/RG.2.2.30997.58087.

Jani, S. & Shah, T. (2018). *Applications of Blockchain Technology in Banking & Finance*. Doi: 10.13140/RG.2.2.35237.96489.

Janssen, M., Weerakkody, V., Ismagilova, E., Sivarajah, U., & Irani, Z. (2020). A framework for analysing blockchain technology adoption: Integrating institutional, market and technical factors. *International Journal of Information Management, 50*, 302–309. Doi: 10.1016/j.ijinfomgt.2019.08.012.

Java. (2021). History of blockchain. *JavaTPoint*. https://www.javatpoint.com/ history-of-blockchain.

Jesus, E. F., Chicarino, V. R. L., de Albuquerque, C. V. N., & Rocha, A. A. de A. (2018). A survey of how to use blockchain to secure Internet of Things and the stalker attack. *Security and Communication Networks, 2018*, 1–27. Doi: 10.1155/2018/9675050.

Jha, N., Prashar, D., Khalaf, O. I., Alotaibi, Y., Alsufyani, A., & Alghamdi, S. (2021). Blockchain based crop insurance: A decentralized insurance system for modernization of Indian farmers. *Sustainability, 13*(16), 8921. Doi: 10.3390/su13168921.

John-Pierre, M. (2016). The Rogers adoption curve & how you spread new ideas throughout culture. https://medium.com/the-political-informer/ the-rogers-adoption-curve-how-you-spread-new-ideas-throughout-culture-d848462fcd24.

Karanjia, B., Lakshman, S., & Goswami, S. (2017). *Blockchain technology in India: Opportunities and challenges*. Associated Chambers of Commerce and Industry of India, pp. 1–8.

Khatri, N. & Budhwar, P. S. (2002). A study of strategic HR issues in an Asian context. *Personnel Review, 31*(2), 166–188. Doi: 10.1108/00483480210416856.

Kim, K., Lee, G., & Kim, S. (2020). A study on the application of blockchain technology in the construction industry. *KSCE Journal of Civil Engineering, 24*(9), 2561–2571. Doi: 10.1007/s12205-020-0188-x.

Koncheva, V. A., Odintsov, S. V., & Khmelnitski, L. (2019, December). Blockchain in HR. In *International Scientific and Practical Conference on Digital Economy (ISCDE 2019)*, pp. 504–507. Atlantis Press.

Korpela, K., Hallikas, J., & Dahlberg, T. (2017). *Digital Supply Chain Transformation toward Blockchain Integration*. Doi: 10.24251/HICSS. 2017.506.

Laurence, T. (2017). *Blockchain for Dummies*. John Wiley & Sons.

Laydon, B. (2019, December). *Digitalization and decision making*. International Society of Automation, NC, USA. https://www.isa.org/intech-home/2019/november-december/columns/digitalization-and-decision-making.

Leon Zhao, J., Fan, S., & Yan, J. (2017). Erratum to: Overview of business innovations and research opportunities in blockchain and introduction to the special issue. *Financial Innovation, 3*(1), 9. Doi: 10.1186/s40854-017-0059-8.

Lowry, D. (2006). HR managers as ethical decision-makers: Mapping the terrain. *Asia Pacific Journal of Human Resources, 44*(2), 171–183. Doi: 10.1177/1038411106066394.

Malhotra, A. (2022, February 14). The rise of blockchain in India and its future. *Analytics Insight*. https://www.analyticsinsight.net/the-rise-of-blockchain-in-india-and-its-future/#:~:text=56%25%20of%20Indian%20businesses%20are,blockchain%20ecosystem%20around%20the%20nation.

Malhotra, A. & Puhan, B. (2022, April 1). Taxation, legality of cryptocurrency in India 1 April 2022. *Asia Business Law Journal*. https://law.asia/taxation-legality-cryptocurrency-india/.

Marsal-Llacuna, M.-L. (2018). Future living framework: Is blockchain the next enabling network? *Technological Forecasting and Social Change, 128*, 226–234. Doi: 10.1016/j.techfore.2017.12.005.

McCartney, S., Murphy, C., & Mccarthy, J. (2020). 21st century HR: A competency model for the emerging role of HR Analysts. *Personnel Review, 50*(6), 1495–1513. Doi: 10.1108/PR-12-2019-0670.

Mishra, H. & Venkatesan, M. (2021). Blockchain in human resource management of organizations: An empirical assessment to gauge HR and non-HR perspective. *Journal of Organizational Change Management, 34*(2), 525–542. Doi: 10.1108/JOCM-08-2020-0261.

Moffitt, M. L. & Bordone, R. C. (eds.). (2005). *The Handbook of Dispute Resolution*. Harvard Law School.

Moffitt, M. L., & Bordone, R. C. (eds.). (2012). *The Handbook of Dispute Resolution*. John Wiley & Sons, NJ.

Muhr, J., & Laurence, T. (2017). *Blockchain fur Dummies*. John Wiley & Sons, NJ.

Nakamoto, S. (n.d.). Bitcoin: A peer-to-peer electronic cash system. www.bitcoin.org.

NIC. (2022, March 31). Centre of excellence for blockchain technology. MeitY-Government of India. https://www.nic.in/blockchain/.

Olivas-Lujan, M. R. (2019). *Blockchains 2019 in e-HRM: Hit or Hype?* (pp. 117–139). Doi: 10.1108/S1877-636120190000023010.

Pal, A., Tiwari, C. K., & Haldar, N. (2021). Blockchain for business management: Applications, challenges and potentials. *The Journal of High Technology Management Research*, 32(2), 100414. Doi: 10.1016/j.hitech.2021.100414.

Pichlak, M. (2016). The innovation adoption process: A multidimensional approach. *Journal of Management & Organization*, 22(4), 476–494. Doi: 10.1017/jmo.2015.52.

PON STAFF. (n.d.). What are the three basic types of dispute resolution? What to know about mediation, arbitration, and litigation. Retrieved October 10, 2022, from https://www.pon.harvard.edu/daily/dispute-resolution/what-are-the-three-basic-types-of-dispute-resolution-what-to-know-about-mediation-arbitration-and-litigation/.

Prager, F., Martinez, J., & Cagle, C. (2021). Blockchain and regional workforce development: Identifying opportunities and training needs. In *Blockchain and the Public Sector*, pp. 47–72. Springer, Cham.

Pratik. (n.d.). HR analytics & HR strategy improvisations from an HR practitioner's POV — Why high performers leave the organization? Retrieved May 8, 2022, from https://thebrew.in/hr-analytics-hr-practitioner-pov-declutter/.

Rejeb, A., Rejeb, K., Simske, S., & Treiblmaier, H. (2021). Blockchain technologies in logistics and supply chain management: A bibliometric review. *Logistics*, 5(4), 72. Doi: 10.3390/logistics5040072.

Reyna, A., Martín, C., Chen, J., Soler, E., & Díaz, M. (2018). On blockchain and its integration with IoT. Challenges and opportunities. *Future Generation Computer Systems*, 88, 173–190. Doi: 10.1016/j.future.2018.05.046.

Rogers, E. (2007). Everett M. Rogers — Diffusion of innovations and more. https://nhokanson.wordpress.com/2007/07/12/everett-m-rogers-diffusion-of-innovations-and-more/.

Romano, D. & Schmid, G. (2017). Beyond bitcoin: A critical look at blockchain-based systems. *Cryptography*, 1(2), 15. Doi: 10.3390/cryptography 1020015.

Russell, C. and Bennett, N. (2015). Big data and talent management: Using hard data to make the soft stuff easy, *Business Horizons*, 58(3), 237–242. https://doi.org/10.1016/j.bushor.2014.08.001.

Salah, D., Ahmed, M. H., & Eldahshan, K. (2020). Blockchain applications in human resources management: Opportunities and challenges. *ACM International Conference Proceeding Series.* pp. 383–389. Doi: 10.1145/3383219.3383274.

Saundry, R. A. & Wibberley, G. (2014). *Workplace Dispute Resolution and the Management of Individual Conflict — A Thematic Analysis of Five Case Studies.*

Schuetz, S. & Venkatesh, V. (2020). Blockchain, adoption, and financial inclusion in India: Research opportunities. *International Journal of Information Management, 52,* 101936. Doi: 10.1016/j.ijinfomgt.2019.04.009.

Schuler, R. & Jackson, S. (2001). HR issues and activities in mergers and acquisitions. *European Management Journal, 19*(3), 239–253. Doi: 10.1016/S0263-2373(01)00021-4.

Schulte, S., Sigwart, M., Frauenthaler, P., & Borkowski, M. (2019). *Towards Blockchain Interoperability* (pp. 3–10). Doi: 10.1007/978-3-030-30429-4_1.

Sharma, R., Mithas, S., & Kankanhalli, A. (2014). Transforming decision-making processes: A research agenda for understanding the impact of business analytics on organisations. *European Journal of Information Systems, 23*(4), 433–441. Doi: 10.1057/ejis.2014.17.

Shrier, D., Wu, W., & Pentland, A. (2016). *Blockchain & Infrastructure (Identity, Data Security).*

Shukla, M., Lin, J., & Seneviratne, O. (2021). *BlockIoT: Blockchain-based Health Data Integration using IoT Devices.*

Sivasankaran, M. S., & Suganya, T. (2021, May). Full fledged automated human resource management software suite. In *Journal of Physics: Conference Series*, Vol. 1916, No. 1, p. 012163. IOP Publishing.

Sun, L. Y. & Pan, W. (2008). HR practices perceptions, emotional exhaustion, and work outcomes: A conservation-of-resources theory in the Chinese context. *Human Resource Development Quarterly, 19*(1), 55–74. Doi: 10.1002/hrdq.1225.

Tan, T. M. & Salo, J. (2021). Ethical marketing in the blockchain-based sharing economy: Theoretical integration and guiding insights. *Journal of Business Ethics,* 1–28.

Taylor, S. (2011). *Contemporary Issues in Human Resource Management.* Kogan Page Publishers, London.

Thakur, V., Doja, M. N., Dwivedi, Y. K., Ahmad, T., & Khadanga, G. (2020). Land records on Blockchain for implementation of Land Titling in India. *International Journal of Information Management, 52,* 101940. Doi: 10.1016/j.ijinfomgt.2019.04.013.

Tsvetkova, L. A. (2017). Prospects of development of blockchain technology in Russia: Competitive advantages and barriers. *The Economics of Science, 3*(4), 275–296. Doi: 10.22394/2410-132X-2017-3-4-275-296.

Verma, S. & Sheel, A. (2022). Blockchain for government organizations: Past, present and future. *Journal of Global Operations and Strategic Sourcing.* Doi: 10.1108/JGOSS-08-2021-0063.

Walger, C., Roglio, K. D. D., & Abib, G. (2016). HR managers' decision-making processes: A "reflective practice" analysis. *Management Research Review,* *39*(6), 655–671. Doi: 10.1108/MRR-11-2014-0250.

Wang, H., Ma, S., Dai, H.-N., Imran, M., & Wang, T. (2020). Blockchain-based data privacy management with Nudge theory in open banking. *Future Generation Computer Systems, 110,* 812–823. Doi: 10.1016/j.future.2019.09.010.

WEF, W. E. F. (2020). *Bridging the Governance Gap: Interoperability for Blockchain and Legacy Systems.*

Yaga, D., Mell, P., Roby, N., & Scarfone, K. (2019). *Blockchain Technology Overview.* Doi: 10.6028/NIST.IR.8202.

Yiannas, F. (2018). A new era of food transparency powered by blockchain. *Innovations: Technology, Governance, Globalization, 12*(1–2), 46–56. Doi: 10.1162/inov_a_00266.

Zhang, H., Zhang, G., & Yan, Q. (2019). Digital twin-driven cyber-physical production system towards smart shop-floor. *Journal of Ambient Intelligence and Humanized Computing, 10*(11), 4439–4453. Doi: 10.1007/s12652-018-1125-4.

Part II

The Stakeholder Approach

Chapter 5

Technology-Enabled Future of School Education: Policy Priorities and Economic Models for Rural India

Neelakshi Saini[*] and Shanker Prakash[†]

Chandigarh University, Chandigarh, India

[*]neelakshi_saini@rediffmail.com

[†]shanker.e10381@cumail.in

Abstract

Information and Technology Communication (ICT) is a blessing for students in the education sector. The education sector is facing many challenges due to the COVID-19 pandemic. Even as the urban areas have progressed rapidly in use of technology for online classes and work for home, in rural areas there are barriers despite the interest of the teachers and students to accept the new technology. For example, poor network connectivity, electricity problems or low income to afford these facilities. In this chapter, we discuss the overview of the education system in India, the importance of ICT and challenges faced by ICT in India and what national policies are on ICT in school education.

Introduction

India is a developing country and most of the population of India is living in rural India. According to the Indian Constitution Act, 2009, compulsory and free education is compulsory for the age group of 6–14 years. In 2005–2006 83.13% of schools offering elementary education (Grades 1–8) were managed by the government and 16.86% of schools were under private management (excluding children in unrecognized schools, schools established under the Education Guarantee Scheme and in alternative learning centres). Of those schools managed privately, one-third are "aided" and two-thirds are "unaided". Enrolment in Grades 1–8 is shared between government and privately managed schools in the ratio 73:27. However, in rural areas this ratio is higher (80:20) and in urban areas much lower (36:66) (Little & Lewin, 2011). In the 2011 Census, about 73% of the population were literate, of which 81% are male and 65% are female. The National Statistical Commission surveyed literacy to be 77.7% in 2017–2018, of which 84.7% are male and 70.3% are female (National Statistical Commission, 2018).

Much of the progress, especially in higher education and scientific research, has been credited to various public institutions. Enrolment in higher education has increased steadily over the past decade, reaching a Gross Enrolment Ratio (GER) of 26.3% in 2019 ("All India Survey on Higher Education", 2018–2019). As per the Annual Status of Education Report (ASER) 2012, 96.5% of all rural children between the ages of 6–14 were enrolled in school. This is the fourth annual survey to report enrolment above 96%. India has maintained an average enrolment ratio of 95% for students in this age group from year 2007 to 2014. As an outcome the number of students in the age group 6–14 who are not enrolled in school has come down to 2.8% in the academic year 2018 (Annual Status of Education Report, 2018). In January 2019, India had over 900 universities and 40,000 colleges. Information and Communication Technology (ICT) is one of the rapidly developing technological fields in global society (Siemen, 2007). Central and State Governments and NGOs are allocating huge amounts for the development of ICT and rural education. However the level of improvement in accessibility of ICT in rural schools did not reached the expected level ("ICT Enabled Rural Education in India", 2012). As its name suggests, ICT consists of tools that handle information and produce, store and disseminate information. ICT comprises of both old and new tools. Old tools include radio, TV, Telephone. New tools comprise computers, satellites, the Internet and wireless technology (Kaur, 2021).

Importance of ICT in Education

Easy to access

The spread of ICT has made it easily accessible anywhere. During COVID-19, the students and teachers learnt in innovative ways through ICT. ICT make it possible in every area of the country, especially in rural areas, for children to continue to receive education and learn new things. The popularity of ICT has increased since the outbreak of the pandemic.

Online learning

During the pandemic, everyone was sitting in the homes and through different tools like Zoom, Google Meet, and Microsoft Teams, students could easily access and benefit from online education from their teachers.

Enhance skill development

As a result of ICT, it is now possible for everyone to enhance their skills by sitting anywhere in any parts of the globe. It also promotes high-level thinking and everyone can now solve any problem in different ways.

ICT is a part of the curriculum

Now ICT plays a very important role in the life of all human beings and it is an important part of education. Now every school's authorities are make it a compulsory part of the curriculum.

Improves ICT literacy

A few years ago, very few people were aware of ICT and its advantages. Now, after it has been included as a part of curriculum, ICT literacy rate has improved.

Challenges of ICT in Rural Areas

Poverty

In India, many people still have to work very hard for their daily earnings. To provide them with internet connectivity is a big challenge because they don't even have mobiles to access the Internet.

Lack of infrastructure

In villages, there is a lack of infrastructure like electricity and poor installation of Internet towers. Without them, communication cannot be possible from both sides.

Illiteracy

The literacy rate in the villages is very low as compared to urban areas because these people are less aware about the new things which are happening around them.

Technical literacy

Due to low literacy levels, people also have low technical literacy. They have no awareness about Internet, technology and what the uses of technology are in education. The government has launched many projects, but in rural areas people are least interested in this type of technology adoption.

Costly

India is a developing country where poor people still struggle to earn their livelihood. For them to utilize internet connectivity is a big challenge because they do not even have mobiles with which to access the internet.

Adopting new things is a big challenge

It is human nature that people do not accept new things at once. They are happy with their existing situations and do not want to learn new things because that needs more time and effort.

Language barrier

The language barrier is also a big challenge in remote areas. People cannot even read and write their own regional language properly, so how is it possible for them to understand English? This is the reason technology is useless to them.

National Policies on ICT in School Education

High level policy guidelines are made to prepare the Indian young for future challenges.

ICT literacy and competency enhancement

This policy defines ICT on the basis of levels. A student or teacher is introduced to ICT on the basis of stage of schooling. These levels may be changed according to the change of technology from time to time.

Stage 1: Basic

In the basic level, the basics of computers and use of tools and techniques, how to operate a computer and manage, store and retrieve data are taught. Basics also include input and output devices and data processing tasks; connecting to the Internet; using e-mail and web surfing; using search engines; keeping the computer updated and secure; operating and managing content from external devices (sound recorders, digital cameras, scanners, etc.); connecting, disconnecting, operating and troubleshooting digital devices.

Stage 2: Intermediate

Create and manage content using a variety of software applications and digital devices; using web sites and search engines to locate, retrieve and manage content, tools and resources; install, uninstall and troubleshoot simple software applications, etc.

Stage 3: Advanced

Use different software applications to enhance one's learning — database applications, analysis of data and problem solving, computing, design, graphical and audio–visual communication; undertake research and carry out projects using web resources; use ICT for documentation and presentation; create and participate in web-based networks for cooperative and collaborative learning; become aware of issues of cyber security, copyright and safe use of ICT and take necessary steps to protect oneself and one's ICT resources.

ICT curriculum for teachers

A model curriculum for ICT in Education (CICT) will be developed at the National Level and states will be encouraged to adopt/adapt it.

States will develop an ICT literacy curriculum and appropriate course materials mapped to the stages mentioned above for uniformity. These will be in the form of self-instructional materials, enabling students and teachers to process them on their own. The ICT literacy programme will endeavour to provide a broad set of generic skills and conceptual knowledge and not focus on mastering the use of specific software applications.

The Boards of Secondary Education will develop a suitable scheme of evaluation. ICT would be an additional subject together with the award of a certificate of proficiency.

A dedicated teacher with appropriate qualification will be engaged in each school. This teacher will also function as the ICT coordinator of the school where ICT literacy is to be imparted. With the growth of infrastructure in the school, a suitably qualified technical assistant may also be provided.

Enabled teaching–learning process

ICT enabled teaching–learning encompasses a variety of techniques, tools, content and resources aimed at improving the quality and efficiency of the teaching learning process. Ranging from projecting media to supporting a lesson, to multimedia self-learning modules, to simulations and virtual learning environments, there are a variety of options available to the teacher to utilize various ICT tools for effective pedagogy. Each such device or strategy also involves changes in the classroom environment, and its bearing on effectiveness. Availability of a wide range of such teaching–learning materials will catalyze transformation of classrooms into ICT-enabled classrooms.

Teachers will participate in selection and critical evaluation of digital content and resources. They will also be encouraged to develop their own digital resources, sharing them with colleagues through the digital repositories.

Elective courses at higher secondary levels

States will initiate the process of launching/creating courses in different areas of ICT for the higher secondary stage. The courses will factor in the requirements of students of different streams, including academic and vocational streams

Courses will be modular in design to enable students to select appropriate software applications based on current needs of higher education and job prospects. Courses will be revised frequently to keep pace with emerging trends in ICT.

An ICT Lab attendant/technical assistant with appropriate qualifications will be appointed to manage the ICT/Multimedia Resource lab.

ICT for skill development (Vocational and job oriented area of general education

Job-oriented courses in ICT will be developed and established for students of the vocational stream at the higher secondary level by linking them with the needs of ICT-enabled industries/establishments in the neighbourhood. The scope of these courses would be a broad-based ICT literacy. It will not be limited to ICT-based occupations, but will inform and enhance productivities in a wide range of other occupations (for example, accounting, office automation, office communication, data handling and data processing, desktop publishing, graphics and designing, music and video, etc). This will also include courses on cyber security.

The courses will be modular and students will be provided a wide range of choices, catering to a variety of job options, hardware and software platforms, tools and resources. Appropriate mechanisms to counsel students in selecting career paths and courses will be developed simultaneously. The courses will be in conformity with the National Vocational Education Qualifications Framework (NVEQF).

The courses will be frequently revised and updated in order to maintain relevancy to changing requirements of the job market and emerging trends in technology. Hence, it will also be imperative to conduct such courses in close liaison with industry.

The institutions offering vocational courses will be required to integrate ICTs in their teaching–learning process.

An open learning system will be developed permitting students to continue to reskill themselves. Conventional restrictions of age and previous qualifications will be suitably reworked to facilitate an open system. Where feasible, online and distance modes will also be explored. Lateral and vertical mobility will be established among the courses with multiple entry and exit options.

A system of on-demand evaluation and certification, to enable students to obtain timely qualifications, will be developed.

ICT for children with special needs

Use of ICT will catalyze the cause and achieve the goals of inclusive education in schools

ICT software and tools to facilitate access to persons with disabilities, like screen readers, Braille printers, etc., will be part of the ICT infrastructure in all schools. Special care will be taken to ensure appropriate ICT access to students and teachers with special needs.

All teachers will be sensitized to issues related to students with special needs and the potential of ICT to address them. All capacity-building programmes will include components of ICT-enabled inclusive education.

All web-based interfaces developed for the programme including digital repositories, management information systems, etc. will conform to international guidelines for accessibility. 4.6.5 Accessibility norms will be adopted as per the world wide web consortiums. Web-based digital repositories with W3C compliance will address the lack of availability of resources for persons with disabilities. Digital content and resources, for the exclusive use of persons with disabilities, talking books for example, will also be developed and deployed.

The absence of appropriate vocabulary for different subject areas in the different Indian languages and the unfamiliarity of the cultural context can make digital communication and resources inaccessible to students and teachers across the country. Efforts will be initiated to develop appropriate word lists and dictionaries in Indian languages and wide spread translations will be encouraged.

ICT for open and distance learning

Open and Distance Learning with the use of ICT opens up alternate possibilities for students who have dropped out, cannot continue formal education or are students of the non-formal system of education. Existing formal systems of education will be strengthened with ICT-based instruction available in Open and Distance Learning Systems so as to cater to the needs of such learners.

Present Open Schooling systems (e.g. National or State Level Open Schools) will be strengthened by harnessing ICTs innovatively. Access to e-books, digital learning resources, Digital Repositories (with relevant learning resources), etc. will be developed by these institutions as student support services. This will also be used for online capacity building for open and distance teacher training.

All Open and Distance Learning Systems will be automated and provide online all services including admissions, examinations, e-Accreditation and grievance redressal on the lines of the National Institute of Open Schooling.

The proposed mentoring system for students involving expert teachers will be extended to these students also. Online courses, online on demand exams, digital repositories and content, media broadcasts planned through DTH/satellite-based, open learning systems allowing multiple entry and exit points, opening out the school resources to non-formal students, guidance and counselling, will result in effective use of ICT for open and distance learning.

ICT for school management

States will adopt or adapt an e-governance and automated school administration programme for schools, build capacities for its implementation and deploy school-based Management Information Systems (MIS). These MIS will be integrated with the proposed state wide web-based School Education Management Information System. A school wide local area network enables automation of a variety of processes. Beginning with library automation, locally cached offline access to internet resources, office automation, maintenance of records, student tracking, resource planning, using the existing ICT infrastructure will increase efficiencies. At the same time, savings in cost, time and effort will also accrue. The school wide local area network will be used to facilitate this automation.

School Management Information System

A Nation Wide Network will be established in which schools, teachers, students, school managers, and the community at large participate. This implementation will include the School Management Information Systems (School MIS); digital repositories of tools, content and resources;

professional development and continuing education platforms; and guidance, counselling and other student support services.

School MIS will emerge as a single window clearing house on all information related to the secondary school system. The information will facilitate research and analysis activities and guide decision-making at different levels in the education system, contributing to enhanced efficiencies.

The scope of information to be collated by the MIS will be broad and include student and teacher tracking, particularly for their academic needs. The norms will also define standards of technology including language fonts, word processors, technical dictionaries, etc. Open standards facilitating universal access to information, content and resources will be ensured.

ICT Infrastructure

There will be two types of Infrastructure:

(1) Core ICT Infrastructure
(2) Enabling Infrastructure

Hardware

States will establish state-of-the-art, appropriate, cost-effective and adequate ICT and other enabling infrastructure in all secondary schools.

Based on the size of the school, needs of the ICT programme and time sharing possibilities, states will define an optimum ICT infrastructure in each school. Not more than two students will work at a computer access point at a given time. At least one printer, scanner, projector, digital camera, audio recorders and such other devices will be part of the infrastructure.

Each school will be equipped with at least one computer laboratory with at least 10 networked computer access points to begin with. Each laboratory will have a maximum of 20 access points, accommodating 40 students at a time. The ratio of total number of access points to the population of the school will be regulated to ensure optimal access to all students and teachers.

In composite schools, exclusive laboratories with appropriate hardware and software will be provided for the secondary as well as higher secondary classes.

In addition, at least one classroom will be equipped with appropriate audio–visual facilities to support ICT-enabled teaching and learning.

Appropriate hardware for Satellite terminals will be provided to selected schools in a progressive manner.

In addition to the laboratory, computer access points with internet connectivity will be provided at the library, teachers' common room and the school head's office to realize the proposed objectives of automated school management and professional development activities.

ICT-enabled education can be significantly enhanced and the range of classroom practices expanded with the introduction of digital devices like still and video cameras, music and audio devices, digital microscopes and telescopes, digital probes for investigation of various physical parameters. These will also form a part of the infrastructure. States will make appropriate choices and promote the use of such devices in classrooms.

Network and connectivity

All computers in the school will be part of a single local area network to enable optimum sharing of resources. Each school will be serviced with broadband connectivity capable of receiving streaming audio and video, a range of digital learning resources and interactive programmes. The number of computers given internet connectivity will be governed by the available bandwidth, in order to ensure adequate speeds. A mechanism to have offline access to internet content will be set.

Teachers and students will be educated on issues related to the safe use of internet Firewalls and other security measures will be implemented to guard the school network against cyber attacks and misuse of the ICT facilities. Appropriate guidelines for network security will be developed.

Software

A software environment favouring a pedagogy of learning which promotes active learning, participatory and collaborative practices and sharing of knowledge is essential to nurture a creative society. Free and Open Source Software — operating system and software applications will be preferred in order to expand the range of learning, creation and sharing.

A wide variety of software applications and tools, going well beyond an office suite, is required to meet the demands of a broad-based ICT literacy and ICT-enabled teaching — learning programme. Graphics and animation, desktop publishing, web designing, databases, and programming tools have the potential of increasing the range of skills and conceptual knowledge of the students and teachers. A judicious mix of software applications will be introduced in schools.

Creation and widespread dissemination of software compilations, including specialized software for different subjects, simulations, virtual laboratories, modelling and problem solving applications will be encouraged. These will be distinct from multimedia packages and digital learning resources.

Enabling infrastructure

The enabling infrastructure required to efficiently maintain the ICT facility will be defined, established and maintained.

Regular and regulated supply of electricity, appropriate electrical fixtures, adequate power backup and support, including alternate sources of energy, where needed, will be ensured. Students and teachers will also be trained in the safe use of electrical outlets and fittings.

Physical facilities like an adequately large room, appropriate lighting and ventilation, durable and economic furniture suitable for optimization of space and long hours of working will be established. Alternate layouts and arrangements facilitating interactions among students and with the teacher will be encouraged.

Adequate safety precautions and rules for use will be established. Each laboratory will be equipped with a portable fire extinguisher and students and teachers trained in its use. An appropriate fire drill will also be implemented.

All the equipment and resources will be secured from theft and damage. They will also be covered under an appropriate insurance policy against theft and damage.

Implementing and Managing the Policy

Programme Monitoring and Evaluation Group (PMEG)

The PMEG of the Department of School Education & Literacy, Ministry of HRD, Government of India, will be tasked with the overall responsibility of guiding the implementation of the ICT programme in schools across the country. The PMEG may set up task groups and invite institutions or established professionals with substantial expertise in that sector to develop norms, specifications, guidelines, evaluation reports, white papers, etc. to guide the states in implementing the ICT programme.

Inter-ministerial group

An Inter-ministerial Group consisting of members from the Ministry of HRD, Ministry of Communications and Information Technology, Ministry of Information and Broadcasting, Department of Space, Department of Science & Technology, Ministry of Power, Ministry of New and Renewable Energy, Ministry of Labour, Ministry of Rural Development and such other ministries dealing with issues related to education will be set up and tasked with the responsibility of guiding technological choices and specifying cost-effective and optimum infrastructure and connectivity.

The group will also review the state-of-the-art technology, connectivity and inter-sectoral convergence based on its relevance to educational ICT goals, feasibility of implementation in the school sector, appropriateness in terms of finance, environmental footprints, need for training and learning curves for use and managing the system. The group will regularly review technological choices and guide the states in making informed investments, maximizing the educational benefits.

Technology choice reviews will include standards and norms for computer configuration, input and output devices like scanners, printers and projectors, operating systems and system software applications including virus scans, productivity applications and educational software, power conditioning equipment, and other digital equipment like camera and audio recorders. It would also include norms for Edusat terminals. Norms for pricing of enabling infrastructure like telephone, internet, and electricity will also be considered and states will be guided in establishment and management of the infrastructure.

The Group will review, from time to time, ICT and education related issues emerging out of Acts and Policies in other sectors, particularly relevant to security, copyright and effective use of ICT and guide states accordingly.

National and state level agencies role of states

The states will have a two-fold task:

* Define norms, standards, guidelines and frameworks to implement the policy in an effective manner;
* Facilitate and monitor the implementation of the policy in an effective manner.

These tasks will include:

* A programme of action, an appropriate road map and a feasible time line;
* Guidelines based on national standards and norms for infrastructure, implementation processes at various levels, capacity-building programmes, monitoring and evaluation criteria, targets, etc.;
* Framework for development, selection, evaluation, deployment in repositories, and use of digital content;
* Facilitation of widespread participation of all stake holders, including community and private partners in various aspects of the ICT programme implementation of the policy in an effective manner;
* Development, deployment and maintenance of infrastructure and digital repositories;
* Development and phased implementation of an appropriate capacity-building framework mobilization of resources including from private and community sources;
* Development of an appropriate legal and regulatory framework;
* Monitor and evaluate the implementation.

These actions will be in conformity with Guidelines issued by the Central Government.

Norms, standards and procedures

In order to ensure uniform and high standards of ICT, optimum utilization and cost-effective implementations, states will adapt standards and norms suggested by the inter-ministerial group at the national level for all aspects of the ICT implementation, in particular the technology mix, specifications of equipment, selection of software and connectivity, selection and deployment of digital resources and capacity-building programmes.

Prevailing norms in the states will be utilized to phase out, dispose of or exchange old and obsolete equipment. Care will be taken to minimize avoidable upgradation and generation of electronic waste.

States will draft SLA for procurement, installation, operation and maintenance procedures, and draw up appropriate agreements with the vendor/agency. The MoUs/agreements will involve strict compliance clauses to ensure quality of equipment and service and minimum downtime. Appropriate Guidelines for SLA developed by the Inter-ministerial Group will form the basis

Models of ICT infrastructure

Build, Own, Operate and Transfer (BOOT) models for ICT infrastructure may be used to maximize coverage of the programme in schools in the shortest possible time. Different combinations of services like equipment only and equipment + manpower will be tried out and the appropriate combination, based on feasibility and cost-effectiveness, adopted by the states. Based on prevailing depreciation and obsolescence norms, the states may also choose to use a build, own and operate (BOO) model to avoid out of date/obsolete equipment in schools.

In view of increasing capacities of regular teachers in integrating ICT and capacity-building programmes for teachers, an attempt will be made by states to phase out the requirements of a separate teacher for ICT, except at the +2 level, where ICT is introduced as a separate subject. The states will avoid (and phase out) outsourcing of teacher recruitment to BOOT agencies.

States will explore the possibilities of sharing the infrastructure partly or wholly with the community to extend education or train youth after school hours or similar purposes. Care will be taken to ensure that such usage does not compromise the school's educational or ICT programmes. The BOOT agency and/or the school may also utilize it for augmentation of resources. States will try out and establish appropriate community partnership models for optimum utilization of infrastructure and resources, while ensuring safety of school property.

Regulatory measures

Access to the Internet enhances the risk of inappropriate content reaching children and compromising privacy and identity of individuals.

Evolving appropriate advisories for regulating access, monitoring internet activity and education including privacy and security of students and teachers will be taken up at the instance of the Advisory Group. Heads of schools and teachers will be trained in appropriate security and regulatory measures.

Incentives

The states will draw up an appropriate incentive scheme for teachers, students and schools to recognize, showcase and promote initiative and talent. Easy loan schemes for procuring ICT equipment and resources, awards, professional support packages, and a variety of similar incentives will be considered. States will also explore the possibility of partnerships and sponsorships with Government and Private agencies like Banks, Corporations and Charitable Institutions (SMARTNET, 2012).

Some Examples of Enhancing the Quality of Education in Rural India Through Digital Learning

(1) Noida-based Schoolnet has created an integrated digital solution linking in-school teaching–learning with after-school services through personalization of content and a hybrid model of delivery of quality education. Schoolnet's mission is to expand lifelong learning opportunities for all, and democratize education by harnessing the power of technology and ecosystem partnerships. Schoolnet wanted to bring various types of content together — multimedia, animation-based, simulation-based and others. The idea was to bring in elements of the constructivist and blended approaches, with theories of multiple intelligence in the development of pedagogically sound content (Apurva, 2021).

(2) In a small school in Nashik, Maharashtra, most of the students are drawn towards their coming annual day practice, running around for speakers and costumes. However, amidst all this chaos, there is one classroom where the students are engrossed in navigating through a tablet and solving a math quiz (Gangakhedkar, 2020).

(3) The Indian Institute of Technology Madras (IIT-Madras) Parvartak Technologies Foundation has partnered with an education provider to bring computer science literacy to students in Government schools in the remote, rural areas of Tamil Nadu. The partners successfully set up two Rural Technology Centres earlier this week and plan to establish more centres this year. The two Rural Technology Centres were inaugurated in the Kanayama Chatham and Seetha Jeri villages of Tiruvallur district, around 60km from Chennai. After assessing the students, the centres will teach basic digital literacy and the basics of programming. The IIT-Madras Pravartak Technologies Foundation will provide the project with financial and technical support. Students from Government schools in Classes 9–12 will learn about advanced technologies like drones, 3D printing, robotics, artificial intelligence (AI), animation, webpage design and hardware-based programming (IET India, 2018).

(4) Ajodhya, July 20, 2018: Saraswathi Seva Foundation (SSF), a non-profit organization committed to serving the underprivileged communities using knowledge tools and networks to support a sustainable

foundation of the society, with support from the Institution of Engineering and Technology (the IET), launched a STEM-C (Science, Technology, English, Mathematics and Computer) Programme to create "Tech Awareness Events" in schools. The programme aims to promote project-based learning (PBL) in schools and organizes STEM-C classes for thousands of under-privileged children in eastern Uttar Pradesh and in its next step, plans to support/assist students in making small technology-related projects. While SSF supplements school teaching with the best-in-class teaching resources using digital equipment, it has taken Robots, Humanoids, Segway, Multi-copters, Arduino, Micro:bits, Raspberry Pi, etc. to demonstrate and conduct DIY (Do it Yourself) sessions with the students under its "Tech-skill the Youth Program" (TSYP). STEM-C initiative combined with "Tech-skill the Youth Program" will give the youth skills to build micro-enterprises, develop a scientific temper for further research or develop tech-savvy employees for SMEs and large enterprises (Raj, 2022).

Conclusion

ICT plays a very significant role in the field of education. It helps the students and teachers learn different tools in an effective way. ICT helps in improving the literacy rate in the field of technology and it also plays a major role in the economy.

References

Annual status of education report. (2018). 47.
Apurva, P. How this enterprise is enhancing the quality of education in rural India through digital learning. (2021, October 19). https://yourstory.com/socialstory/2021/10/schoolnet-education-rural-india-digital-learning/am.
Gangakhedkar, S. (2020, March 2). What Ed-tech looks like in rural Maharashtra's schools. https://thebastion.co.in/politics-and/what-ed-tech-looks-like-in-rural-maharashtras-schools/.
Roy, N. K. (2012). ICT enabled rural education in India. *International Journal of Information and Technology, 2.* (2012, October 5).
IET India (2018). Bringing project based learning and latest technologies to rural schools in India. https://india.theiet.org/news-media/news/press-releases-2018/bringing-project-based-learning-and-latest-technologies-to-rural-schools-in-india/.

India, D. (2018–2019, January 17). All India Survey on Higher Education 2019, New Delhi: Department of Higher Education, Ministry of Education, Government of India.

Kaur, M. (2021, January 4).What is ICT in education and its importance. Vinay Prajapati.

Little, A. W. & Lewin, K. M. (2011). The policies, politics and progress of access to basic education, *Journal of Education Policy*, *26*(4), 477–482.

National Statistical Commission (2018). Annual Report 2017–18, New Delhi: Government of India.

Raj, S. D. (2022, February 15). Tech centres to boost digital literacy and opportunities in rural Tamil Nadu, India. https://opengovasia.com/tech-centres-to-boost-digital-literacy-and-opportunities-in-rural-tamil-nadu-india/.

Siemen, I. J. (2007, November). Managing Director. ICT for Development and Education. p. 47.

SMARTNET (2012, March 23). National Policy on information and communication.

Chapter 6

Public–Private Partnerships in EdTech for Transforming Rural India: How Start-Ups are Shaping the Post-COVID Landscape

Aparna Saluja

USB, Chandigarh University, Chandigarh, India

aparna.e8363@cumail.in

Abstract

Rural India faces severe technology deficits as it is struggling to fulfil even the basic infrastructural necessities such as provision of power, water, resilient health care facilities, roads, education system, etc. To cover these gaps, Government of India is actively taking initiatives to bring sophisticated technology for rural development. This is evident from the use of High Yielding Variety (HYV) seeds in agricultural activities, introduction to the concept of organic farming, digitalization of education in primary and secondary schools in rural areas, sophisticated technologies encouraging digital financial transactions, technological skill development for artisans, traders, etc., for enhancing productivity of village and cottage industries, technological upgradation for establishing strong infrastructure at the rural level, etc.

This chapter aims to highlight the enabling trends and challenges in providing technology education for rural development in India, especially during the pandemic situation. The purpose of this chapter is to understand the role of public–private partnerships in imparting education about sophisticated technology in rural India, initiatives taken by the Government by introducing various schemes for technology education and encouraging start-ups to invest in technology innovation for rural people to overcome the difficult times.

Introduction

Education is the essence of development not only for the human mind but also the whole society, communities and economies at large. Education has the potential to increase the ability and knowledge of the rural population in India, allowing them to make more informed decisions about their agricultural activities, markets and other sectors of the economy. The Government has taken several initiatives to promote education, especially in rural areas. The implementation of the National Education Policy, which ensures imparting of quality education to all children, who are the future of our country, is an example of one such initiative by the Government. The 2019 National Education Policy (NEP) aims to solve the challenges that are faced by children, especially those living in rural areas, by extending RTE (Right of Children to Free and Compulsory Education Act) to children aged 3–18. One of the reports recommended using Edtech to enhance learning through apps, online student communities, and course delivery that goes beyond "chalk and talk".

Due to technological improvements, India's educational environment has altered considerably during the last decade. The COVID-19 epidemic has pushed previous Edtech efforts to provide students with an engaging and immersive learning experience through digital platforms, hence overcoming the shortcomings which were faced during the traditional class room teaching era. Due to a lack of infrastructure, such as electricity and Internet connection, quality education has traditionally been scarce in rural sections of the country, but this is changing post the pandemic.

Edtech platforms are slowly but steadily gaining traction in rural India, opening up new opportunities. Collaboration with governmental and non-governmental organizations and institutes has tremendously aided the adoption of Edtech in rural India, leading to the rise of public—private partnership in this area. These enterprises are creating initiatives to cater to the less privileged segments of the student population, notably those enrolled in government and affordable private schools, in both rural and underdeveloped metropolitan regions. Some Edtech businesses are bringing in artificial intelligence to bridge the gap between human and computer language, making it easier for students, teachers and parents to connect. A recent surge in digital literacy in the rural areas has helped people face difficult social and economic issues during the challenging times of the pandemic.

During the pandemic situation, many start-ups emerged as well and took the opportunity to expand in the untapped areas of rural education. Through innovation and pivots, these start-ups not only helped rural people fight against the deadly virus, they also created awareness about using the sophisticated technology to improve one's livelihood.

However, there are certain challenges that are being faced by the new ventures and the Government in implementing the advancement of technology education in the rural sector. This chapter highlights the role of public—private partnerships in Edtech for transforming the lifestyle of the rural people, and the emergence of various start-ups that have invested in technology innovation for rural people to overcome difficult times. Furthermore, this chapter also discusses the challenges and problems faced by the Edtech companies in transforming rural India.

Selected Indian Academic Perspectives on Edtech Developments

- *Korreck (2019) analyzed* the Indian start-up ecosystem and challenges faced by them in rural areas. She examined the current situation of the Indian start-up ecosystem with three objectives:

  (Continued)

(Continued)

to provide insight into the growth drivers and motivations of Indian company founders, to identify obstacles that these businesses face, and to outline the pillars that support them.

- *Verma & Singh (2014)* concluded that ICT (Information and Communication Technology) is a critical component of rural development. It is simple to boost development by utilizing ICT. People in rural places may be more interested in ICT if they are more aware that it can boost production and increase efficiency. Increased productivity can boost the country's economic growth.
- *Anurag (2021)* noted the challenges in education faced by India as well as the role that technology can play in bridging the gap between learning and teaching on a large scale.
- *Amirullah (2014)* examined the public–private partnership and the future of ICT in developing rural India. Furthermore, he emphasized that ICT plays an important role in facilitating the rural areas towards sustainable development.
- *Mukherjee (2011)* stated that recent advances in technology have opened a multitude of development options in every conceivable field and rural people are adopting the technological trends. However, there are certain challenges in embracing the technological tools, but these problems can be resolved by creating awareness.
- *Rekha (2019)* investigated the role of sophisticated technology in the upliftment of the rural sector and the efforts taken by the Government to encourage the spread of information communication and technology in the rural sectors.
- *Ananth & Karti (2013)* demonstrate the application of technology in India to transform rural areas towards development for sustainable and profitable livelihood. The advancement of technology has led to increase in the productivity and efficiency of the rural sector.

Edtech Start-Ups for Rural India

During the pandemic, technology-induced education matured, and with it, educational disparity inside the system rose. A huge dent in education was created by COVID-19, especially for the underprivileged sections.

Due to school closures, educational systems were forced to quickly design and implement new ways of remote learning, such as radio, television and several other sorts of Internet tools. To overcome this dent, many Edtech start-ups emerged for helping the rural schools and are running the show in the rural market post the pandemic. Entrepreneurs devised solutions for students on a budget who cannot afford expensive memberships.

Edtech businesses and companies began to think about how to close the gap between students who can afford high-tech education and those who cannot. Edtechs are generating high-quality e-content in local languages to address the diversity of Indian languages and reach more students across the country. They're also establishing digital classrooms and merging education systems and technology to deliver skill development courses, virtual labs, and virtual vocational training. Edtechs are developing frameworks for assessments in the digital age for students who are unable to commute, as well as ensuring a consistent user experience through multi-mode access to education via mobile apps, web portals, TV channels, radio and podcasts, so that education is not limited to a single device. To reach the majority, chatbots have been placed in commonly used programmes such as WhatsApp and Telegram. With the help of tailored content recommendations, accurate and dynamic assessments, and doubt-solving sessions, these interactive chat-based systems aid adaptive learning. These platform-based solutions have the advantage over some of the other options available in that they can run at moderate Internet rates and do not take up space on a device.

Here are few start-ups that are making **education affordable for students**, especially living in rural areas:

WhatsApp-based learning by ConveGenius

ConveGenius is an Edtech Social Enterprise founded by Jairaj Bhattacharya and Shashank Pandey with the goal of bringing excellent education to over 100 million poor students in India and closing the learning gap. A simple application, such as Whatsapp, can be used to access the platform. In addition to being inexpensive, 2G/3G internet services can be used in places with limited connectivity. For effective home learning, ConveGenius provides tailored evaluations and remedial lessons.

Dhurina Ventures Private Limited

A Haryana-based Edtech firm was launched in June 2019 by four friends: Sachin Sardana, Ajay Kumar, Murari Singh and Sanjay Singh. Aspirants from Tier II and III cities, suburbs and rural areas can access online counselling, classes and resources for state, regional and central level competitive examinations, bridging the learning gap between Bharat and India.

BYJU's

BYJU's has partnered with Isha Vidhya, a non-governmental organization (NGO) based in Coimbatore, with the goal of empowering and providing children from all walks of life with equitable learning opportunities. Isha Vidhya and BYJU's will deliver digital learning tools to poor youngsters in Tamil Nadu and Andhra Pradesh as part of the cooperation. BYJU's programme would make the country known for high-quality school education that is accessible and cheap to everybody, particularly rural youngsters.

Learning Delight

It is a Rajkot-based Edtech company that aims to make rural education more feasible and applicable It established a smartphone application to deliver free education to youngsters, particularly those from low-income families. Learning Delight has impacted the education systems of around 10,500+ schools in rural and semi-urban parts of Gujarat, and it has now moved to Rajasthan. Through its mobile application, it provides free access to content for children in grades 1 through 10.

Edtech Start-Ups for the Agriculture Sector

The pandemic worked as a catalyst, forcing various industry sectors, including agri-tech, to develop and come up with swift solutions to get past the lockdowns' uncertainty. As farmers couldn't meet their peers in person due to a lack of access to on-the-ground consulting services, many farmers turned to online portals to discuss their crop and cattle difficulties. The number of agricultural and cattle-related enquiries on agri-networking platforms grew by 30% as a result.

According to Bain & Co, India's agri-tech business is predicted to rise to $30–35 billion by 2025. As a result, the agri-tech start-up sector has been attracting investor interest for some time. However, it was difficult to foresee how quickly digitalization, supply chain improvements, big data, machine learning, AI, data analytics, IoT and other technologies would be adopted. The pandemic increased the uptake of technology and made it evident to investors.

For decades, Indian farmers have relied on traditional ways. Now, agri-tech companies are using technology disruption to help with farm output growth and improvement, supply chain interventions, post-harvest waste reduction, and a variety of other innovations. A substantial majority of farmers willingly turned to tech integrations as a result of the pandemic. The supply chain is now considerably more efficient, regardless of the situation, thanks to technology improvements. Farmers can choose from a number of suppliers and items, evaluate the available price alternatives, quality and diversity, and then make a decision using input e-commerce. Farmers who sell their produce on such platforms, on the other hand, receive the best offer price.

According to AgFunder's "India Agrifood Startup Investment" report, which was prepared in collaboration with Omnivore, investment in farm tech start-ups in India increased to $527 million across 119 agreements in the financial year 2020–2021 (FY21). Over the last few years, funding for on-farm technology has significantly increased in India, both in terms of quantities raised and the number of transactions closed. This is largely because of the COVID-19 outbreak, which caused problems in the country's agrifood value chain, which start-ups and investors rushed in to fix.

Few Agritech start-ups for farmers that changed their lives during the pandemic situation

AgriBazaar

AgriBazaar, as a full-stack agritech player, has replaced the physical *mandi* (marketplace) with an e-*mandi* aggregator model, in which buyers can place orders for a purchase when a farmer registers and uploads his produce. AgriBazaar handles the logistics of collecting up the food from the farmers' doorsteps and transporting it to the purchasers' warehouse once the transaction is completed. Buyers pay a transaction fee, but farmers don't have to pay anything extra to sell their produce.

Unnati

It is a cutting-edge financial start-up that helps farmers all around the country with their entire farming lifecycle. The company, which is data-driven, assists farmers in becoming entrepreneurs by providing services such as working capital, procuring the appropriate seeds, fertilisers and pesticides for crops, harvesting and selling the crops virtually.

eFeed

The Lucknow-based start-up aims to educate farmers about localized animal nutrition, animal dietary needs, as well as how to meet them using locally sourced supplies. eFeed's motto is to provide the correct information to farmers about animal nutrition and right way of feeding cattle that will lead to increase in the quantity of milk. eFeed first establishes contact with these farmers using social media platforms such as WhatsApp or through its physical outlets.

BharatAgri

It is a farming technology platform with a mission of bridging the gap between technology and agriculture in India, with the aim to reach out to maximum Indian farmers, provide them with knowledge about the systematic implementation of the scientific techniques and to create awareness about the advancement of technology to the rural farmers.

Edtech Start-ups for Rural Health

According to latest health data, India's rural population was 903 million in 2021, and by the end of 2022, it is expected to reach 905 million. This shows that the majority of the country's population lives in rural areas. However, it is evident that death rates are at an all-time high as a result of insufficient facilities. The Government's push to promote technology deployment, telemedicine, and telehealth, as well as the Make in India initiative, is propelling the sector forward and ensuring that rural areas have access to high-quality healthcare. Ayushman Bharat Health, Infrastructure Mission, and Jan Arogya Yojana are all aimed at providing state-of-the-art health care. According to an Invest India report, the Government has approved 100% FDI under the automatic method to invest in establishing hospitals. Furthermore, under automatic channels in medical device production, 100 percent FDI is permitted. Doctors are being trained, MBBS and post-graduate seats are being doubled, and hospital investments are increasing to fulfil the country's growing demand for health care employees.

The size of the market, which is estimated to reach INR485.4 billion by 2024, makes health care an enormous real opportunity to scale. With increasing investments, health care service providers, start-ups and the industry as a whole are gaining the necessary support to reach hitherto untapped areas. According to Invest India's report, total investments in healthtech businesses have increased by 45.06 percent. During the COVID-19 epidemic, when patients and doctors wanted to reduce in-person contact for routine appointments, telehealth became a more significant means of providing healthcare. Telehealth refers to the use of telecommunications technology and other electronic data to aid with remote clinical healthcare services, including as education, administrative activities and peer discussions. One of the most common images of telehealth is a patient speaking with a healthcare professional who is stationed remotely through videoconference.

Few Edtech start-ups that are bringing health care to rural India

My family first

In the next two years, My Family First plans to open 500 Digitally Enabled Smart Health (DESH) clinics around the country to connect patients in remote villages and towns with medical specialists in major cities. The organization, which began operations in mid-2021, has already opened 30 DESH clinics through franchising across Uttar Pradesh, Jharkhand and Madhya Pradesh. This start-up uses digital technology and Internet of Things-based gadgets to connect doctors in cities with patients in the rural hinterland, addressing the problem of a shortage of skilled doctors in villages and semi-urban areas. Patients can receive the greatest medical advice at cheap pricing directly at their doorsteps, eliminating the need to go to cities.

AI Health Highway

AI Health Highway is an Indian Institute of Science (IISC) incubated start-up founded by Dr Satish S Jeevannavar, Dr Radhakrishna S Jamadagni and Anuj Pandit in 2019. Its goal is to reduce the burden on hospitals by developing a web app for COVID-19 self-screening to help identify low, mid and high-risk groups who may be susceptible to the coronavirus based on demography. Its COVID-19 pre-screen and triage tool is freely accessible on the company's website, and it offers solutions based on COVID-19 risk assessment scores that are related to clinical symptoms, comorbidities and contact history. This is mostly for the rural population, who have limited access to high-quality health care.

Medishala

Medishala, a Patna-based healthtech firm, intends to close the gap between urban and rural healthcare by sending doctors to people rather than the other way around and enabling inexpensive care delivery. This healthtech start-up offers two services: telemedicine, which allows patients to consult doctors online from the comfort of their own homes, and a digital clinic, which allows patients to visit a nearby Medishala centre where attendants can assist them in connecting with doctors online using IoT equipment.

Rural Transformation with the Help of Public–Private Partnership in Edtech

Rural areas in India still lack access to fast internet connections and e-services that are available to the country's urban population. For a long time, India has promoted the concept of Digital India, which has been particularly successful in the country's urban areas, despite the fact that there has always been a digital divide between the urban and rural populations. In order to address this issue, the Union Cabinet has devised a plan. For bringing about the rural transformation in India, the Government is focusing on public–private partnerships. For instance, Bharat Net recently stated that it will expand its connectivity and services to about 3.61 lakh villages across 16 Indian states. The broadband link would provide high-speed data and enable greater access to e-services provided by various government agencies in rural India. It would also allow rural residents to participate in online classrooms, over-the-top (OTT) media service, e-commerce, skill development, telemedicine, and other broadband-related activities.

The Union Cabinet has announced that this expansion will be carried out using a Public–Private Partnership model, which will allow entrepreneurs to participate in the bidding process and provide their services in connection setup. Not only is the broadband service being created, it is also being upgraded, maintained, operated and used under the new strategy. The company that receives the tender will be responsible for everything.

Furthermore, under the Innovation and Agri-entrepreneurship Development Programme component of the Rashtriya Krishi Vikas Yojana (RKVY), the Centre has invested INR 118.65 crore in about 800 start-ups to fuel innovation in the fields of artificial intelligence (AI), internet of things (IoT), information and communication technology (ICT), and blockchain technology in the agriculture sector. The move is part of the Government's effort to modernize the agriculture and related industries. With supportive government initiatives in the healthcare industry, public–private partnerships are on the rise. Ayushman Bharat–Pradhan Mantri Jan Arogya Yojana (AB-PMJAY) was created with the goal of providing universal healthcare to 50 million Indians by 2030. Technology has shown to be the most effective means of achieving such a large-scale expansion in healthcare services. To assist in bridging the gap, new-age health IT start-ups are partnering with various government entities and NGOs.

As a result, the future of Edtech is bright, but it hinges on the sector's capacity to quickly adapt to changing circumstances and provide personalized solutions across a wide range of categories. Online learning is here to stay in the current educational system. To maintain the momentum, the industry must continue to innovate in order to profit from the void caused by the closing of traditional classrooms. In the classroom, this innovation will encourage critical thinking, collaboration and creativity. Immersive technologies such as Augmented Reality and Virtual Reality can be used to bring these advancements in.

Challenges Faced by the Edtech Start-ups in Transforming Rural India

Rural areas in India face numerous obstacles and problems; they are still underdeveloped, the rural masses face poverty and unemployment, and they are illiterate, making it difficult for them to seek out better future opportunities on their own. These issues and obstacles can be addressed by making efficient use of technology in rural regions.

- *Inadequate infrastructure and poor accessibility*: Poor internet connectivity continues to be a big issue, particularly in rural regions. For innovation-driven learning, high-speed internet is required. For the vast majority of people, online education remains a pipe dream. This is a depressing reality in which residents in large cities have exclusive access to excellent learning tools that were supposed to be available to all citizens of the country. The longer this issue persists, the more Edtech firms will be harmed.
- *There are only a few persons with technological skills*: The isolated lifestyle does not appeal to those who come from towns or cities, therefore existing teaching staffs are forced to teach subjects in which they have not majored. Existing teachers may not be digitally proficient, and those who are will be in charge of all tech-related activities, placing a significant pressure on them.
- Farmers in India who are illiterate have less opportunities to try recent technologies. Farmers find difficulties in adopting the complex technology in agriculture. Precision agriculture adoption has been hampered by a lack of knowledge and devoted education among farming communities. Many of the pricey instruments and tools used in digital farming are out of reach for small and marginal farmers. Because of the expensive cost and maintenance of sophisticated technology, they are rarely employed or even available. Adoption of technology advancements is hampered by the high operational costs of machines and tools. Still, the majority of farmers stick to the traditional methods of farming and are not ready to adopt the sophisticated technology.
- In India, a key challenge with rural education is a lack of equipment and ICT (Information and Communication Technology) resources. According to the current study, the quantity of computers, the number

of topics kids learn online, and exposure and initial experience with technology are all lower among rural students in India. A large section of the rural populace continues to lack the necessary internet capacity as well as the ability to recognize devices and digital terminologies. Another important concern is the lack of supporting infrastructure, such as a consistent supply of electricity and access to high-speed internet. There is also lack of expertise among teachers in rural areas to handle digital platforms.

- *Language barrier*: In India, about 85% of the people do not speak English. Due to a lack of standardized content in Hindi and other regional languages, the uptake of online courses is delayed. Standardized digital content that covers every major curriculum from K-12 to higher education appears to be a long way off. Curation of any high-quality content from open sources will increase costs and will necessitate a coordinated effort from the Government. From a blended learning perspective, the syllabus must also be re-contextualized.
- The absence of proper infrastructure is the most serious challenge for the rural healthcare system. The existing healthcare centres in rural areas are under-financed. Basic concerns such as sanitation, health, nutrition and cleanliness, as well as health care regulations, the value of medical services, their rights, financial support alternatives, and the necessity for effective waste disposal facilities must be informed. It is critical to instil in them a desire to seek medical help. Moreover, due to illiteracy among farmers they are not aware about the latest technological trends in the health sector.
- Lack of funds is one of the biggest barriers to the adoption of technology by small traders and craftsmen. The technical tools are expensive therefore it becomes a major concern for small craftsmen to instil sophisticated technology in their profession. Moreover, due to lack of training and absence of supporting infrastructure facilities, they are unable to embrace the technological tools of their profession.
- Internet issues are still major concerns in adopting digital banking for many rural people, especially living in a backward region. Furthermore, the challenging task for the Government is to create awareness about the virtual transactions among the rural people as many of them are not educated and they find the virtual banking system complex and find it difficult to use technological tools for transactions.

Suggestions and Recommendations

To adopt the technological changes in the rural sector, especially in agriculture, the Government needs to put in place an effective framework, including suitable regulations and programmes, to fully realize ICT's already well-known potential. Moreover, Edtech platforms are slowly but steadily finding their way into rural India, bringing new opportunities with them.

Collaboration with governmental and non-governmental organizations and institutes aided the adoption of Edtech in rural India. The Edtech startups are building activities in both rural and underdeveloped metropolitan regions aimed at catering to the less privileged segments of the student population, particularly those enrolled in government and affordable private schools. In order to gain popularity, they could offer low-cost multilingual platforms to the rural people that can be operated on limited bandwidth while yet providing access to high-quality material. To encourage this, the Government might provide tax breaks to these businesses. Furthermore, innovative techniques can be implemented to make online education more engaging and dynamic. The country's rural communities can benefit from the vital infrastructure supplied through public–private partnerships. For instance, schools in remote areas should be equipped with digital learning tools, and alternative energy sources such as solar panels should be deployed.

Conclusion

Rural India's digital education hurdles can be overcome by providing affordable and accessible e-learning options. To propel digital education in rural India, it is necessary to consider content standardization, facilitating all essential amenities and services in government schools through a PPP (public–private partnership) model, up-skilling teachers by providing them with customized teacher-training programmes on online education, blended learning in schools, and the advancement of initiatives in the digital learning space by NGOs and corporate social responsibility (CSR) wings of organizations. Aside from that, all stakeholders should work together to develop innovative pedagogies, accessible educational gadgets, adequate infrastructure and a high-quality environment to support the spread of digital learning in rural India.

Furthermore, Edtech platforms are slowly but steadily making their way into rural India. Rural users can work together to address problems and take advantage of new opportunities. Students' learning can be adapted to their own needs thanks to technology. Edtech apps can track students' progress and behaviour throughout the course and provide real-time individualized feedback. Educators can save time by using these platforms to assess their pupils depending on the feedback they receive. In locations where teacher-to-student ratios are uneven, Edtech apps can provide these students with access to a number of job opportunities in a variety of sectors, as well as increase their confidence. Edtech startups are not only focusing on sophisticated technology in rural transformation, but also helping rural youth in generating employment opportunities. Just Opportunities, Quickr Jobs and Kaam 24 are three free sites that offer jobs accessible for blue-collar employees that the trained rural people can use to advance their careers. As a result, Edtech has successfully revolutionized the rural educational scene and generated opportunities for rural residents.

References

Korreck, S. (2019). The Indian startup ecosystem: Drivers, challenges and pillars of support, Observer Research Foundation. India. Retrieved October 21, 2022, from https://policycommons.net/artifacts/1352732/the-indian-startup-ecosystem/1964890/. CID: 20.500.12592/7435mm.

Verma, P. & Singh, A. (2014). Multifaceted impact of technology on rural development. *SSRN Electronic Journal*, 5, 7015–7021.

Chapter 7

Integrating Diverse Approaches of Informal Sector for Sustainable E-waste Management

Georg Jahnsen*, Shweta Dua*, Priyanka Porwal[†] and
Navita Mahajan[‡,§]

*Deutsche Gesellschaft für Internationale
Zusammenarbeit (GIZ) GmbH, Germany

[†]Frametrics Consulting Private Limited, India

[‡]Amity University, Noida, India

[§]navitamahajan07@gmail.com

Abstract

Various forms of informal activities, particularly in developing countries, have long played an under-recognized but significant role in e-waste management. Although the informal sector plays a pivotal role in the collection, dismantling, recycling and resource recovery of precious resources, as a societal responsibility, the integration of the informal sector will ensure the formalization by providing them the health benefits, secured income and legalization of their work. This will help in uplifting their socio-economic status, thereby enhancing compliance with e-waste rules.

The present case study is about an initiative or a campaign on awareness by the Ministry of Electronics and Information Technology, Government of India with the name 'Awareness Programme on Environmental Hazards of Electronic Waste' under the 'Digital India Initiative'. The campaign was built to enhance outreach and advocacy around the environmental and health hazards of improper disposal of e-waste in the country.

Launched in 27 States and 3 Union Territories of India, with involvement of all stakeholders as a part of the system, the campaign was executed and made a huge success through various digitalized initiatives like developing an IEC framework, websites, mobile applications, conducting workshops, activities, training the trainers and campaigns across cinema halls, creating logos, mascots, posters, leaflets and banners, etc. The mass awareness program witnessed a huge success with coverage to more than 200 million viewers, conducting around 600 workshops, with participation of 300,000 stakeholders and 6,000 government officials.

Introduction

Living in a world whose boundaries between the physical and digital are constantly evolving has created a dynamic platform for the way humans live and behave. The disruptive technologies and innovations have majorly replaced manual processes since the early 20th century. Not only human beings, organizations and industries, too, have undergone this transition process from traditional, physical environments to digital platforms through the introduction of new technologies and the redesigning of existing systems. Migration to digital platforms has broken away the legacy of manual processes and opened the opportunity for digitally enabled economic environments. This digital revolution has enlarged human capacity, thought processes, systems designing, institutional knowledge, intelligent solutions and a resilience for the future.

In the 2030 agenda for Sustainable Development Goals (SDGs), where the focus has been on attaining 17 sustainable goals, digitalization in every sphere will be one of the major successes. Benefiting everyone socially and economically through the various mechanisms of technology facilitation, public, private and civic society linkages are going to be the key focus areas all over the world (*The Digital Agenda of BMZ, report*). In India, there has been a paradigm shift towards digitalization and, furthermore, the focus of the Indian Government towards digitalization by launching the Digital India Mission aimed at enhancing infrastructure and empowering citizens through digital availability at their doorstep. The Digital India Mission, which was started with the vision of transforming India into a "Digitally Empowered Knowledge Economy", is a key success factor for using ICT in an effective and efficient manner by achieving the public end by digital means (Singh & Maurya, 2017). Digital India is bound to have massive impact on the Make in India program for the hardware and electronics goods because of the creation of an ecosystem for its demand (Gaur, 2016).

The growth in the IT and communication sector, with the emphasis on the digitalization, has enhanced the usage of the electronic equipment exponentially. As per IAMAI (Internet and Mobile Association of India), the E-com sector itself has grown by 34% (CAGR) since 2009 (Anooja, 2015). The India Electronic Industry is estimated to reach $400 billion by 2025, with the electronic and consumer appliances industry becoming the 5th largest in the world by 2025, as per the reports of the Government of India on Electronic System Design and Manufacturing (Investindia, 2021 report). However, the growing consumerism and rapid urbanization have led to a rapid increase in the consumption of electrical and electronic items. The Indian consumer electronics market is expected to grow by double digits over the next few years, with estimates of 18% by 2025, as the domestic manufacturing is expected to grow faster, says a *Business Today* report from 2020. It has been observed that digital technologies are evolving at a faster pace with easy access to and usage of electrical and electronic equipment by consumers. Its affordability has allowed the steep growth of digital products such as mobile phones and laptops and other electronic gadgets, however, the end-of-life materials, once they are discarded, pose a huge environmental and health hazard. The result of advancing technology of old laptops, mobiles, televisions and other electronic devices is the creation of large quantities of electronic waste, which are a major growing concern because of the toxicity of the by-products. Undoubtedly, the increase in consumption of electronics has also led to production of large electronic waste due to increase in discarded devices.

The Global E-waste Monitor 2020 report says that across the entire world, about 53.6 million tonnes (MT) of e-waste was generated in the year 2019–2020, with India ranked 3rd (after China and USA) in e-waste generation, approximately having generated 3.23 million MT/annum e-waste during that period. The e-waste in India is expected to rise to 5 million MT by 2021, as per reports from the Associated Chambers of Commerce and Industry of India (ASSOCHAM), and if COVID-19 interventions are not taken seriously, e-waste is bound to increase globally reaching 100 million MT by 2050, as per the report from MONGABAY. Although India is the third largest generator of e-waste in the world, its per capita contribution is much lesser, about 2.4 kg as compared to the top two countries like China (10.1 MT) and USA (6.9 MT), as per the UN report on e-waste management in India. Computers only generate around 70% of India's e-waste, while telecom equipment contribute 12% (Neha & Deepak, 2019). The global e-waste is expected to increase 30% between the year 2020–2030 as per UNU (United Nations University) information prepared for the Global E-Waste Monitor Report, 2020.

The e-waste in the form of discarded, life-ended old appliances, obsolete ICT equipment, broken consumer electronics products, electronic components, consumables parts and spares of electrical goods, all consist of harmful and toxic chemicals such as Lead, Mercury, Cadmium, Chromium-VI, Polybrominated Biphenyl (PBB) and Polybrominated Diphenyl Ether (PBDE) besides precious metals like gold, silver, copper, and platinum. These are mostly reported to be dumped, rather than appropriately treated for reuse purposes. UN Global E-waste Monitor 2020 has reported a worrisome scenario that only 17.4% (9.3 Million MT) of e-waste was recycled globally, therefore posing a situation where all the valuable metals like gold, silver, platinum, cobalt, palladium, and germanium are either being dumped or burned with very little resource recovery. It is noticeable that e-waste contains about 69 elements of the periodic table (*Times of India*, 2020), so there is a strong need for development of a well-structured strategy for installing regulatory and economic measures for efficient management.

In India, the installed capacity of e-waste dismantling and recycling is 1.06 million MT per annum as per the Central Pollution Control Board, March 24, 2021, which is less than one-third of the capacity in comparison to the generation of e-waste. The collection, dismantling, and the resource recovery of the substances are majorly done only by the informal sector up to the extent of 90% and they are carried out without any appropriate protection or protective equipment, hence causing serious health hazards. Over 90% of the e-waste generated is treated and processed in urban slums of the country through unprotective mechanisms by untrained workers with dangerous procedures which are hazardous to not only their own health but the environment as well (Monika & Kishore, 2010). As per ASSOCHAM, about 80% of e-waste workers in Indian are suffering from various types of respiratory problems related to breathing, irritation, coughing, etc. (Deepak, 2020). Therefore, there is a pressing need to properly manage the e-waste in a scientific and sustainable manner to recover high-value materials, safely disposing toxic or non-recyclable materials without compromising the health and safety of the informal sector and recovering materials, which are reintroduced back into the production cycle.

Digitalization as an Enabler of the Circular Economy

Today's digital era has brought a complete revolution in businesses, markets and consumption patterns and that has been a game changer forthe private players or entities in the digital sector. The traditional manual processes have been replaced by cloud services, IoT, AI, digital applications and a wider variety of competitive apps to address the consumer needs. The consumer's needs also have been transformed with time, wherein availability of several applications or electronic tools have eased the processes. However, this digital transformation has also triggered the concern for sustainability by the consumers and the manufacturers for shifting from linear economy to circular economy benefiting the digital transformation. It has been observed that there is a growing demand for products and services that are both sustainable as well as durable.

With a paradigm shift from linear (wherein resources are extracted, transformed, utilized and discarded) to a circular economy wherein in the focus is more on closing the loop by incorporating in practice the reuse, repair, recycling, recovering and redesigning of the product.

Figure 1 elaborates that consumption of raw materials must be minimized by reusing the resources or substituted by materials with low environmental impact. The big companies like BMW and Apple are using AI

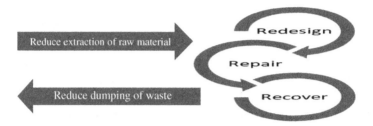

Figure 1.   Circular Economy Approach Towards Digital Transformation

technology that can recover the material after the product is discarded thereby reducing the utilization of virgin natural resources, thereby applying the circular economy principles. It also explains how the product designing should be focused on eco-design wherein environmental impact is considered during the design process, adopting the key principles of circular economy, i.e. resource recovery and recycling. Therefore, it is very important that circular economy and digitalization are complementary as both are based on the principles of improving efficiency and being economical. Digital transformation showcasing the circular economy principles enables the adaptability of the current market and furthermore provides the solutions that are sustainable, resource efficient and economical.

The main principles of the circular economy are designing a product that relies minimally on non- renewable resources and considers the holistic approach of both supply and the value chain. This means maximizing the life span of a product, its components, reusability and recovery. Circular economy adopts the principles by innovative design aspects (with a focus on value addition, resource extraction and recovery), manufacturing, delivery, and reuse of products in ways that are efficient, cost effective and sustainable, both economically and environmentally (Valenturf & Purnel, 2019).

Societal role in e-waste management

Recycling and the related issue of sustainable development are increasing in importance around the world and its efficiency depends not only on the education and cooperation of the people but also on cooperation among

As per the articles published by *Times of India*, February 21, 2019, a study was conducted on 54 electronic goods companies for maintaining adherence to compliances of EPR, as per E-waste (Management) Rules, 2016. It was found that only seven out of the 54 could be rated good, having initiated the measures of taking-back discarded e-material, 13 were assessed average, while 29 were below average. It was surprising that five electronic brands were not complying with Extended Producers Responsibility (EPR) standards and there was no mechanism in place to take back electronics products from the consumers in exchange. Out of all companies surveyed, 60% of them had no information on their helpline numbers related to take-back setups. Only four companies were found to have formal collection centres set up. This shows that in spite of E-waste (management) Rules, 2016, in India the ground realities have not changed much, and companies are still hesitant to set up effective take-back systems. The serious loopholes are the lack of information centres and collection setups, which shows there are hardly any serious efforts by companies.

Source: Article by Jasjeev Gandiok, "Policy Gone Waste: Failure to take back discarded e-goods for disposal", *Time of India*, February 21, 2019.

industrial waste generators, distributors and the government (Oliviera *et al.*, 2012). The challenges to sustainable management of e-waste are immense, but civil society must address the responsible management of existing e-waste and gradually phase out these electronic toxins. The problem of e-waste has forced environmental agencies of many countries to innovate, develop and adopt environmentally sound options and strategies for e-waste management, with a view to mitigating and controlling the ever-growing threat of e-waste to the environment and human health (Wath *et al.*, 2010). Building consumer awareness through public awareness campaigns is the most appropriate attribute for raising consumerism, and the roles citizens can play (Pinto, 2008). The opportunity to recycle e-waste is massive when only 17–18% of electronics used on this

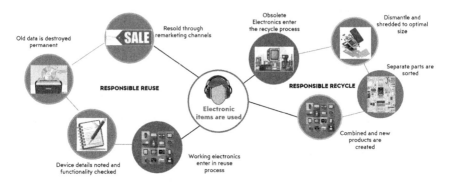

Figure 2.   Societal Role in E-Waste Handling

Source: www.omrsolutions.com.

planet are responsibly recycled when arriving at the end of their lives. The government and all the stakeholders like manufacturers, retailers, consumers, recyclers and others that are part of the electronic ecosystem are learning to be part of the solution to clean up the rear end of technological revolution. The contributions that society can make are based on responsible reuse and responsible recycling (see Figure 2). The outcomes of both approaches are managing of e-waste handling mechanisms efficiently.

Every institution, at every level, is responsible for ensuring that technological advancements do not jeopardise environmental and human health. To this purpose, whenever possible, handling e-waste should be a primary organizational priority and a major campaign topic. India is only in the early stages of developing fundamental sustainability practices, and it lacks the infrastructure and resources to adequately treat e-waste. Furthermore, e-waste must be viewed as a priority in light of critical connected concerns such as the private employment, informal sector, children's engagement, poverty and human health. While the obstacles of long-term e-waste management are significant, civil society can and must promote effective e-waste management.

Key stakeholders

The key stakeholders who are engaged in e-waste management value chain are categorized as primary and secondary. The broad classification of actors is basically the decision/policy makers (Ministry of Environment, Forest, and Climate Change-MoEF, Central Pollution Control

Board-CPCB), dismantlers and recyclers of e-waste, and bulk consumers/ consumers (Bank, Public Sector Undertaking-PSU, etc). Primary stakeholders comprise those stakeholders who are directly affected by the rules:

- State Pollution Control Boards (SPCBs) and Pollution Control Committees (PCCs)
- Producers and Manufacturers
- Producer Responsibility Organization (PRO)
- Dealers
- Refurbishers
- Collection centres
- Informal sector.

Secondary stakeholders comprise those whose involvement in e-waste management value chain is indirect:

- Non-Government Organizations (NGOs)
- Ministry of Micro, Small and Medium Enterprises (MSME)
- Department of Environment
- Academics.

E-waste value chain management

As shown in Figure 3, many key stakeholders (producers, dismantlers, recyclers, PROs, etc) are responsible for collection, transportation, recycling of the material that helps in resource recovery thereby reducing the waste entering into landfills and contributing towards managing e-waste. These actors have also been able to develop competitive advantages for themselves in terms of specific areas of expertise to handle different material flows for end-of-life materials.

Figure 4 details out the material flow and value chain for discarded e-waste materials. The value chain is basically the post-consumer e-waste management value chain, and comprises stakeholders such as dealers/ retailers, the informal sector, collectors, dismantlers, refurbishers and recycling/material recovery operations for metal and plastics mainly.

In India, more than 90% of the informal sector is involved in the collection, dismantling and recovery of metals and play a substantial role in e-waste management; however, the informal sector is not recognized and

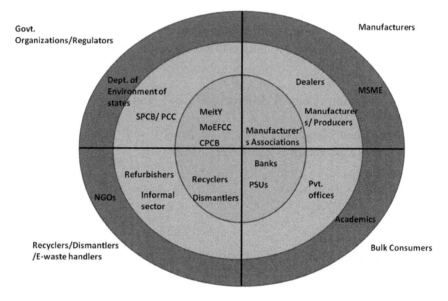

Figure 3.   Key Stakeholders

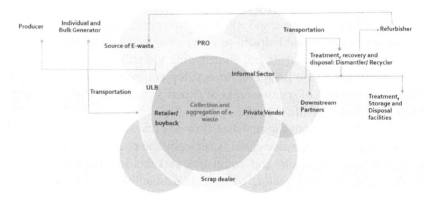

Figure 4.   E-Waste Value Chain Management System

given proper attention. The informal sector has a strong network, which helps in the collection of materials, but the crude methods adopted for recovery of the materials pose hazard to health and environment. As mentioned, the entire collection from all stakeholders in the e-waste value chain is done through the informal sector and it is a source of livelihood for them, but the unprotected methods of extracting metals leads to health and occupational hazards; therefore it is very important, and the need of the hour, to integrate and mainstream the informal sector into the formal system. There are several approaches that can be adopted to integrate the informal sector, as follows:

Mainstreaming informal into formal system

Informal sector could be formalized through establishing Producer responsibility organizations (PROs). As prescribed in the E-waste Rules, producers or manufacturers have to comply with the collection and recycling targets and abide by the Extender Producers Responsibility as mentioned in the rules. To conform and meet the recycling or collection targets, large manufacturers of electrical and electronic devices are delegated to outsource the responsibility of recycling or collection target to PROs. These PROs are specialized compliance service providers that manage e-waste on behalf of producers or manufacturers to fulfil their targets as prescribed based on the products sale or manufactured and brought in the market. For smooth functioning and efficiency in meeting the targets, it is very important to get the desired quantities of e-waste from the market. Since it is a well-known fact, the informal sector is very proficient in the collection of e-waste as more than 90% of collection is still done by the informal sector. Considering this fact, the informal sector can play a very important role when they collaborate formally with PROs to achieve their collection targets. With this arrangement and collaboration with the PROs or formal recyclers, the informal sector can improve their working conditions along with competitive economic or market benefits. Additionally, informal workers through this collaboration could get proper protective equipment and access to health schemes, proper ID, social and economic security and other benefits. Furthermore, this arrangement will broaden the access to the collection of valuable materials, which earlier they were not able to reach, which will lead to an increase in revenue generation. At the same time, safe and better working conditions for the informal sector will reduce the environmental and health hazards.

Involvement of Government to formalize the informal sector

Development of Common Facility Centre (CFC) for informal sector

Common Facility Centre (CFC) model has been introduced by The Ministry of Micro, Small and Medium Enterprises (MSME), Government of India (GoI), under the Cluster Development Scheme, which promotes enhancing of the productivity levels, competitiveness, and capacity building of micro and small enterprises. Under this model, the informal sector can also be formed as clusters and constituted into an association. The association can apply to leverage CDP-CFC scheme of the GoI. This scheme provides legal and safe work infrastructure for the cluster and will create micro-entrepreneurs in the e-waste sector, which will provide a solution to integrate the informal sector in the formal chain. Apart from formalization, this will create legal businesses and bring security to them and their families' livelihood. The formal sector lacks collection facilities, thereby leading to the rudimentary recycling process by the informal sector, which processes the e-waste in an unscientific and unsustainable manner, posing a threat to the environmental and human health. The cluster development scheme will be the win–win model for the informal sector, the producers/manufacturers and the Government. The materials can be collected by the informal sector and the infrastructure development under the scheme will enhance the recycling of e-waste in a safe and secure manner. This will also help in implementation of the E-waste (management) Rules, prevent treatment of e-waste in hazardous ways, and avoiding adverse impacts on the environment. This model will also promote the following:

- *Collection, segregation, transportation, dismantling for recycling in a safe and secure manner*
- *Inventory of generated e-waste for the State*
- *Resource recovery and circular economy by integration of material into the product value chain*
- *Transparent mechanism of data (input and output)*
- *Implementation of Extended Producers Responsibility*

- *Formalization of the informal sector*
- *In-house infrastructure development*
- *Occupation health and safety of the workers*
- *Skill enhancement and capacity building of informal sector*
- *Upscaling of development of technology, provided by the Government.*

For the successful development of this model, a stakeholder mapping is required as shown in Figure 5.

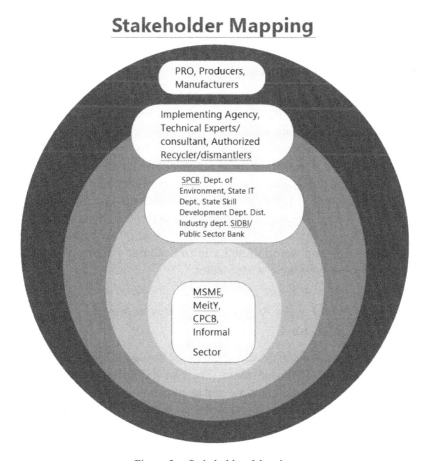

Figure 5.   Stakeholders Mapping

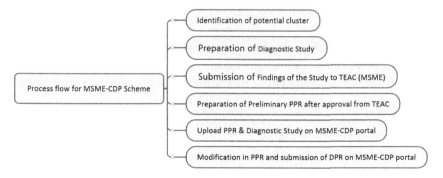

Figure 6.   MSME-CDP Scheme

Figure 6 lists the steps to be followed for applying MSME-CDP scheme.

Access to the recycling technology

A recycling technology has been developed by the Center for Materials in Engineering Technology (C-MET), a scientific society of the Ministry of Electronics and Information Technology, GoI. This low cost and small-scale technology solution can be provided to the informal sector. The Ministry of Electronics and Information Technology and State Government of Telangana have now jointly created a Center of Excellence at C-MET, Hyderabad, which hand-holds start-up companies and informal units, offering a technology and scientific recycling culture, which will be propagated and proliferated so that it can be best used by the country to extract materials and achieve resource efficiency as well as a circular economy in the e-waste sector.

Skill development and entrepreneurship development of the informal sector

Skill and entrepreneurship development could be a good model to integrate the informal sector in formal chain. The GoI has initiated a certification programme in e-waste dismantling and segregation of e-waste. Under this programme, informal sector clusters will be identified in various parts of the country. The programme will support in providing skills on e-waste dismantling procedures so that more material can be extracted from e-waste in an environment friendly manner. Such training programmes may also help in opening up livelihood options for the informal sector.

The training programme needs to focus on dismantling of the e-waste equipment and segregation of the various components like PCBs, valuable industry grade plastics, other electrical/electronic components, etc., so that the bulky equipments may be conveniently and economically transported to the Recycling Plants or reused in the industry.

These skill development programmes have been initiated in several states by the Ministry of Electronics and Information Technology, which aims to create a sustainable model to integrate the informal sector in the formal chain.

Establishing protocols and providing incentivization to foster formalization of the informal sector

To ensure the transparency and strengthen formal–informal collaboration, it is very important to create protocols and a platform for monitoring that will enable stakeholders to comply with. These protocols could be established and integrated in the form of tri-/bi-partite agreements, Memorandum of Understanding (MoUs), Joint Declaration of Intent with clear focus on roles and responsibilities, activities to be carried out, monitoring and evaluation mechanisms, codes of conduct, and nodal point of contact between the partnering organizations for ensuring communication and transparency. The informal sector needs to be made an integral part of such arrangements and should clearly be instructed on the safe standard working conditions for collection, dismantling, recycling, reliability and agreed prices for the e-waste collection and dismantling, Also the code of conduct should clearly ensure that the involvement of children in collection and dismantling of e-waste is discouraged.

Furthermore, an incentivization mechanism needs to be established that encourages them to collect and channel requisite amount of e-waste towards authorized recyclers. The incentives can be monetary or non-monetary in nature. Monetary incentives can be in the form of weight-based payment methods for waste collected or providing fixed salaries paid on a monthly basis.

Non-monetary incentives could be in the following forms:

- *Access to public or private services like health care and education (e.g. trainings in sustainable e-waste management)*
- *Support to formalize as an individual or a group (forming an association of scrap workers)*

- *Access to financial services (e.g. opening of a bank account, mobile money accounts, insurances)*
- *Provision of Protective gear or uniforms for collectors or groups of collectors*
- *Provision of ID-Cards*
- *Advocacy of workers' rights*
- *Certificates of compliance with the system*

Capacity building

It plays a significant role in improving the competitiveness of the informal sector and helping them to overcome the several challenges faced during the collection and dismantling of e-waste: The informal sector has access to materials through value chains and for recycling of e-waste now proper recycling mechanisms need to be established in the country. For streamlining this process, strategic as well as systemic processes are to be established and maintenance of work ethics and building of team work are to be encouraged.

- Hands-on training on dismantling of e-waste and extracting components is required so that environmentally sound recycling can take place.
- Human resources for administrative and accounts work are required to get the tax revenues and other legal process required by them.
- By formalizing the informal sector, they can continue their livelihood. This can be provided by supporting them in the form of training on skill development (soft skill development as well as skills on dismantling procedures to extract more materials from e-waste), various subsidies, government schemes, tax revenues, etc. to work in a safe and healthy environment.

A digital platform to create champions in e-waste dismantling

Application of digital tools are providing new opportunities to connect the informal collectors to the formal system. The registration of informal collectors, aggregators on the public domain and in the digital platform will improve the outreach, communication and management of large networks. The database in the centralized domain will help in ensuring the accountability and transparency of e-waste flows in the overall value chain. Furthermore, the informal sector, who could be the certified trainees under skill development programmes, may be working as resources for other stakeholders like producers, dismantlers, recyclers, PROs, etc. A government platform may be created to approach this certified informal sector. This can create job opportunities for this sector and other stakeholders will also be able to avail these manpower resources through this digital platform.

The following study elaborates the need for the capacity-building programme on a large scale for all stakeholders and showcases how regular mass awareness and capacity-building programmes benefit the overall value chain and management of e-waste in a sustainable and scientific manner.

Study Background

Need for capacity-building programme including awareness generation of all stakeholders on e-waste management

Rapid growth of the electronic industry and high rate of obsolescence of electronic products leads to generation of huge quantities of electronic waste (e-waste). The recycling of e-waste in non-formal units by unscientific, unhealthy and non-environmentally friendly methods is the key challenge in our society. Like other parts of the world, India is also facing serious challenges due to growing generation of e-waste and the lack of awareness of its environmental, social and economic aspects, among various stakeholders. The channelization of e-waste for proper recycling and establishing a system of accountability in e-waste management would only happen if effective awareness could be established among all stakeholders, including the consumers, manufactures, recyclers, young generations in schools, colleges as well as the government and corporate sectors. The public awareness campaigns should aim to not only achieve safe e-waste disposal, but also to reduce e-waste consumption. Therefore, an urgent need was felt by the decision-makers to hand-hold the stakeholders for scientific and sustainable e-waste management.

The Ministry of Electronics and Information Technology (MEITy), GoI, has recognized the fact that awareness is required considering the high stakes of everyone involved at various stages. Therefore, in partnership with the National Association of Software and Service

Companies (NASSCOM) Foundation, the Manufacturers Association of Information Technology (MAIT), Consumer Electronics and Appliances Manufacturers Association (CEAMA), PHD Chamber of Commerce and Industry (PHDCCI) and National Institute for Electronics and Information Technology (NIELIT) launched an awareness initiative in 2015 with the name **"Awareness Programme on Environmental Hazards of Electronic Waste" under the "Digital India Initiative"**, which seeks to enhance outreach and advocacy around the environmental and health hazards of improper disposal of e-waste in the country.

Methodology

Phase-wise implementation

The multi-stakeholder programme was targeted to reach across the length and breadth of the country so that stakeholders could be apprised of the challenges that are posed due to indiscriminate disposal of e-waste and its management by the informal sector. It was initiated in two phases:

Phase-I: In Phase I of the project, 10 states were identified across the country:

- Madhya Pradesh
- Bihar
- Uttar Pradesh
- Pondicherry
- Orissa
- Manipur
- Assam
- Goa
- West Bengal
- Jharkhand

    Along with identification of cities, key stakeholders were identified based upon the application of the E-waste Management and Handling Rules, 2011. It also included stakeholders who were responsible for managing e-waste as a part of their livelihood but did not fall within the ambit of the rules. The different stakeholders, for instance, schools, colleges, RWAs, bulk consumers, refurbishers, dealers, informal sectors, manufacturers, etc., were identified in the programme where outreach and advocacy efforts could be focussed for bringing the desired outcomes.

The awareness was generated through several ways and different media as well as tools were used to create awareness among each stakeholder in the value chain. Under the programme, the following strategies and tools were created:

- Develop an IEC framework for the website and mobile application and conceptualize the identity of the programme through a logo, a mascot, posters, leaflets, banners and other such collaterals
- Conduct workshops and activities with stakeholders across different cities identified
- To know the quantum of generated e-waste per annum in the identified 10 states covered
- Conduct a training of trainers with identified ambassadors who would then spread the message of e-waste and create awareness in these cities and states across the country
- Conduct a campaign across cinema halls in 10 states to enhance outreach on e-waste disposal and its proper management

Phase-II: Here, additional 17 states and 3 Union Territories (UTs) were covered:

- Andhra Pradesh
- Andaman and Nicobar Islands
- Chhatisgarh
- Daman and Diu
- Delhi
- Gujarat
- Haryana
- Himachal Pradesh
- Karnataka
- Kerala
- Lakshadweep
- Maharashtra
- Meghalaya
- Punjab
- Rajasthan
- Sikkim
- Tamil Nadu

- Telangana
- Tripura
- Uttarakhand

The project design of Phase II aimed at making the programme sustainable to ensure that once the support from the government ends, it would still be carried on by interested stakeholders in the private sector. Many factors contributed to this, including the advent of the E-waste Management Rules, 2016, the institutionalization of Extended Producers Responsibility (EPR) and the enhanced compliance and monitoring by the State Pollution Control Board (Spcbs), Pollution Control Committees (PCCs) and Central Pollution Control Board (CPCB).

Work packages

The lessons learnt from Phase I of the project were used to design Phase II. As listed in Table 1, seven work packages were designed to maximize outreach and creating capabilities, while ensuring monitoring and evaluation by an independent agency. The broad components or activities undertaken for every work package comprise the following:

Impact of awareness program

The awareness programme turned out to be a huge success, considering that the MEITy had hoped to reach out to close to 600,000 stakeholders by the end of Phase II; the outreach achieved was more than twice this figure. The unique selling proposition (USP) of the programme was the active participation of several industries in terms of outreach, which has been created through the support of different stakeholders including PROs, recyclers and industrial associations.

The positive impact of the countrywide awareness programme initiatives, which were a huge success, is listed as follows:

Formalizing the informal sector — Creating the demand

Informal actors across the cities where the programme was conducted have expressed willingness to access technology that has been developed

Table 1.   Activities Work Packages

Work Packages (WPs)	Activities Undertaken
WP1	Two components: 1. Development of content for the SWAYAM/Diksha platform, which is operated by the Ministry of Human Resource Development (MHRD), GoI. 2. Creating awareness using social media so that outreach could be enhanced extensively.
WP2	Upgradation of the content and incorporating of the changes as per project requirement.
WP3	Create resources and build capacities at the local level so that they could be used in the future for conducting capacity building with support from private partners and state departments. Training of trainers was conducted in the identified 20 cities so that trainers could be developed for different stakeholders including, schools, colleges, RWAs, the informal sector, refurbishers and bulk consumers. The names of these trainers are put up on the project website (greene.gov.in).
WP4	Create awareness with stakeholders through conducting activities and workshops at local levels in 20 cities across the country. Follow-up activities were also to be conducted in 10 cities where the programme had been conducted in Phase I of the project
WP5	Develop standard methodology for National level and State level inventory
WP6	Create awareness through the use of small films in cinema halls as had been done in Phase I. Small films were featured right after the National Anthem was played before the start of the feature film in cinema halls across 20 cities
WP7	Monitoring and evaluation of all packages stated above by an independent agency so that the impact of the project could be measured as per set indicators and outputs.

by the MEITy. After the intensive programme on outreach, awareness generation and technological options, there has been an increase in the number of registered Dismantlers and Recyclers with the CPCB.

• *Creating Ambassadors for driving the change*: The attitude of stakeholders towards e-waste has also seen changes over the course of the project. Children and youth have turned out to be ambassadors of change as they have taken upon themselves to drive the agenda for environmentally sound management of e-waste.

• *Sustainability through adoption by Industrial sector*: The largest PROs in the country have come forward and have started using the mascot of the programme, GreenE, in their awareness programmes which they have been conducting on behalf of their Producers.

• *Enhanced demand for compliance — Building Capacities*: Regulators in states have also developed auditing mechanisms so that compliance monitoring can take place on a regular basis. The National Institute of Electronics and Information Technology, an arm of the Ministry of Electronics and Information Technology, has been at the forefront of developing tools that can assist the compliance authorities in proper implementation of the E-waste Management Rules, 2016.

• *Start of a Movement — Driving Change*: The interest which has been generated by the programme across stakeholders has been provided a fillip by industry, which has come forward to support and sustainably run the programme going ahead. PROs have been provided the support of the Digital India logo as well as the GreenE Mascot.

• *Creating the potential for employment*: The e-waste sector in India has the potential to employ lakhs of people in the informal sector and provide them livelihoods that ensure security, safety and dignity to live as per the standards. Active industrial participation has also allowed to bring the focus on the urgent need for development of infrastructure for recycling and dismantling in the country so that environmentally sound disposal of e-waste can take place.

Key achievements of the awareness programme

The awareness programmes have had some of the major implications that were dispersed throughout and benefited all the stakeholders involved in e-waste management.

• Under the programme, around 600 Workshops and activities were organized in various states, and more than 300,000 lakh participants from schools, colleges, RWA, manufacturers, informal operators, etc. and 6,000 government officials participated (see Figures 7 and 8).

- The mass awareness among youth of the country was created through cinema halls and more than 200 million viewers have been reached in nearly 3,000 cinema halls (see Figure 9).
- The programme in Phase II saw industry come forward to contribute to the initiatives in creating awareness, which was also part of their compliance requirement under extended producer responsibility as stated in the E-waste Management Rules, 2016.
- The programme was designed to ensure that it would be sustainable as well as leading to direct action, which allows for e-waste to move into the formal chain for its environmentally sound disposal. Activities, workshops, coupled with collection drives allow for safe disposal of e-waste by stakeholders. Furthermore, trainers across cities were being equipped with skills to engage with different stakeholders in order to ensure that activities and workshops could be conducted to build capacities and create outreach on ways and means for safe disposal of e-waste. These trainers can be adopted by producers, PROs, SPCBs as resources that can create awareness on e-waste disposal at a miniscule cost in the future.

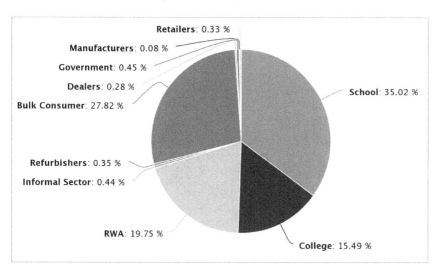

Figure 7.   Percentage of Participants Achieved

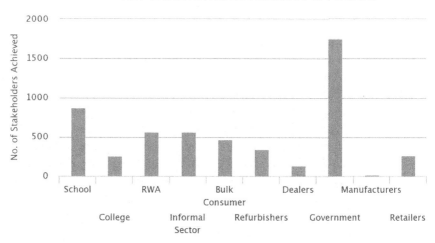

Figure 8.   No. of Stakeholders Achieved

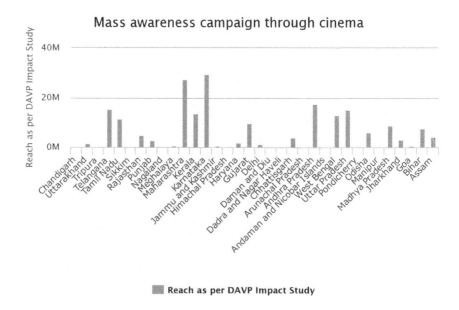

Figure 9.   Mass Awareness Campaign through Cinema

Study Limitations

The awareness initiative highlights the importance of vision, strategic planning and implementation of outreach and awareness generation activities for different stakeholders in managing e-waste responsibly and sustainably. However, there were certain limitations of this awareness campaign, such as:

* Reservations initially from the informal sector, industries and state governments to ensure active participation.
* Creating an enabling environment for stakeholders to gather at one platform to make the programme successful.

Conclusion and Future Recommendations

Every institution, at every level, is responsible for ensuring that technological advancements should not jeopardise environmental and human health. Although through this awareness initiative the best maximum practices were taken up to integrate all stakeholders to access the capacity building in effective e-waste collection mechanisms in the country, still there is scope for further research on how these activities should be taken up in the future.

Inclusive Steps for Integrating Informal Sector in E-waste Management for sustainability

Figure 10 lists steps for integrated management of sustainability.

* Engagement of all stakeholders (producers, consumers, bulk generators, dismantlers, recyclers) in e-waste value chain for active participation thereby ensuring responsible collection and its sustainable management.
* Integration of informal sector in the formal system as they are the backbone of collection, sorting and dismantling, thought they are not recognized and not given any incentives or proper infrastructure. Therefore, it is important to provide them proper training, incentives like health security, access to the material and legalization that would encourage them to be more efficient towards sustainable e-waste management.
* A collaborative approach to engage public and social enterprises to associate with e-waste handlers should be made available. The

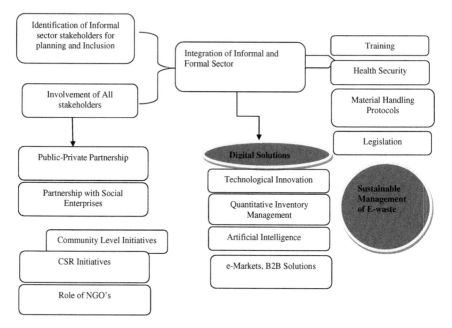

Figure 10.   Inclusive Steps for Integrating Informal Sector in E-waste Management for Sustainability

activities can be taken up in public–private partnership to associate informal sector through organized mechanisms with suitable financial inclusions. At the very basic level, the door-to-door awareness programmes apart from facilitations for collections can be run by NGOs or other bodies to maximize resource recovery and minimize waste. The funding for the similar initiatives can be provided by concerned public bodies. The NGOs can also set up collection centres in a satellite mechanism for e-waste handling and fair prices can be provided to handlers through them.

- The e-waste handlers should also be provided with awareness on safety and protective gear mechanisms to avoid any exposure to health hazardous metals, radiations or sharp wires. NGOs, social media, backward extension workers can play a very important role here to educate all stakeholders involved at various levels in e-waste handling mechanism. The training and extension programmes should be aimed to build capacities for achieving best safe handling practices.
- The treatment and recognition of e-waste handlers in the informal sector as legitimate service suppliers or contributors have to be

channelized. Some of the inclusive steps can be providing identification cards to informal sector e-waste handlers, signing contracts with them, formalizing their addresses and places and listing them as identified sources for the services.

- Strengthening e-waste online marketplaces in B2B model — specifically, installing sophisticated e-waste identification by AI can be a great leap towards it. There has been recent research on e-waste handling through a mobile robot that performs segregation based on arm lift mechanism with 96% accuracy. RFID Tags, IoT sensors, AI Equipped programmes, cloud-based e-waste handling programmes, Trash Bot Robots, using computer vision and machine learning programmes are few technological innovations that may be saviours in the sector, if implemented at the grassroots level stepwise.
- The concerned regulatory authorities at prime level should form exclusive organizations to collect and track information about e-waste production along with recycling. The reporting of these organizations has to maintain speed and accuracy to trace accountability, transparency and fix the responsibility.
- Prior to discarding any electronic equipment, one must be aware to securely erase all confidential material from any device, also the redundant electronic equipment may be donated rather that discarded.
- Innovative technological solutions should be adopted for material usage during the manufacturing of the product, enhancing the longevity as well durability of the product through eco-design, which can promote repair, refurbishment and recovery of the material after end-of-life of the product.
- Standardization of the inventorization methodology for the quantitative analysis of e-waste generation so that appropriate infrastructures could be established for recycling units in the country.

Appropriate measures to be adopted by the manufactures for right to repair, recovery and recycling of the end-of-life product to ensure responsible and sustainable management of e-waste.

References

Anooja, A. (2015). Digital India with E-commerce revolution in rural India: Transform India digitally and economically. *Engineering International, 3.* Doi: 10.18034/ei.v3i2.771.

Das Gautam, *Business Today*. (2020, May 7). https://www.businesstoday.in/current/economy-politics/make-in-india-consumer-electronics-manufacturing-to-grow-at-18/story/390876.html.

Gaur, A. D. & Padiya, J. (2016). A Study Impact of 'Digital India' in 'Make in India' Program in IT & BPM Sector. In *Fourteenth AIMS International Conference on Management*, pp. 325–331.

Monika & Kishore, J. (2010). E-waste management: As a challenge to public health in India. *Indian Journal of Community Medicine: Official Publication of Indian Association of Preventive & Social Medicine, 35*(3), 382–385. Doi: 10.4103/0970-0218.69251.

Pinto, V. N. (2008). E-waste hazard: The impending challenge. *Indian Journal of Occupational and Environmental Medicine, 12*(2), 65.

Report by The Federal Ministry for Economic Cooperation and Development (BMZ), Division of Public Relations, Harnessing the digital revolution for sustainable development, The Digital Agenda of BMZ.

Singh, A. K. & Maurya, S. (2017). A review of digital India programme and comparative study of E-governance initiatives around world. *Asian Journal of Research in Business Economics and Management, 7*, 1. Doi: 10.5958/2249-7307.2017.00125.6.

Wath, S. B., Vaidya, A. N., Dutt, P. S., & Chakrabarti, T. (2010). A roadmap for development of sustainable E-waste management system in India. *Science of the Total Environment, 409*(1), 19–32.

Websites

http://www.sustainabilityoutlook.in/content/e-waste-management-india-new-rules-old-problems-756361.

www.greene.gov.in.

www.investindia.gov.in/sector/electronic-systems.

Chapter 8

Exploring the Growth of India's Foreign Direct Investment Equity Inflow amid COVID-19 Outbreak

Ifeanyi Mbukanma[*,‡] and Ravinder Rena[†,§]

*Department of Economics and Business Sciences, Walter Sisulu University, Mthatha Campus, South Africa

†DUT Business School, Durban University of Technology ML Sultan Campus, Durban, South Africa

‡imbukanma@wsu.ac.za

§ravinder.rena@gmail.com

Abstract

The COVID-19 pandemic has spread at an alarming pace, infecting millions and bringing several global economic activities to a halt, as various countries have tightened regulations and steps to monitor and control the spread of the virus. In this context, this study was conducted to explore the growth of India's Foreign Direct Investment (FDI) equity inflow amid the COVID-19 outbreak. This was based on the fact that previous studies found FDI as an engine that creates opportunities for employment development, increases productivity, increases domestic economic stability through introducing expertise and technologies, strengthened infrastructure, boosts exports, and contributes to long-term economic growth in countries around the world.

To achieve this objective, an in-depth review of current and previous literature from journals and periodic publications of legitimate organizations, both local and international, on the evolution and the trend of the COVID-19 pandemic and its impact on India's FDI was conducted. However, the findings revealed a significant drop in net FDI flows globally, but a sustained growth and significant increase in India. Secondly, key sectors such as services, computer software and hardware, telecommunications, trading, automobile, construction development, chemicals and pharmaceuticals were revealed to have attracted the maximum FDI inflow to India amid the COVID-19 pandemic. Therefore, it was recommended that a cohesive policy that further strengthens FDI by identifying and creating incentives for other main industrial sectors could further promote the continued attractiveness of FDI to India.

Introduction

The economy of India is one of the contemporary world's top emerging economies. It was considered fragile five decades ago, but no longer. Since 2014, it has emerged as one of the world's leading international destinations with a substantial increase in FDI. However, most of the economic activities that promoted this economic growth in India were halted as the world experienced an unprecedented surge of coronavirus, also known as the COVID-19 pandemic. The COVID-19 pandemic was first identified in Wuhan, China, in late 2019 and started spreading worldwide. At first, maximum cases were initially detected in China, but the infection spread over Europe, America and worldwide. The COVID-19 pandemic is a global shock involving a concurrent disruption of demand and supply in the integrated world economy (Mbukanma, Ravinder & Ifeanyichukwu, 2020; Nicola *et al.*, 2020). The virus has reduced labour availability and output on the supply side, as companies have been disrupted, resulting from lockdown regulations implemented to control the spread of the virus. On the demand side, consumer consumption and business investment are constrained by layoffs and loss of income, the burden of sickness, quarantine, unemployment and declining economic prospects.

Accordingly, India is the second most affected country in terms of infection rate globally, with the number of infected individuals hitting above 43 million and deaths over 500,000 in April 2022. Extreme doubt about the course of the virus, duration, severity and effect of the pandemic has led to a downward cycle of a declining market and consumer morale. It has also worsened global financial conditions, leading to employment cuts and continuous investment and economic development reduction. As the tolls of infection and fatality escalate, global devastation is evident, representing the world's biggest economic shock in decades. Consequently, different nations have started requesting financial assistance from the International Monetary Fund (IMF) to support the financial shock caused by the pandemic. As a result, reserve banks around the globe have initiated aggressive policies to cut interest rates and roll out massive stimulus measures to help manage the impact of the pandemic that has rocked global economic activities and the financial market (Ozili & Arun, 2020). It is evident that the pandemic has affected different countries differently, going by their level of vulnerability before the outbreak of COVID-19. To this end, advanced, emerging and developing countries across the globe are evaluating and counting the cost of the pandemic in terms of the impact it has caused in different sectors of the economy in the striving to reactivate a cross-sectional economic growth and development. Hence, the objective of this study was engineered in this context to evaluate the impact of the COVID-19 pandemic on India's FDI equity inflows.

Method

This study utilized a literature review strategy. The choice of research strategy was informed by the objective of this study, as the key emphasis was on the survey and assessment of past works of literature to unfold logically and up to date issues as they concern the spread of the coronavirus and its impact on India's FDI equity inflows. Although there are varieties of literature review methods in this context, including narrative review, vote counting, meta-analysis and descriptive analysis of literature (King & He, 2005), a descriptive analysis of literature was used for the benefit of this study. Thus, the descriptive analysis of literature mainly summarizes and synthesizes accessible studies on a specific subject field.

However, due to the limited number of empirical research as it concerns up to date logical analysis of the current global information on the pandemic, a detailed descriptive analysis of previous literature was conducted, which aids in revealing current issues, challenges and impacts of COVID-19 on the Indian economy as well as the response of FDI inflows to the trend of the virus. Thus, various COVID-19 articles gathered from various significant and applicable websites, journals, newsletters and magazines were considered in extracting information for the descriptive analysis.

Review of Related Literature

The unprecedented outbreak of coronavirus in late 2019, leading to a global pandemic in 2020, has triggered public health crisis globally, with underlining evidence of negative impacts on social and economic activities. A detrimental effect has been felt globally from the ripple effect of COVID-19, which continues to plunge the global economy in several ways. In the quest to manage and reduce the spread globally, different economies have enforced several measures, which have affected economic activities worldwide (Chakraborty & Maity, 2020; Nicola *et al.*, 2020). Consequently, FDI decisions by firms globally were disrupted significantly due to several measures adopted by nations to control the spread of the virus. The inevitable impact on FDI flows will depend on the success of both these public health and economic policy responses by the different nations (OECD, 2020). In essence, FDI is a long-term investment partnership between a resident entity and a non-resident entity, which typically includes a significant managerial impact on the investment firm by the investor (Mbukanma & Rena, 2021; Arain *et al.*, 2020; Zameer *et al.*, 2020).

Over the years, these systematic long-term investment partnerships have helped boost economic growth and development in advanced, emerging and developing economies. It has also helped promote industrial revolution through the transfer of technology, industrial robotization and digital advancement in production and investment across the globe (Singh, 2019). On the contrary, the surge of COVID-19 has created uncertainty in global investment, which has continued to affect FDI inflows across economies as the global FDI collapsed in 2020, dropping 42% from $1.5 trillion in 2019 to an estimated $859 billion in 2020

(UNCTAD, 2021). According to the UNCTAD report, the concentration of the decline in FDI was on developing economies, where FDI equity flows dropped by −12% (an estimate of $616 billion), while developed economies recorded a drop of −69% (an estimate of $229 billion) and transition economies recorded a drop of −77% (an estimate of $13 billion). The United States also recorded a sharp decrease in FDI flows to −49% (an estimate of $134 billion), while China cemented their lead on FDI, with other Asian countries benefiting.

However, the United Kingdom (UK) and other European countries have also experienced a heavy drop in FDI inflows. Ironically, India being the second most affected country by COVID-19, received an increased rate in FDI inflow, hitting a rise of 13% (an estimate of $57 billion) in the year 2020, as an investment in the digital economy continues to witness growth (UNCTAD, 2021). Other than equity investments, there has been a significant rise in the inter-corporate debt of FDI firms, which covers borrowing or leasing among affiliated direct investment firms. Consequently, the streamlining of the policy mechanism for external commercial borrowings (ECBs) since January 2019 has enabled all companies eligible for FDI to raise ECBs, and other relaxations, such as widening the spectrum of end-use resources, have resulted in increased FDI flows of US$8.3 billion in 2019–2020, three times the amount a year earlier (Reserve Bank of India, 2020).

The framework of India's FDI policies

FDI is considered a significant source of non-debt financial capital for economic growth and development. Therefore, the Indian government needs to attract and encourage FDI to complement domestic resources, technology and skills for accelerated economic growth and development. Thus, over the last few decades, there have been significant shifts in approaches and policies related to FDI in India, together with improvements in the country's industrial policy and foreign exchange status. These policies are embedded in a consolidated framework, updated every six months to monitor and keep pace with the regulatory changes. However, the policies are formulated in different phases (see Table 1), which address the issues as it concerns the requisite policies that will enhance the growth of FDI in India.

Table 1.   Major Features of FDI Policy in India

Phase	Category	Features
Phase I 1950–1967	Receptive attitude	Non-discriminatory treatment to FDI; No restrictions on remittances; Indians having ownership and control.
Phase II 1967–1980	Restrictions	Restrictions on FDI without technology. More than 40% not allowed. FDI controlled by FERA (foreign exchange regulation act).
Phase III 1980–1990	Pro-business approach: gradual liberalization	Export oriented units allowed higher FDI. Liberalization in the procedure of remittance and royalty in technical fees. Faster channels for FDI clearance created.
Phase IV 1990–Onwards	Open door policy	Liberalized policy framework for foreign trade, foreign exchange and technical collaborations. Core and infrastructure sectors: FDI was welcomed and FERA replaced with and FEMA (Foreign exchange management act). It was not necessary for FDI to be accompanied with technology. FDI was encouraged through mergers and acquisitions in services and financial sector, non-banking financial companies and insurance, etc.
Phase V 2014 Onwards	Open door policy and promotion of selective sectors of national interest	Promoting FDI selectively in several sectors. Focus on FDI for job creation and domestic manufacturing. Raising FDI in defence sector from 26% to 49%. Full Indian Management and control through FIPB route. Development of smart cities and reduction in FDI from 50,000 square meters to 20,000 square meters with a three year post completion lock in. FDI in manufacturing through automatic route. Manufacturers allowed to sell through retail including e commerce platforms. Raising for FDI in the insurance sector from 26% to 49%., Civil aviation raised from 74% to 100%. FII/FPI allowed to invest in Power exchanges through primary market. Overseas investment up to 49% in the insurance and pension sectors under the automatic route. 100% FDI in asset reconstruction companies through the automatic route. Construction development eligible for 100% FDI under the automatic route. Limit for investment by foreign portfolio investors (FPIs) in central public sector enterprises, other than banks, listed in stock exchanges raised from 24% to 49%. Investment limit for foreign entities in Indian stock exchanges will be enhanced from 5% to 15%.

Source: DIPP (2020).

The early phase of the policy primarily addresses the receptive attitude that provides foundations for foreign investment attractions. However, the liberation efforts started in 1980, with industrial policy statements in 1980, 1982 and 1983. The procedures for formulating FDI policies in India involve a coherent contribution of the Department of Industrial Policy and Promotion (DIPP) and Ministry of Commerce and Industry with procedural instructions issued by the Reserve Bank of India. Thus, these policies are reviewed ongoing and measured for further liberalization with a regulatory framework consisting of Acts, Regulations, Press Notes, Press Releases and Clarifications (DIPP, 2020).

In the 1990s, when the economy was in a crucial stage and needed macro-economic stabilization and economic reform, FDI emerged as the most preferred option for mobilizing financial resources. As a result, up to 51% of FDI's equity in specified industries was authorized by the Reserve Bank of India under the automatic approval route. Indeed, since the liberalization effort in the third phase of the policy, FDI flows to India have steadily increased and are an essential part of foreign capital, as FDI infuses long-term sustainable resources in the economy and contributes to technology transfer, strategic sector development, increased innovation, competition and job creation, among other benefits. Thus, the fourth and the fifth Phases of the policy framework incorporate significant policies that have caused a long-run and most recent attraction of foreign firms to invest in India. However, though a list of investment sectors exists for investment by foreign firms, investment is prohibited in gambling, lottery, the business of chit fund, housing and real estate, trading in transferable development rights, atomic energy, manufacturing of cigars, cheroots, cigarillos and cigarettes, of tobacco or of tobacco substitutes, to mention but few (DIPP, 2020).

Growth of India's FDI inflows amid COVID-19 pandemic

Developed and developing countries are expected to contribute to economic growth more than domestic investment (Ketteni & Kottaridi, 2019; Dunning & Lundan, 2008, p. 316). FDI is widely regarded as a vital component to stimulate economic growth and integrate the economy into the global environment. It is also considered one of the essential platforms through which nations can access global finance. However, the surge in the COVID-19 pandemic created absolute uncertainty in the investment environment, where major economic activities were put to a halt in the efforts to control the spread of the virus. International borders were closed, businesses were disrupted and shut down, investors counted their losses, and jobs were lost. Perhaps, in this kind of hostile economic environment, FDIs are less expected because of the level of vulnerability of most economies. Many economies around the globe were experiencing contractions, and projections were made on further economic contractions in advanced, developed, emerging and developing economies.

According to the Department for Promotion of Industry and Internal Trade (DPIIT), the Indian economy received significant growth in its FDI in 2021, attracting a percentage growth of 19% (over $500 million), a milestone in the Indian economy amid the high level of uncertainty created by the COVID-19 outbreak (see Table 2).

The increased rate of India's FDI inflow during this unprecedented time, as presented in Table 2, shows a structural growth in crucial sectors of the Indian economy compared to other emerging economies that have shown the highest level of vulnerability during this pandemic. However, the effort of the Indian government since the year 2000 by implementing major FDI reforms has helped ensure that the country becomes an increasingly desirable and investor-friendly destination (Singh, 2019). Although the growth trend as presented in Table 2 seems to fluctuate, absolute consistency has been the brain behind Indian reforms that have kept the pace of FDI attractions to India even amid the coronavirus pandemic. Accordingly, the investment climate in India has changed and improved significantly since the opening up of the economy in 1991, and more improvement has been made since 2014 (Singh, 2019).

In addition, the relaxation of FDI criteria has played a crucial role in rising FDI in various sectors of the Indian economy. The new FDI policy framework provides two routes for foreign companies to access the country: the government route and the automatic route. Under the government route, prior investment approvals are required and must be authorized by the corresponding administrative agency or department. On the automatic route, the investor does not need an investment authorization from the Government of India. However, up to 100% of FDI will be allowed on both routes. It could be argued that India's existing FDI policy framework has provided coaching and significant leverage on the havoc and uncertainty created by the COVID-19 outbreak. As a further weakening

Table 2. Indian's FDI Equity Inflows between 2000–2021 (US$ million)

S. No.	Financial Years 2000–2020	Amount of FDI Equity Inflows	Percentage Growth over Previous Years
1	2000	2,463	—
2	2001	4,065	+65%
3	2002	2,705	–33%
4	2003	2,188	–19%
5	2004	3,219	+47%
6	2005	5,540	+72%
7	2006	12,492	+125%
8	2007	24,575	+97%
9	2008	31,396	+28%
10	2009	25,834	–18%
11	2010	21,383	–17%
12	2011	35,121	–64%
13	2012	22,423	–36%
14	2013	24,299	+8%
15	2014	29,737	+22%
16	2015	40,001	+35%
17	2016	43,478	+9%
18	2017	44,857	+3%
19	2018	44,366	–1%
20	2019	49,977	+13%
21	2020	59,825	+19%
22	2021	84,835	+42%
Cumulative Total (From April 2000 to March 2022)		614,779	

Source: DPIIT (2022).

situation in FDI growth more contractions are expected globally, more significant efforts are required by the government of India to sustain the existing growth in FDI by further addressing individual sectors of the economy.

Table 3. Sectors Attracting Highest FDI Equity Inflows to India (US$ million)

Ranks	Sectors	2018–2019 (April–March)	2019–2020 (April–March)	2020–2021 (April–September)	Cumulative Inflows	% of Total Inflows by Sector
1	Services Sector	9,158	7,854	2,252	84,255	17%
2	Computer Software & Hardware	6,415	7,673	17,554	62,466	12%
3	Telecommunications	2,668	4,445	7	37,278	7%
4	Trading	4,462	4,574	949	28,543	6%
5	Construction Development: Townships, housing, built-up infrastructure and construction development projects	213	617	118	25,780	5%
6	Automobile Industry	2,623	2,824	417	24,628	5%
7	Chemicals (Other than Fertilizers)	1,981	1,058	437	18,077	4%
8	Construction (Infrastructure) Activities	2,258	2,042	377	17,223	3%
9	Drugs & Pharmaceuticals	266	518	367	16,868	3%
10	Hotel & Tourism	1,076	2,938	283	15,572	3%

Source: DPIIT (2022).

However, the importance of addressing individual sectors of the economy was presented in the report of UNCTAD (2021) and Reserve Bank of India (2020) as they emphasized that the increase in India's FDI equity inflows was attributed to the investment in the service sector and digital economy, which includes communication services, retail and wholesale trade, financial services, computer and business services and the manufacturing sector. Cross-border M&A sales were increased by 87% (an estimate of $27 billion). A significant record deal was the acquiring of 10% of Jio Platform by Jaadhu, owned by Facebook (United States) with a value worth $5.7 billion (UNCTAD, 2021). Thus, Table 3 presents 10 top sectors of the Indian economy that attract the highest FDI equity inflow 2018–2020.

Accordingly, the investment in the service sectors also reported a rise in cross-border M&A as well as the digital sector, which also recorded a significant rise. Indeed, the sectorial attraction of FDI represents the quality of multinational investment that a country attracts. Similarly, the sectorial share of investment also indicates the direction of growth in the host nation as it concerns productivity capacity and local economic development. Although it is clearly shown in Table 3 that there is a significant shift of FDI from the manufacturing to services sectors, these developments are primarily attributed to foreign firms' interest, which represents their focus on investment areas with more optimal benefits. However, 29% of India's FDI came through the Mauritius route, followed by Singapore at 21%, the US, Netherlands, and Japan at 7% and the UK at 6% (DPIIT, 2021). However, as the COVID-19 pandemic continues to spread across the globe with lesser optimism about the vaccines from fewer companies, incentives in different sectors of the Indian economy that will attract more FDI need to be sustained. Hence, the sustainability of the relationship and attraction of these foreign firms is key to long-term growth in FDI, which also attracts comprehensive economic growth and development.

Key Findings of the Study

The global economy has experienced several ups and downs recently, struggling with the devastating economic situation that resulted from the outbreak of COVID-19 with lots of uncertainty in the investment environment. However, globalization has helped most economies to survive, as more significant benefits exist in an increased relationship in economic activities and investment between nations. Similarly, FDI has played a more significant role in leveraging most economies by attracting multinational firms to invest in key economic sectors. Thus, in evaluating the growth of India's FDI amid the COVID-19 outbreak, key findings were identified with policy recommendations.

(a) The Indian economy has recently been described as one of the most attractive developing economies globally. In line with globalization, trading partners with India have grown significantly over the last decades, providing more opportunities for various sectors of the economy. Reflecting closely, India's half-trillion-dollar FDI indicates foreign investors' deep confidence in India's strong economic fundamentals, stable political outlook, and sustainable economic growth that generated returns for investors even during the global recession of 2007–2008.

(b) The sectorial attraction of FDI in India has shown a significant shift from the manufacturing sector to the service and digital economy sectors. This has helped to create competitiveness and boost the business's productivity, expanding across the whole network of firms engaged in the production of goods or services that need to be updated to satisfy current consumer demands.

(c) As India battles with the increased rate of the COVID-19 pandemic, existing structural economic policies have helped leverage them from significant economic contraction. Indeed, the global economy has undergone a sharp contraction since the COVID-19 outbreak, and more contractions more contractions are expected, but the Indian economy has demonstrated a positive degree of resilience that poses a non-vulnerable economic policy.

(d) A significant cross-border M&A sale was also recorded in India's economy amid the COVID-19 outbreak, which was less expected considering the backdrop of economic activities around the globe. However, this has shown the level of FDI attraction even during the pandemic period, and that multinational firms were still interested in acquiring investment shares in India.

Conclusion and Recommendation

The objective of this chapter was to evaluate theoretically and unveil the growth of India's FDI equity inflows amid the COVID-19 outbreak. For this purpose, a concise literature review was conducted. From the literature analysis, evidence was unveiled on the growth of India's FDI inflows as FDI was found to be an engine that has promoted economic advancement in India. However, the COVID-19 pandemic was found to have disrupted major economic activities across the globe, as different nations implemented measures to control the spread of the virus. Secondly, the growth trend of India's FDI equity inflows amid the COVID-19 outbreak was revealed, as India's FDI was identified to have attracted a 13% increase from the previous year. This was contrary to many economists in the wake of the coronavirus pandemic, as both advanced, developed, emerging and developing economies were on the verge of collapsing.

Some schools of thought suggest that the attraction of FDI flows in different countries amid the COVID-19 pandemic is highly attributed to how individual countries have managed the pandemic. Besides the service sector, computer software and hardware, telecommunication services, retail and wholesale trade, financial services, construction development, automobile and chemical industries were the highest recipients of FDI, which triggered the rise amounting to over $500 billion. In essence, the existing FDI policy in India was identified as the bedrock that has provided resilience and sustainable attraction of FDI growth during this period of global economic contraction. It was recommended that further strengthening of the FDI policy by identifying and creating openings for other critical industrial sectors will further sustain the continuous attraction of FDI to India.

References

Arain, H., Han, L., Sharif, A., & Meo, M. S. (2020). Investigating the effect of inbound tourism on FDI: The importance of quantile estimations. *Tourism Economics*, *26*(4), 682–703.

Chakraborty, I. & Maity, P. (2020). COVID-19 outbreak: Migration, effects on society, global environment and prevention. *Science of the Total Environment*, *728*, 138882.

DIPP. (2020). Annual report on consolidated FDI policy. https://dipp.gov.in/sites/default/files/FDI-PolicyCircular-2020-29October2020_0.pdf.

DPIIT. (2022). Quarterly fact sheet of FDI. https://dpiit.gov.in/publications/fdi-statistics.

Dunning, J. H. & Lundan, M. (2008). *Multinational Enterprises and the Global Economy*. Cheltenham: Edward Elgar Publishing.

Ketteni, E. & Kottaridi, C. (2019). The impact of regulations on the FDI-growth nexus within the institution-based view: A nonlinear specification with varying coefficients. *International Business Review, 28*(3), 415–427.

King, W. R. & He, J. (2005). Understanding the role and methods of meta-analysis in IS research. *Communications of the Association for Information Systems, 16*(1), 32.

Mbukanma, I. & Rena, R. (2021). Relationship between foreign direct investment and tourism: A conceptual review of South Africa context. *Researchers World, 12*(1), 55–67.

Mbukanma, I., Ravinder, R., & Ifeanyichukwu, L. U. (2020). Surviving personal financial strain amid COVID-19 outbreak: A conceptual review of South African context. *Acta Universitatis Danubius. Œconomica, 16*(6), 175–190.

Nicola, M., Alsafi, Z., Sohrabi, C., Kerwan, A., Al-Jabir, A., Iosifidis, C., Agha, M., & Agha, R. (2020). The socio-economic implications of the coronavirus pandemic (COVID-19): A review. *International Journal of Surgery, 78*, 185.

OECD. (2020). Foreign direct investment flows in the time of COVID-19. https://www.oecd.org/coronavirus/policy-responses/foreign-direct-investment-flows-in-the-time-of-COVID-19-a2fa20c4.

Ozili, P. K. & Arun, T. (2020). Spillover of COVID-19: Impact on the global economy. *SSRN Electronic Journal, 3562570*. Doi: 10.2139/ssrn.3562570.

Reserve Bank of India. (2020). Annual report on economic review. https://www.rbi.org.in/scripts/AnnualReportPublications.aspx?Id=1286.

Singh, S. (2019). Foreign Direct Investment (FDI) inflows in India. *Journal of General Management Research, 6*(1), 41–53.

UNCTAD. (2021). Investment trends monitor. https://unctad.org/system/files/official-document/diaeiainf2021d1_en.pdf.

Zameer, H., Yasmeen, H., Zafar, M. W., Waheed, A., & Sinha, A. (2020). Analysing the association between innovation, economic growth, and environment: Divulging the importance of FDI and trade openness in India. *Environmental Science and Pollution Research, 27*, 29539–29553.

Part III
The Knowledge Partnership Approach

Chapter 9

Indian Fintech Companies: Scope and Challenges

Seema Garg[*], Pranav Tewari[*,†] and Navita Mahajan[*,‡]

*Amity International Business School, Amity University, Noida, India

†pranav.tewari@s.amity.edu

‡nmahajan@amity.edu

Abstract

The goal of this study is to examine the opportunities and difficulties that exist in the financial technology business. It provides an overview of the history of the fintech industry in India, as well as an assessment of the current situation of financial technology in the country's financial sector. Financial technology allows the digitization of transactions, which makes them safer for the end user. Fintech is enabling cheaper operational costs and a more user-friendly graphical user interface, for financial technology services in India. It is changing the attitudes and behaviours of persons in the Indian financial sector.

Introduction

Fintech is "a cross-disciplinary subject that mixes finance, technology management, and innovation management" (Leong, 2018). A fintech company focuses on financial technology and services. In the financial technology industry, a fintech company provides alternatives to traditional banking services and nonbanking finance services. Fintech is a relatively new concept in the financial industry, having emerged as a result of the financial crisis. In today's industry, every single participant is introducing tech-enabled solutions that cater to end-customer wants while also enhancing efficiency and influencing the market space to produce a win–win situation. Fintech in India is particularly favourable due to the country's unrivalled youth demographic, which is continually increasing in size. Collaboration and innovation are becoming increasingly common, driven by established banks, well-known technological companies, and even regulatory groups operating in the market.

The word "fintech" was coined by a New York banker in 1972 to describe the field of financial technology. Fintech relates mainly to small start-up companies, which develop innovative technological solutions in such areas as online and mobile payments, big data, alternative finance and financial management. Such firms provide services such as payment options; online marketplace lending; mobile applications; financing; foreign exchange and remittances; investments; distributed ledger technology; digital currencies; mobile wallets; artificial intelligence and robotics in finance; crowd funding; insurance and wealth management, among other things (Digital Finance Institute, 2016). They use technology to supply financial services more efficiently. A new type of service has evolved in the 21st century, and it is known as on-demand. Mobile payments, loans, money transfers and even asset management are some of the techniques that new start-up companies are attempting to replace the existing transaction system with in order to make it more efficient and cost-effective, such as using technology in financial areas as diverse as mobile payments; loans; money transfers and even asset management. Financial transactions involving peer-to-peer technology, such as online lending, peer-to-peer payment technology and peer-to-peer lending, are examples of how technology is being used in financial transactions.

Fintech is an umbrella word that refers to both new technology-enabled financial services and the business models that support such services. Another way to put it is that the term "fintech" can be used to refer to any innovation that is related to how organizations are seeking to better the process of providing, receiving and utilizing financial products and services, among other things. Figure 1 compares Fintech with Banks.

Fintech vs Banks

Comparison Table

Characteristics	Fintech	Banks
Definition	Is a term used to describe new technology that automates and improves the delivery of financial services	Refers to financial institutions that is licensed to accept deposits from its customers and make loans
Purpose	Focus on making the customer experience seamless through convenience, functionality, personalization and accessibility	Focus on security and the management of financial risks.
Potential coverage	Has a larger market distribution due to the use of technological trends and advancements such as smartphones	Has a limited market distribution
Structure	Has organizational structures with fewer barriers to trends which encourages innovation	Has a rigid organizational structure that may restrict quick rolling of innovation changes
Technological reliance	Relies heavily on technology	Does not rely heavily on technology advancements
Target customers	Targets the unbankable such as those with low credit ratings	Targets customers with proven track records as well as strong credit ratings
Collateral	Has lenient and flexible collateral requirements	Banks have strict collateral requirements

DB Difference Between.net

Figure 1. Difference between Fintech and Banks

Source: DifferenceBetween.net.

While the COVID-19 crisis has had a disproportionately negative impact on developing economies such as China and India (Huong, Puah & Chong, 2021), it has forced legacy financial institutions in developed economies to clarify their strategies, develop new capabilities and transform their cultures as a result of the economic downturn. The forced rethinking of financial institutions' strategic decisions and markets is opening the door to new opportunities for strategic alliances with fintech start-ups with a long track record of success. As the digital transactions have exploded, the Indian fintech industry is rising to become one of the world's most important participants in the global economy.

Indian fintech start-ups are finding success in one of the world's fastest-growing marketplaces, with a population of more than 1.2 billion people. In order to provide basic connectivity, the telecommunications network was used first, which was then followed up with a landmark project known as Digital India, which connected 250,000 gram panchayats across the country (Broadband highways). Using this infrastructure, fintech companies could increase their reach into the unbanked population by delivering products that were similar to those offered by traditional financial institutions. In November 2016, the Indian government announced the demonetization of cash, which accelerated the use of digital transactions even further. Financial technology is one of the fastest-growing areas in the world today, thanks to the numerous start-ups, e-commerce enterprises and technological corporations operating in this domain throughout the world. In recent years, finance technology has caused significant disruption in the financial services industry, providing significant challenges to traditional financial institutions such as banks, credit unions, insurance companies and central banks, as well as regulatory bodies. A great interest in the subject has also been indicated by academics, financial institutions and research organizations, among other groups.

Generally speaking, the term "digital" is considered to be the most significant aspect in addressing the expectations of online customers. With India aiming to be a cashless society, the entry-level players such as Paytm of India are altering the financial services industry with a digital payment system. Many factors are contributing to the exponential growth of the digital payment sector, including the convenience of paying with a smartphone, the rise of non-banking payment institutions (payments banks, digital wallets and so on), progressive regulatory policies and increasing consumer readiness to use the digital payment platform, among others. In addition, favourable policy framework changes and government initiatives, such as the introduction of new payment systems, such as the Unified Payments Interface (UPI) and Aadhaar-linked electronic payments, as well as the improvement of the digital infrastructure, are important factors driving digital payments.

In India, the use of digital payments is quickly increasing. After demonetization, a surge in digital payments and wallets occurred, and this trend has continued to dominate the country's payments scene. India is one of the world's most important mobile phone markets, accounting for more than a quarter of global sales in the sector. India is not only home to one of the world's oldest and richest cultures, it is also home to some of the world's most innovative financial technology solutions. According to the recently published Indian Fintech Report, India has surpassed the United States as the world's second-largest fintech ecosystem in terms of size. Furthermore, for the first time in 2019, Indian fintechs outperformed Chinese fintechs in terms of raising financing. A large number of the world's largest financial institutions, top financial technology and services companies, and global banking and financial services conglomerates are establishing branches in India. It is also possible to trace the origins of several fintech businesses in Silicon Valley back to India.

The country is well-positioned, in part because of a solid talent pipeline of easy-to-hire and inexpensive technology workers, despite the fact that India's growth tsunami is not yet on the same scale as that experienced by its global competitors. Financial technology services have profoundly altered the way in which businesses and consumers perform their daily operations. As a result of the widespread acceptance of these practises, India is becoming an increasingly attractive market for businesses from all sectors. Aside from that, through innovation in new businesses, India represents a significant untapped market for budgetary administration that has yet to be discovered.

The government has taken a number of steps to boost investment inflows into the fintech sector. The scheme known as the Pradhan Mantri Jan Dhan Yojana (PMJDY) aims to increase financial inclusion in India by assisting beneficiaries in opening new bank accounts, enabling them to receive direct benefits transfers and providing them access to a variety of financial services applications. As a result, fintech firms have been able to develop technology products that are appealing to India's enormous consumer base. In addition to providing the public with access to government digital services, Aadhaar (the unique biometric identification system) improves the availability and openness of social benefits, including financial support to those in need. Fintech has now shifted to more consumer-based services and is used in various sectors including retail banking, education, investment management and non-profit, just to name a few. Functions which incorporate fintech include depositing cheques with smart phones, money transfers, managing investments, applying for credit and any assistance that does not require technology.

Most popular Fintech companies in India

- *National Stock Exchange (NSE)*: The National Stock Exchange of India (NSE) is a stock exchange that services a number of cities and towns across India. The headquarters of the company is in Mumbai, Maharashtra, India.
- *IndusInd Bank*: IndusInd Bank is a Mumbai-based Indian new generation bank that was established by the Government of India in 1994 to serve the needs of its customers. The company is based in Gurgaon, Haryana, India.
- In addition, *Paytm Payments Bank* is a mobile-first bank that does not require customers to maintain a minimum balance or pay digital transaction fees. The headquarters of the company is in New Delhi, Delhi, India.
- *MobiKwik*: In addition to its operations in consumer payments, payment gateways and financial services, MobiKwik is India's most prominent fintech platform. MobiKwik is an Indian mobile payment company with its headquarters in Bangalore. The company is based in Gurgaon, Haryana, India.
- *PhonePe*: PhonePe is a mobile payments application that enables users to send and receive money in real time. The company is based in New Delhi, Delhi, India.
- *Mahindra Finance*: Mahindra Finance primarily serves the rural and semi-urban areas of India, and it provides financing for the purchase of utility vehicles, tractors and automobiles, among other things. The company is based in Mumbai, Maharashtra, India.

Segments in the Indian Fintech Industry

The Indian fintech business is increasingly focussing on lending to both consumers and small and medium-sized enterprises (SMEs). At the same time, this market has expanded to cover more typical financial services such as financial insurance, personal finance and gold loan services. Let's take a look at a few segments in the fintech industry in India.

- *PayTech*: Using services such as payment gateways, card networks, application programming interface (API) and payment security, PayTech Fintech companies in India are able to access this sector. A number of consumer-centric services are available, including third-party application providers (TPAP), prepaid cards/Wallets, bill payments, QR code payments, payment aggregators and point of sale (POS). Business-centric services include corporate cards, business-to-business payments and invoice payments, to name a few examples. Paytm, PhonePe, MobiKwik and Google Pay are some of the most prominent players in this market segment.
- *LendTech*: In the field of lending technology, the following are included: lenders and providers of Buy Now Pay Later (BNPL) services, AML and anti-fraud technology, data interchanges, marketing and insurance services for products and services such as personal loans, salary loans, gold loans, vehicle loans, student loans and peer-to-peer lending. Google Pay, M-Swipe and Razor Pay are all attempting to establish themselves as important financing systems for both customers and merchants, respectively.
- *InsurTech*: Insurtech is the use of technological breakthroughs in the insurance industry in order to achieve cost savings and increased efficiency in the current insurance business paradigm. It is responsible for much more than just providing digital communications. Using it, carriers may better manage their adjusters' schedules while also increasing the efficiency and efficacy of their adjusters. This is true for both direct-hire personnel and third-party contractors working together. Claims processing, a sales platform, underwriting risk management, insurance infrastructure APIs and a policy administration system are all examples of services that can be provided by fintech in the insurtech industry. Policy Bazaar is the market-leading provider in this field.
- *WealthTech*: Wealthtech is a combination of money and technology that provides digital solutions to improve personal wealth management,

investment and portfolio management for individuals and businesses. Digital payment methods, e-KYC via Aadhaar, online money transactions and online investment reports have all grown in popularity, paving the way for the development of a completely automated asset management system. For example, using Big Data, artificial intelligence and deep learning to analyze investment alternatives, improve portfolios and manage risks are all instances of improvements in the financial industry. Zerodha and Small Case are two well-known start-ups in the wealthtech sector of the fintech industry.

- *RegTech*: Regtech is a type of technology that is used in the financial industry to manage regulatory processes. Its key responsibilities include monitoring, reporting and compliance with regulatory requirements. Data breaches, cyber-attacks, money laundering and other fraudulent activities have all increased as a result of the widespread usage of digital products. By utilizing big data and machine learning technologies, it lowers the risk of the compliance department by giving real-time data on money laundering operations that are conducted on the Internet.

- *Digital payments*: Neo banks provide a variety of banking products easier and faster to use, including payment gateways, payment processing, cash delivery, Internet payments and a variety of other banking solutions. API providers and aggregators, banks with open APIs, banking as a service and core banking are just a few examples of fintech services that are being used in digital banking today. Paytm, PhonePe, RazorPay, and other fintech businesses in India are at the forefront of the digital payments revolution.

Figure 2 illustrates the structure of the fintech in India.

Future of Fintech

According to estimates, the value of global fintech investments was US$310 billion in 2022 and is estimated to double by 2025. As of November 2021, there were 10,755 fintech (financial technology) start-ups in the Americas, making it the region with the most fintech start-ups globally. In comparison, there were 9,323 such start-ups in the EMEA region (Europe, the Middle East and Africa) and 6,268 in the Asia Pacific region. India is among the fastest growing fintech markets in the world

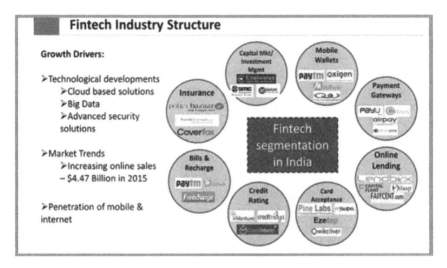

Figure 2.   Structure of Industry

Source: Shrivastava (2021).

Figure 3.   Techniques of Fintechs

and there are 6,636 fintech start-ups in India. Figure 3 illustrates major techniques of the fintech in India. Below we discuss a few of them.

- *Blockchains*: Traditionally, transactions required the approval of a third party before they could be completed. Then there were blockchains, which eliminated the need for third-party reconciliation while also providing cryptographic security. Bitcoins, which are decentralized digital currencies that employ blockchain technology, have already gained popularity. In the long run, blockchains are predicted to go far beyond bitcoins and payment transactions to include the financial industry, as well as several other sectors such as media, telecommunications, travel and hospitality.
- *Alternate lending*: Alternative financing arose as a result of the traditional banking industry's inability to make a profit lending to small

businesses. Fintech entrepreneurs took advantage of this opportunity by venturing into peer-to-peer (P2P) lending and developing web platforms that brought lenders and borrowers together at cheaper interest rates, among other things. This trend is expected to continue, and other alternative lending avenues, such as crowd funding, are expected to become more prevalent in the future.

- *Robo advisory*: In the past, intermediaries played a major role in the relationship between the stock market and the public. Many times, this resulted in transactions that were not traceable and were inefficient. Robo advising will make the stock market more accessible, transparent and traceable, as well as provide greater value addition to the more savvy investors who will benefit from it.
- *Digital payments*: Fintech start-ups have improved the speed and convenience of making payments. Mobile wallets have already displaced traditional wallets in a number of instances, and their use will continue to grow as better and faster payment options become available. And, yeah, ATMs will be rendered obsolete as well. Other segments like alternative lending and personal finance are also estimated to increase significantly by 2026.
- *Insurance sector*: On the Internet, we can find a variety of insurance marketplaces where consumers can evaluate their insurance policies and make educated purchasing decisions. With the help of data-driven automation, fintech will continue to usher in a technological revolution throughout the insurance value chain, resulting in not only lower operating costs, but also a greater range of products accessible on the market.

The emergence of fintech and the development of the digital marketplace drew the attention of a number of organizations. Financial technology is a vital subject because digital connectivity is a critical component of sustainability and productivity (Anshari *et al.*, 2019). Furthermore, fintech services enable the execution of business transactions from any location at any time. Innovative methods to extend banking services to customers and investors through mobile phone applications are used by Fintech companies, which provide higher-quality, higher-value solutions (Anshari *et al.*, 2019). These technologies and services help to meet market demands for areas that are underserved in terms of financial services (Guild, 2017). As a result, fintech has boosted the flexibility and efficiency of financial services. The main promise of fintech is the prospect of time and cost savings through the use of digital technology (Bofondi, 2017).

India's government planning arm, NITI Aayog, estimates the Indian fintech business value to be US$31 million. The Reserve Bank of India (RBI) has introduced a new idea of a "regulatory sandbox". This concept allows these companies to test their goods and services on a select group of consumers prior to their wider distribution. Shaktikanta Das, the Governor of the Reserve Bank of India, has emphasized the importance of the establishment of a supervisory and regulatory framework that will be followed by these companies (Dubey & Shukla, 2020).

There are two main differences between the credit scoring algorithms employed by fintech lenders and those utilized by traditional lenders. Using intermediaries, a higher quantity of information can be collected and used. In addition to traditional data sources, fintech credit platforms may make use of non-traditional data sources such as insights acquired from social media activity and the digital footprints of users (Jagtiani & Lemieux, 2018). Using machine learning techniques to extract non-linear information from variables is the second difference between the two approaches.

In contrast, the most important impact of India's fintech revolution has been felt by the landscape of small and medium-sized firms (SMEs) (SMEs). Small enterprises with no bank records or credit histories are now able to acquire much-needed access to funding for the first time, thanks to the growth of innovative alternative lending platforms. Also being expanded is the Goods and Services Tax Network (GSTN), which now has a registered base of more than 9.2 million MSMEs who are expected to file monthly returns on a continuous basis. GSTN data can be checked as a result of the matching concept, and it provides a deeper and more comprehensive insight of the nature of the organization, so supplementing conventional financial data. Improved underwriting processes would be enabled by more precise verification and validation of transactional information, which would in turn improve the efficiency and coverage of newer fintech lending models such as flow-based lending, vertical-based lending, and ecosystem-based lending, among others (Mittal & Monika, 2020).

Fintechs can assist in the introduction of more efficient and inclusive business models, as well as the expansion of the pool of financial service providers. The huge potential of FinTech to establish a more egalitarian financial system and to drive economic growth is also becoming increasingly well known and acknowledged. According to a study conducted by the McKinsey Global, emerging markets might see a $3.7 trillion increase in GDP by 2025 if they fully embrace digital financial services. According to research, countries with higher levels of financial inclusion had higher GDP growth rates and lower levels of income inequality than their counterparts (Kapadia, 2019).

Barriers in Fintech Businesses

Fintech, despite the fact that it offers tremendous potential, faces a difficult road ahead. The following is a list of potential stumbling barriers on the route of fintech businesses:

1. Entry and performance in the Indian market are difficult due to the stringent regulatory structure. There are numerous formalities that must be completed prior to the company beginning operations.
2. In addition to the unbanked population, a lack of adequate infrastructure in terms of Internet connectivity, and a low literacy level, there are other challenges to overcome. Even today, a sizable section of the Indian population (48%) lacks access to bank accounts, which are essential for making purchases on the Internet. People have bank accounts, but they continue to have problems with limited Internet connectivity, which causes the transaction to take longer to complete even though they have bank accounts in place. Consequently, people are more likely to prefer making cash transactions rather than making an online purchase. In spite of the fact that having a bank account and Internet access are both extremely beneficial, the bulk of the Indian population still lacks the financial literacy essential to taking advantage of these resources.
3. Makeovers are difficult because they require a shift in the conservative mentality of merchants and customers who conduct their daily transactions in cash. At this stage of their lives, it is difficult to suddenly shift their old habits and introduce them to new channels of payments because the vast majority of the elderly have been carrying out these transactions in cash for a lengthy period of time.

4. Due to the government's failure to provide support, when it comes to protecting their interests in the Indian financial markets, fintechs are hampered by a severe lack of governmental backing and incentives. Especially for new fintech players, this can be quite demotivating. Fintechs play a critical role in promoting economic growth and should be provided with all of the resources they require to succeed.

Conclusion

The fintech industry is transforming the face of financial services in India. The financial sector in India has been reformed as a result of the Aadhaar card, eKYC, UPI and BHIM integration. Following the abolition of the 500 and 1,000 rupee notes, it has been stated that digital transactions in India have increased by up to 22%. FinTech start-ups such as Paytm witnessed a 435% increase in visitors to their websites and mobile applications. Many fintech start-ups have sprung up in India as a result of this, as there are numerous chances for growth.

In the past, financial services were available in India, but they were only available at a gradual pace. Purchasing and selling stocks necessitated numerous phone calls to a broker. Obtaining loan approval was a time-consuming process that necessitated numerous trips to bank branches. A paper copy of your bank statement had to be requested if you wished to check your account balance. And to pay your utility bills, you had to go to one of the many physical branches that were scattered across the city. All of these services are now available at the touch of a finger on a smartphone. The amount of time saved and the number of productive hours gained is a significant benefit for both the individuals engaged and the greater society as a whole. These advancements have been made possible because of the fintech ecosystem in India, which comprises a dynamic yet focused group of companies, both new and old, that have attentively observed client problem areas and given beautiful solutions.

In response to the fintech possibility, traditional cash-driven Indian economies have reacted favourably, which has been fuelled in part by a surge in e-commerce and smartphone penetration. It also lays a significant emphasis on and encourages the development of the fintech industry, in addition to encouraging the dissemination of innovative ideas and technologies that are relevant to the fintech business.

References

Anshari, M., Almunawar, M. N., Masri, M., & Hamdan, M. (2019). Digital marketplace and FinTech to support agriculture sustainability. *Energy Procedia, 156*, 234–238. Doi: 10.1016/j.egypro.2018.11.134.

Bofondi, M., Carpinelli, L., & Sette, E. (2017). Credit supply during a sovereign debt crisis. *Journal of the European Economic Association, 16*(3), 696–729. Doi: 10.1093/jeea/jvx020.

Dubey, A. & Shukla, U. N. (2020). Expectations of FinTech startups and regulatory sandbox in India: An empirical study. *International Journal of Business Innovation and Research, 1*(1), 1. Doi: 10.1504/ijbir.2020.10030659.

Guild, J. (2017). Fintech and the future of finance. *Asian Journal of Public Affairs, 10*(1). Doi: 10.18003/ajpa.201710.

Huong, A. Y. Z., Puah, C. H., & Chong, M. T. (2021). Embrace Fintech in ASEAN: A perception through Fintech adoption index. *Research in World Economy, 12*(1), 1. Doi: 10.5430/rwe.v12n1p1.

Jagtiani, J. & Lemieux, C. (2018). Do fintech lenders penetrate areas that are underserved by traditional banks? *Journal of Economics and Business, 100*, 43–54. Doi: 10.1016/j.jeconbus.2018.03.001.

Kapadia, S. (2019). A perspective on financial literacy and inclusion in India. *SSRN Electronic Journal*. Doi: 10.2139/ssrn.3396241.

Leong, K. (2018). FinTech (Financial Technology): What is it and how to use technologies to create business value in Fintech way? *International Journal of Innovation, Management and Technology, 2*, 74–78. Doi: 10.18178/ijimt.2018.9.2.791.

Mittal, S. & Monika. (2020). Accounts receivable: Payable impact on each other with special reference to financial performance — A study of small cap companies. *SEDME (Small Enterprises Development, Management & Extension Journal): A Worldwide Window on MSME Studies, 47*(4), 362–373. Doi: 10.1177/09708464211055532.

Shrivastava, D. (2021). Fintech Industry in India: History, Growth, And Future. https://startuptalky.com/fintech-industries-in-india/

Websites

https://economictimes.indiatimes.com/news/economy/finance/budget-digitisation-initiatives-could-lead-to-10-7-billion-spend-on-technologyservices/articleshow/89458330.cms?utm_source=contentofinterest&utm_medium=text&utm_campaign=cppst.

http://www.differencebetween.net/business/difference-between-fintech-and-banks/#ixzz7Q9GzaSUZ.

https://doi.org/10.1142/9789811271786_0010

Chapter 10

Innovative and Technology-Led Strategies Adopted by Start-ups in India during COVID-19 Pandemic

Kumar Mukul[*,§], V Padmaja[†,¶], Jayadatta S[‡,||],
Yashaswini Murthy[†,**] and Megha Balasubramanyam[†,††]

[*]CMS B-School, Jain (Deemed-to-be) University, Bangalore, India

[†]Ramaiah Institute of Management, Bangalore, India

[‡]KLE Society's IMSR, BVBCET Campus, Vidyanagar, Hubli, India

[§]dr.kumar_mukul@cms.ac.in

[¶]padmaja@msrim.org

[||]jayadattaster@gmail.com

[**]yashaswini@msrim.org

[††]meghab@msrim.org

Abstract

Entrepreneurs constantly need to innovate and come up with effective strategies to meet the ever-dynamic business environment and novel challenges thrown by it. COVID-19 pandemic has tested the innovative capabilities of entrepreneurs to the maximum. The challenges during the pandemic have been more pronounced for the start-ups who are vulnerable anyhow and also resource starved in most cases, unlike well-established organizations. Start-ups rely on their unique approaches to make optimum use of their limited resources and sustain in competitive and uncertain scenarios. Unique situations like the recent COVID-19 pandemic draw the best out of the entrepreneurs to survive and come out as winners.

The present study focuses on innovative strategies adopted by entrepreneurs to survive and grow during the pandemic crisis. The research suggests that the survival and growth rates increase when innovative strategies facilitated by latest technological tools are adopted.

Innovative strategies including creative utilization of available resources, maximizing the "human capital" opportunities available, adopting the technology in effective ways, coming up with constant product and process innovations, reaching out to the market in novel ways, and utilizing conventional and virtual social networks helped start-ups in their struggle for survival and growth.

Introduction

The economic impact of the COVID-19 outbreak left the world completely rattled and as industries continue to face the successive waves of this pandemic, start-ups and entrepreneurs have been struggling to survive. The business environment was overwhelmed with unprecedented uncertainty for a long duration due to the COVID-19 induced pandemic and lockdowns, across the globe. This had serious repercussions on the business firms in general and start-ups in particular. With limited customer base, restricted revenue, changing investment patterns, and dynamic business model expectations during the crisis period, the start-ups had to rethink their business strategies and leaders had to set new pathways for their ventures. Periods of crisis can drastically affect organizations and can threaten their survival (Doern *et al.*, 2019) and start-ups have not been spared from this.

Entrepreneurs must start thinking of making start-ups more resilient and devise strategies to survive and sustain during situations such as the COVID-19 pandemic. Different start-ups came up with distinct action plans and strategies to tackle the situation and each had its own significance and success rate with regard to the contribution to the firm's survival. The start-ups which thrive on generation of new ideas and permeate innovation as well as search for quick answers to society's challenges (Spender *et al.*, 2017) may have their continuity threatened by the pandemic (Kuckertz *et al.*, 2020). Innovative start-ups are taking new steps to keep active in the crisis and are trying to overcome the challenges (Ketchen & Craighead, 2020; Kuckertz *et al.*, 2020; Barbulescu *et al.*, 2021). It is necessary that start-ups explore numerous ways to continue making efforts fostering innovation, to ensure their survival and even to identify new opportunities (Davila, Foster & Jia, 2010). In this direction, the present study aims to analyze the strategies adopted by start-ups to overcome the severe impact of the COVID-19 pandemic and consequent lockdowns.

Objectives of the Study

The following objectives have been framed for the purpose of the study:

  (i) To explore the innovative approaches used by start-ups
 (ii) To highlight the use of latest technology to respond to the business challenges presented by the pandemic
(iii) To discuss the various leadership approaches which worked for startup entrepreneurs
 (iv) To identify the use of networking and social media to mobilize resources in response to business challenges during COVID-19
  (v) To explore the future possibilities being created by start-ups using these unique strategies.

Methodology

The methodology used for the research is secondary data research with a focus on innovative strategies adopted by start-ups during the COVID-19 pandemic. Case instances have been quoted to support the discussion and illustrate the themes emerging from the literature review. The literature review was done through research articles search using major databases like EBSCO, JSTOR, Proquest, SpringerLink, ScienceDirect, SAGE, Elsevier and Google Scholar. Some major search topics include: start-ups during COVID-19 pandemic, survival strategies of start-ups during COVID-19 pandemic, innovative strategies of start-ups during COVID-19 pandemic, social entrepreneurship during

COVID-19 pandemic, leadership of start-ups during COVID-19 pandemic, use of networks and social capital during crisis situations like the COVID-19 pandemic, social entrepreneurship and the crisis situation, role of effective leadership in case of start-ups during COVID-19, role of start-ups and social entrepreneurship in addressing social issues, role of start-ups during pandemic situations in the Indian context and similar topics.

Table 1 depicts the major research papers referred to during the study to build the discussion around the major themes of social entrepreneurship, social capital and the role of social capital in helping social entrepreneurship during the COVID-19 pandemic. These themes later helped in the formulation of propositions. The table systematically lists the themes of discussion, the authors whose works were referred to and cited, the year of those published works and the essence of those papers.

Discussion

Challenges faced by start-ups

Start-ups, which are characterized as "temporary entities seeking scalable and repeatable business models" (Blank, 2010), strive to achieve market success and eventually grow into large corporations. A start-up company is an entrepreneurial venture which is typically a newly emerged, fast-growing business that aims to meet a marketplace need by developing or offering an innovative product, process or service. According to Padmaja (2018), a start-up is usually a company, such as a small business, a partnership or an organization, designed to rapidly develop a scalable business model. The pandemic brought to light a huge social concern dealing with not just the people infected, but the millions who were on the verge of contracting the virus.

Due to limited revenue sources and fixed business operation costs, start-ups' liquidity and long-term existence are always in question. Entrepreneurs have to manage with scarce capital at their disposal, and they are constantly under pressure to adapt to changing environmental conditions with restricted resources.

Severe crisis can drastically affect organizations, leading to instability, and can threaten their survival (Doern *et al.*, 2019), and startups have not been spared from this as well. Start-up owners and entrepreneurs must start thinking of how to make start-ups more resilient and devise strategies to survive and sustain during the COVID-19 pandemic.

Table 1. List of Studies Referred to in the Present Research

Sl. No.	Themes	Authors and Years	Essence
1	Start-ups during crisis situations like COVID-19	Doern *et al.* (2019); Spender *et al.* (2017); Kuckertz *et al.* (2020); Ketchen & Craighead, (2020); Barbulescu *et al.* (2021)	• The start-ups may have their continuity threatened by the pandemic. • The start-ups thrive on new ideas, innovation and search for quick answers to society's challenges. • Innovative start-ups are taking new steps to keep active in the crisis. • Start-ups must explore numerous ways for fostering innovation, survival and finding new opportunities.
2	Entrepreneurship and pandemic	Isenberg & Schultz (2020); Bacq & Lumpkin, (2020)	• The pandemic brought to light a huge social concern dealing with not just the people infected, but the millions who were on the verge of contracting.
3	Pro-activeness of firms in uncertain times	Nygren & Olofsson, (2020); Grimsdottir & Edvardsson, (2018); Liu *et al.* (2016)	• Institutions and organizations in both private and public domains are important sources of social capital. • VP-Firms need to be proactive during uncertainties and leverage social capital. • Social capital can be mobilized to ensure the success of an organization and propel its pro-activeness and entrepreneurship.
		Faccin & Balestrin (2018), Nafei, (2016); Nissen & von Rennenkampff (2017);	• By virtue of a bonding that already existed, several proactive measures were initiated by organizations.
		Al Omoush (2020); Grimsdottir & Edvardsson (2018); Petti & Zhang (2011)	• From letting their properties be used as quarantine homes to facilitating employees with better financial assistance, the social capital was demonstrated at various levels.
4	Evidences of innovative entrepreneurial efforts	Bacq & Lumpkin (2019); Tran & Michael (2020)	• Several organizations developed unique ways for easing the crisis situation created by the pandemic. • The focus was on coming up with easy and fast solutions to the problems. • The society, government and the industry were unprepared for what was yet to come, but the SEs were unfazed by the threat it posed and developed innovations that stood the test of the pandemic.

(Continued)

Table 1.   *(Continued)*

Sl. No.	Themes	Authors and Years	Essence
5	Leveraging social media and technology to create an impact	Nassif et al. (2020); Kuchler et al. (2021); Kaur & Chahal (2018); Dwivedi & Pandey (2013)	• Social media enables the connection needed for developing social capital. • Its ability to network and be interactive enables depiction of causes and facilitates the response to the same from like minded people across the globe.
6	Social Entrepreneurship	Corner & Ho (2010); Mair & Marti (2020)	• Social entrepreneurship focuses on addressing social problems by developing viable business models. • The penultimate objective of a social enterprise is the social cause. • All the key elements of setting up a firm such as risk-taking, being proactive and innovation are directed towards achieving greater good.
7	Leveraging social networks during pandemic	Bhatt & Altinay (2013); Trapido (2019); Ogden & Bull (2020); Ding et al. (2020), Kuchler et al. (2020)	• The role of social capital was crucial in speeding up the recovery process among the infected. • Social networking and community involvement served many who were affected in different ways. • The presence of a well-meaning community support system acted as a morale booster in the uncertain times of the lockdown and isolation.
8	Entrepreneurs turn creative	Real life case examples Cotula & Schwartz (2020); Snowden et al. (2021); Oberoi et al. (2019)	• The pandemic encouraged entrepreneurs to be creative and think differently. • Entrepreneurs bring unusual ideas to the table, seeing new patterns and opportunities that others may not perceive. • Creativity is an innate skill of entrepreneurs. • Entrepreneurs use skills and spirit to solve societal problems. • Unique yet thought-provoking ads, slogans and campaigns addressed key issues. • Innovative initiatives of garnering community support were floated by various entrepreneurs at different levels. • Common people from different walks of life ensured greater good was possible despite the challenging times of the pandemic.

In the initial stages of a start-up's life, expenses generally exceed revenues, and for this reason financing often is obtained through bank loans or loans from credit unions. Apart from that, start-ups can receive government-sponsored funding as well as funding from incubators (which can offer both capital and mentorship). If in dire straits, start-ups might consider asking for loans from friends or family. Venture capital is an option for those startups that are able to prove their potential. With venture capital, capital is exchanged for partial company ownership.

Start-ups in India have obtained great interest from all stakeholders in recent years and are being seen as most critical "engines" driving the economy. Their numbers have surged over the last two decades and they are considered as the catalysts yielding economic boom and employment generation. Through innovative approaches, adoption of latest technologies, pragmatic leadership and scalable business models, start-ups have been expected to provide impactful solutions and transforming agents in socio-financial developments in normal times and also help overcome crisis situations like COVID-19 much effectively.

The Indian government has set some guidelines for an entity to be considered as a start-up. Following are the prominent requirements for a firm to be qualified as a start-up as per legal terminology. An entity shall be considered as a start-up if:

(i) It is incorporated as a private limited company (as defined in the Companies Act, 2013) or registered as a partnership firm (under section 59 of the Partnership Act, 1932) or a limited liability partnership (under the Limited Liability Partnership Act, 2008) in India, within ten years of the date of incorporation/registration.
(ii) The entity's annual turnover has not surpassed INR 1 billion in any of the financial years since its incorporation/registration.
(iii) The entity is working on product or process or service innovation, development or enhancement, or it is a scalable business model with a strong potential for job creation or wealth creation (However, an entity formed by the division or rebuilding of an existing business is not regarded a "Start-up").

Start-up Revolution in India

Supportive ecosystem factors in the Indian scenario, such as enterprising young educated, skilful and aspirational youth, financial support through various sources, growing role of incubators, accelerators and facilitators, growing technology, government support, favourable legal and tax regimes and a burgeoning local market, have enabled the Indian start-up community to truly taken off and come into its own. The numbers in Table 2 speak for themselves: from 3,100 start-ups in 2014 to more than 11,500 by 2020, this is clearly not a fleeting fad (the Government of India websites and NASSCOM website). It's a remarkable revolution like never witnessed before. According to the 2019 Start-up Genome Project ranking, Bangalore is one of the world's top 20 startup cities. It is also one of the top five fastest growing startup cities in the world. India presently has the world's third largest startup ecosystem, with 38 unicorns (companies valued at more than $1 billion). Despite the economic disruption caused by the COVID-19 pandemic, the country produced roughly 12 unicorns in 2020. India had 41,061 officially recognized start-ups, and was the world's third-largest tech start-up ecosystem. India's potential unicorns — companies valued at $1 billion or more — have more than tripled from 15 in 2019 to 52 in 2020 making it the world's greatest pipeline of unicorns in the making (NASSCOM, 2020). By 2025, the number of Indian unicorns are expected to reach 95–105. As of March 2021, investments in start-ups accounted for $4.2 billion in capital, growing at an astonishing rate of 40% compared to the January–March quarter of 2020, when the figures were $3.5 billion.

Table 2.   Start-up scenario in India

Sl. No	Total Numbers	Status
1.	41,061	Indian government has recognised 41,061 start-ups
2.	4,70,000	Jobs created by more than 39,000 start-ups
3.	1.75 lakh	Start-up job rose to 1.75 lakh in 2020 from 1.52 lakh in 2019 due to an increase in the number of active recognition of start-ups to 14,784 from 11,694 in the same period
4.	319	Start-ups were granted income tax exemptions till November 2020
5.	38	Unicorns in India, 12 added last year
6.	>40	Start-ups are working in India's space sector

Source: Economic survey 2021 on Start-ups. https://economictimes.indiatimes.com/tech/startups/what-economic-survey-2020-21-says-about-indias-startup-ecosystem/articleshow/80586774.cms

Impact of COVID-19 on Start-ups

Start-up challenges across the globe during the pandemic

The COVID-19 pandemic prompted lockdown and social isolation. The uncertainty about how long the pandemic would last and what solutions could be applied transformed the situation into a riddle that most start-ups couldn't solve. With roughly 1,300 start-ups launched in 2019, the future seemed dismal for the majority of them, given the pandemic's arrival and exit both were unforeseeable. A rapid move to an online or digital format, which would ordinarily require two to three years of planning and strategy, was to be implemented in just a few days. The focus remained on executing necessary expenses, and only the bare minimum was spent to ensure the start-ups' existence. Venture capitalists and angel investors were the most important sources of funding for start-ups. They were quite cautious about the financing ease that existed a year before the outbreak of the pandemic. The flow of money into start-ups slowed dramatically.

Start-ups were, in general, expected to be more vulnerable to the shock of the COVID-19 pandemic compared to established organizations as they engage in high-risk activities, have difficulty obtaining traditional financing, and still have evolving relationships with suppliers and consumers. They rely on a small founding team, structure and culture which are yet to stabilize and are more vulnerable to labour supply disruptions — all these proved to be major hurdles during the pandemic. Start-ups became even more financially vulnerable during the COVID-19 phase of substantial economic uncertainty, with their revenues constantly dwindling with significant decline in demand. They struggled to manage their short-term liquidity needs, which are crucial for start-up survival. The impact of COVID-19 on start-ups is depicted in the following graph, which accounts for the length of time when there was worldwide uncertainty (lockdown).

Start-ups bring unique products or services to the market, and many times, there isn't a well-established market for them. This inhibits the start-up team's understanding of the market. Wilbur Lab, a San Francisco-based start-up studio (that transforms and develops innovative ideas into market-leading enterprises), conducted a study of 150 entrepreneurs last year and found that 77% of them experienced company failures as a result of the pandemic (wilburlabs.com). According to a similar fascinating report based on a study, 30% of surveyed entrepreneurs advocated market research prior to launch, 22% recommended stronger business planning, and 13.5%

Table 3.   COVID-19 impact on Start-ups

Sl. No	Change in revenue of selected start-up sectors since the start of the pandemic	Start-up Sectors
1.	−14%	Blockchain and Crypto
2.	−19%	Gaming
3.	−22%	Social media and messaging
4.	−30%	AI and Big Data
5.	−39%	Agtech and New Food
6.	−43%	Automotive
7.	−59%	Beauty & Fashion
8.	−70%	Travel & Tourism

*Worldwide (between December 2019 and June 2020)
Source: Startup Genome. https://www.statista.com/chart/22134/coronavirus-impact-on-startups/

recommended solid funding to avoid failures. These findings have a substantial impact on the difficulties and survival of businesses, implying the importance of engaging with customers in order to build viable business models based on market data. This has a strong chance of obtaining money as well. Startup Genome (startupgenome.com), a U.S.-based innovation policy advisory and research firm, in its Global Startup Ecosystem Report, reported that four out of every ten start-ups were on the verge of closing due to capital requirements, with only three months' worth of capital left after eighteen months of pandemic until June 2020. Furthermore, since the outbreak of the pandemic, 72% of companies saw a decrease in sales; on average, they lost 32% of their revenue. Approximately 71% of startups cut costs, with 60% laying off employees or lowering compensation (startupgenome.com). Table 3 summarizes the impact of pandemic on startups as reported by Startup Genome and illustrated by Statistica.

COVID-19 pandemic woes in the Indian context

In the Indian context, the announcement of the shutdown on March 23, 2020, could be one of the most memorable in recent memory. It appeared to be one of the safest strategies to keep the general public from becoming infected. The discussion erupted about whether life or livelihood was more important, and without a doubt, life was the most important factor. The government, politicians, police, and the general public worked tirelessly to ensure that people stayed at home as much as possible. The infection propagated in an unpredictable fashion, causing even more havoc. Companies struggled and worked hard to come up with new ways to reach customers who, for the most part, remained at home to protect themselves. Because most consumables were classified as essential, the fast-moving consumer goods (FMCG) industry remained unaffected. For certain products, demand and sales remained unchanged, but sales of personal hygiene products such as hand sanitizers, soaps and shampoos increased dramatically. Since most of the services sectors have collapsed, the segment of self-help, do-it-yourself, ready-to-use and ready-to-eat products exploded. The enterprises that served the larger manufacturing firms were the ones that experienced the most severe losses. Smaller MSMEs battled to stay afloat as production sectors came to a halt due to the mandated lockdown.

According to the survey conducted by Federation of Indian Chambers of Commerce and Industry (FICCI), jointly with the Indian Angel Network (IAN), with a sample size of 250, it was found that:

- Around 70% of India's start-ups were adversely impacted by COVID-19.
- 12% closed down operations since the outbreak.
- Around 60% of start-ups operated with disruptions.
- Only 22% of the start-ups had the cash reserves to meet the fixed cost expenses of their companies over the consecutive three to six months.
- Additionally, 68% of the start-ups had started cutting down their operational and administrative expenses.
- As many as 43% of the start-ups had already started salary cuts in the range of 20–40% over the period of April–June 2020.
- Investment decisions were put on hold for 33% of the start-ups and 10% of the respondents stated that deals have been called off.
- Only 8% of start-ups received funds as per the deals signed before the pandemic. The reduced funding has led start-ups to put a hold on their business development and manufacturing activities, and has resulted in a loss of projected orders.
- More than 70% of start-ups have had to terminate full-time employee contracts since the start of the COVID-19 pandemic.

Creativity and innovation: Start-ups' responses

Individual creativity relies on the employees' ability to build interpersonal relationships and leverage social networks at the workplace, for example by engaging in inter-functional collaboration and pursuing co-creation (Leavy, 2012).

For firms to survive and emerge winners out of crisis situations like the recent COVID-19 pandemic, proactiveness is a necessary requirement. Planning and proactiveness enhance the chances of firms to play critical roles in helping others in their communities. Social capital has an integral part to play in enabling firms to be proactive. It was observed during the COVID-19 crisis that those who were well connected and trusted in communities could easily jump into rescue activities and could swiftly and safely deliver their goods and services to the needy, i.e. those infected or underlockdown or quarantine. This aspect also highlights the role of social capital and social responsibility in business (Nygren & Olofsson, 2020).

Start-ups are increasingly adopting new approaches such as design thinking, lean, and agile, to facilitate creativity and innovation processes (Annosi *et al.*, 2020). The study by Spender *et al.* (2017) suggested that those start-ups which thrive on generation of new ideas, permeate innovation and search for quick answers to society's challenges are able to survive and continue with their business operations.

Social entrepreneurs bring unusual ideas to the table, seeing new patterns and opportunities that others may not perceive (Snowden *et al.*, 2021). Durkin & Gunn (2016) argue that creativity is an innate skill of the social entrepreneur. Oberoi *et al.* (2019) refer to this, claiming that "the inventiveness that employs entrepreneurial skill and spirit to solve societal problems" is not new, but is ahead of the conceptual construct, and is critical to meeting the demands of a changing society.

As Cotula & Schwartz (2020) claim, it is comforting to know that many people are willing to think differently. Just as the tragedies of 9/11 and the global financial crisis prompted fresh thinking and a rebirth in social enterprise (Oberoi *et al.*, 2019), so too are social enterprise and social entrepreneurs confronted with new challenges in the COVID-19 era, allowing society to create a new "normal".

Need for Proactiveness of Start-ups Firms in Uncertain Times

Nygren & Olofsson (2020) observed and felt that during the COVID-19 crisis, those who were well connected and trusted in communities could easily jump into rescue activities and could swiftly and safely deliver their goods and services to the needy, i.e. those infected or under lockdown or quarantine. Organizations constantly use their social networks to obtain ideas, collect information, and learn to recognize and detect new proactive innovations (Grimsdottir & Edvardsson, 2018). Social capital can be mobilized to ensure the success of an organization and propel its proactiveness and entrepreneurship (Liu *et al.*, 2016).

Research by Faccin & Balestrin (2018) suggested that external collaboration is an effective mechanism to generate novel ideas and solutions and being proactive to face big problems and challenges.

The COVID-19 pandemic can be better handled when social capital is high and there has been growing evidence to suggest this. In the initial stages when social distancing, lockdowns and other measures of control were not strictly enforced, people could still reach out to each other and resolve their pandemic-inflicted problems. But in later stages, when the lockdown restrictions were enforced strictly, connecting with people became problematic and access to social capital benefits through the networks also became difficult. In such a restricted environment, technology-mediated networking through virtual means enabled people to keep in touch and exchange resources to overcome the pandemic challenges. This can best be leveraged using various social media platforms for networking. Several researchers have highlighted the involvement of social capital during viral outbreaks (Ding *et al.*, 2020; Trapido, 2019) and mainly in the recent past with the ongoing pandemic (Kuchler *et al.*, 2020).

Influence of Leadership

Leadership has an important influence on employees' psychology and behaviour in the work place. Research studies have shown the influence of leadership style on employees' innovation behaviour, such as transformational leadership (Sheehan *et al.*, 2020; Yang *et al.*, 2021), empowering leadership (Kakhki *et al.*, 2020), inclusive leadership (Ye *et al.*, 2019) and ethical leadership (Lin *et al.*, 2020). Leaders have the important task of providing suggestions, proactively handling the problems that have been reported to them, leading to the innovation process of employees through extra work effort and work commitment.

Moral driven leadership — Coming to fore during the COVID-19 pandemic

Ethical leaders have a positive correlation with positive attitudes and behaviours of employees in the organization (Jha & Singh, 2019). Ethical leadership refers to the behaviour that leaders show in their interpersonal communication and that stimulate the innovation activities of subordinates via two-way communication, strengthening decision-making activities (Nazir *et al.*, 2020). Morally driven leadership summoned greater courage, expressed higher risk-taking behaviour and often drew greater support and resources to help the needy. They garnered goodwill and credibility to serve the needy in crisis situations more effectively — with greater reach and more sustainable ways.

Deloitte (Deloitte's Human Capital Trends, 2019) reported that approximately 86% of millennials believe that parameters to decide the success of a firm should be much broader than profits and that it should be focussed on doing "right" things for the community in which the firm operates. While COVID-19 is posing unprecedented hurdles in the progress of our economy, social enterprises are trying to overcome the lacunae left by administrative and economic failure and create sustainable alternatives for inclusive growth. Social entrepreneurs make a notable difference in the lives of people by facilitating access to livelihood, health, education and other basic amenities for decent living.

Social entrepreneurship is potentially well-suited to respond effectively to new challenges like the COVID-19 pandemic and also "*be the glue*" that holds together multiple solutions emerging from other sources. Despite the numerous unpredictable and novel challenges emerging out of the pandemic situation, the calamity also offers numerous opportunities to social entrepreneurs to come up with innovative solutions for various social issues.

Leaders leveraging their networks — Game changing strategy

There are many cases where entrepreneurs have been able to come up, supported by their networks and their known connections. They leveraged their networks to generate revenues for the funds for the social cause. The resources available through social entrepreneurs' personal and business networks (denoted as "social capital"), include critical information, business opportunities, ideas, financial support, influence, emotional support, goodwill, trust and cooperation (Baker, 2000). Entrepreneurs used their social networks and close relations to their advantage for accessing resources available to them to achieve their goals. While the issues that emerged over the last one year were many, the pandemic has also provided ample opportunities to the innovators to develop solutions to these pertinent issues.

As per research conducted by Nassif *et al.* (2020) the pandemic which resulted in isolation and social distancing encouraged and compelled businesses to look out for alternative channels of communication and means of sustaining the business in the rapidly changing digital environment. Researchers have discussed that e-business implementation is consistent with the shared values, principles and expectations of business partners and other members of social networks (Liu *et al.*, 2016; Oh & Teo, 2006; Son & Benbasat, 2007).

Social capital in the form of networks and ties enables information sharing, resources sharing and collective actions within communities and brings together people of diverse set of backgrounds and preferences towards better outcomes (Seth & Kumar, 2011; Smith, 2006; Kirby & Ibrahim, 2011; Ogden & Bull, 2020). Scholars have shown the importance of social capital during outbreaks such as the ongoing COVID-19 pandemic (Baron & Markman, 2003; Bhatt & Altinay, 2013; Brinckmann & Hoegl, 2011; Ding *et al.*, 2020). Still the literature in this domain suggests a research gap with regard to studies exploring the role of social capital in social entrepreneurship efforts, especially during crisis times like the present COVID-19 pandemic. Such studies are even more scarce in the Indian context (Domenico *et al.*, 2010; Fisher, 2012; Goldstein *et al.*, 2008; Greve *et al.*, 2003; Hasan, 2005; Kuchler *et al.*, 2020; Lin, 2001).

Bacq & Lumpkin (2020) opined that in the present context the COVID-19 situation has illustrated how solutions to complex problems created by the crisis situations are successfully implemented through diverse sets of relationships and vindicates our reliance on social capital networks. Mair & Marti (2006) also highlighted the significance of constant interface between the social context and the social entrepreneurs operating in it. This idea of embeddedness suggests that it is difficult to study the social entrepreneur detached from the social structure or community. Social enterprises find themselves intertwined to the community culture and logically social capital is integral and inseparable from economic considerations.

Some Case Illustrations of Innovative Approaches of Start-ups during COVID-19

As COVID-19 compels businesses around the world to reinvent themselves, entrepreneurs are going inventive to serve communities, from medicine-on-wheels services to recycled face masks. The Ninebee Foundation in Pune started a COVID-19 ambulance service called "Stree Safe" to provide free services to women. "We spread word about the service on social media, and then we started getting two or three calls a day." In a news article, Amarpreet Singh, Founder & Director, Ninebee Foundation, said, "The women are relieved that they do not have to fear for their safety." Sreya Vittaldev, a Bengaluru resident, created a spreadsheet containing contacts of people offering to cook food for those in need and uploaded it on various social media platforms as an example of how social media can be utilized effectively for social service. More than 20 people from various corners of the city quickly volunteered to assist. Another example is Bengaluru resident Abhilash Gowda, who began accumulating contacts of people cooking food for COVID-19 patients in various sections of the city. He was able to reach a big audience in his area by blogging about his projects on social media channels.

These social media channels have been actively used to communicate with individuals as well as collect and mobilize support for another campaign known as the "Mirror Selfie Pledge" challenge. This promotion urges individuals to take a selfie in front of a mirror and then publish it on social media with this caption. This aided in connecting with the campaign's concerned and relevant people — both the victims and the solution suppliers. Breakthrough's "Dakhal Do" (request to intervene) campaign asked individuals to publish their interventions on social media, tagging Breakthrough and five friends and using the hashtag #DakhalDo in the caption. The success of this campaign was due in great part to social media spreading throughout networks and friend circles. Many women have benefited from the programme and have become active "Team Change Leaders", hosting meetings and conversations to raise awareness in their communities. These instances demonstrate how original ideas bolstered by network support magnify favourable outcomes. The distribution of face masks and sanitizers, as well as other COVID-19-related necessities, became simple thanks to the different platforms that were channelled through well-known networks.

Another example of the importance of social capital is the Pune-based start-up Loop Health, which ensures that aid is only a phone call away for beneficiaries. Loop Health assists businesses in providing group health insurance coverage to its employees by providing an in-house team of doctors to care for them 24 hours a day, seven days a week. Loop Health's doctors provide virtual consultations and, if necessary, refer patients to a hospital. Because of the effective usage of social media networks, this virtual consulting could become a reality.

Another intriguing example of social media use is the case of Dr. Aparna Hegde, a Mumbai-based urogynecologist, who heads an organization called ARMMAN, which is dedicated to reducing unnecessary maternal and child mortality and morbidity. This group distributes timely preventative care information to pregnant women and moms of infants every week using mMitra, a free mobile voice service. During COVID-19, these pregnant ladies were subjected to a slew of medical emergencies that went unaddressed.

In this case, the app could attract medical attention via virtual links. COVID-19 made Meghana Narayanan, a young Bangalorean and recipient of the Diana Award, appreciate the necessity of a good insurance coverage for the financially vulnerable sectors of society. She started a social effort called "Project Abhaya", which aims to alleviate the financial burden imposed by inadequate insurance coverage for persons from the poorer sections of society. Currently, her project has benefited around 500 people, with 90% of them being women. Meghana's concept is gaining a lot of traction thanks to social media.

Furthermore, start-up owners stated that the current economic situation is not conducive to creativity. Key partners, customers and investors are all involved in the crisis response, and the uncertainty about how the crisis will unfold discourages any experimentation. When marketplaces are congested, start-ups are compelled to engage in "plateau patterned growth" (Brush *et al.*, 2009, p. 489), which, when combined with hurdles to funding, can have a negative impact on their growth trajectory. Because it produces an external demand to adapt, adversity resulting from a crisis can generate both possibilities and risks, according to the interviewees (Deb *et al.*, 2019). Start-ups have reported being pushed to execute different actions and adopt different behaviours, indicating that some have behavioural skills (Williams *et al.*, 2017). The interviewees also stated that their companies have had to make drastic changes to their organizational architecture as a result of the crisis, which has halted value creation activities and disrupted supply chains. At the same time, some founders reported that the COVID-19 crisis has had little (if any) impact on their businesses, either because their businesses remain relevant despite the crisis or because the firms have put in place measures that bolster their durability (Williams *et al.*, 2017) and make them resilient, albeit such resilience will most likely be temporary.

There were numerous examples of pandemic-related projects that ultimately grew into full-fledged social entrepreneurship businesses. For example, what began as a project to provide basic food to the needy during the nationwide lockdown has evolved into a social company. Dr. Saurabh Jain, MD, of Vardhman Hospital, used social media to set up a langar near Patiala's train station, feeding close to 3,000–4,000 people twice a day and assisting over 1,000 people with basic foodstuffs. However, as the opening up began, he was compelled to close the langar outside the railway station by government order. Recognizing the need, he founded Mahaveer Janhit Rasoi to continue to provide wholesome and hot food to those in need for the low price of INR 10 per plate. Dr. Saurabh Jain's initiative is gaining a lot of traction thanks to social media.

Nehru Yuva Kendra Sangathan (NYKS) Volunteers in Udham Singh Nagar, Uttrakhand, took the initiative to encourage youth to download and use the Diksha and Arogya Setu App for awareness and training. NYKS Volunteers established a method by which each Block Level Volunteer spreads the messages via social media to members of Youth Clubs, Ex-NYKS Volunteers, and other youth wanting to volunteer for COVID-19 pandemic relief. A list of interested youth was compiled based on the input. Later, as a result of the follow-up actions, 3,336 youth downloaded the Arogya Setu app, 425 youth registered for the Diksha app, and 300 youth participated in the iGOT Training. Global Healthcare has introduced a free telemedicine consultation for COVID-19 exams. Global Healthcare was formed in 2010 in response to the enormous demand for healthcare services in India, particularly in rural areas, where it is estimated that more than 28 million people living in remote and underserved areas lack access to cheap and accountable health care. Global Healthcare used social media tools to prevent fear during the COVID-19 epidemic. The free telemedicine consultation is available through phone, as well as through websites and applications. The goal was to avoid panic, provide proper screening, triage and treatment before conditions worsened, and keep the health system from failing.

Many people who loved to cook and feed were rekindled by the lockdown. Many people found their passion in cooking unique dishes and built a company around it, rather than just cooking for the public as a social purpose. Mommy's Kitchen was founded by entrepreneurs like Pratibha Kanoi, a Mumbai-based homemaker. It delivers fresh pizzas to people's doorsteps, and their clientele has grown to over 200 people in just 3–4 months across the city. When the potential of holding sessions was grim, Samera Kumar, a Bengaluru-based dance and yoga teacher, investigated alternative possibilities. She opted to rely on her cooking talents because she didn't know when her job will return. The Brownies Stories, Samera's business, offers a variety of brownies, including fudgy brownies with chocolate ganache, and sea salt and dark chocolate brownies, to mention a few. Samera now delivers to customers not just in Bengaluru, but all over India, thanks to a partnership with a delivery app.

Aanchal Suri's at-home food business in Bengaluru altered focus during the epidemic to provide fresh and authentic meals, recognizing the needs of professionals working from home. From Gatte ki Sabzi to Dahi Waale Aloo to Lauki ke Kofte, Tomato Rasam to Chocolate Almond bread, Aanchal's enterprise Bhaturas to Brownies in Bengaluru delivers delectable home-cooked meals to residents in her neighbourhood.

Spotify, a Swedish company that is the world's leading music streaming service, is an example of a successful business (Guillen, 2020). To make money, Spotify's business model depends on users hearing advertisements before listening to music. As a result of COVID-19, advertisers reduced their expenditure, impacting the company's revenues. By supplying users with podcasts, the company adjusted its strategy and correctly pivoted. This clearly shows that the epidemic gave all businesses an equal chance to succeed, but that success is based on entrepreneurs' rational decision-making. Another failure is Hoop, a UK-based company founded in 2016. Hoop was a leisure and entertainment programme that allowed parents to plan events for their children in their community (hoop.co.uk). COVID-19 had a severe influence on leisure and entertainment activities due to lockdown restrictions. The start-up introduced a new feature that provided online activities for children, but no income was generated as a result, and the company was forced to close. The start-up most likely believed the myth that success in the COVID-19 era was contingent on going online.

Even in isolated regions, abilities can be put to use. The district administration of Chanpatia, a calm town in Bihar's West Champaran district, had awoken to the harsh reality by April-May 2020. Approximately 1.20 million migrant workers have returned home as a result of the nationwide lockdown. The district government placed all personnel in quarantine centres, as was customary at the time. The district administration, led by district magistrate Mr. Kundan Kumar and District Registration and Counseling Centre manager Shailesh Kumar Pandey, made a wise decision to map the skill sets of workers who had worked in textile and garment factories in manufacturing hubs like Surat, Ludhiana, Delhi, Mumbai, and other parts of the country. Following the skill mapping exercise, the administrators judged that the workers were highly gifted and well-trained in their sector of work. Embroidery machines based on cutting-edge technology and laser technology for garment manufacturing were among the skills. To make a living in their own town, the administrators sought the employees' help to start businesses that manufactured ready-to-wear apparel and sarees that were sold across the country and exported to foreign markets. The administrators aided the unit by organizing financing, providing machinery, and locating it in one of the State Food Corporations' unoccupied warehouses in the Chanpatia Block. The units created multiple brands, and their pre-existing skill sets made operations simple for them. The migrant labourers became successful entrepreneurs, earning a whopping 7 crore profit in just a year, despite the pandemic's trials and tribulations. The Chanpatia success story has garnered widespread attention, and the concept is now being copied throughout Bihar. The pandemic has provided an excellent opportunity to observe and study social behavior, social relationships and innovative approaches in times of crisis. While social relationships came to a standstill as a result of the lockdown, the virtual world grew into a new trading and commerce platform. Many online retail companies found business opportunities in times of social crisis and made their way into the homes of millions. They took a clue from existing leaders in the online retail sector like Amazon, Flipkart, Snapdeal and others who had already made shopping and earning money through virtual mode a popular phenomena. These companies leveraged the social media sites to disseminate their business offerings to the communities under lockdown and found new markets. These new emergent players in the online retail domain made many essential commodities available to people which were difficult to get in the open market given the lockdown scenario. Masks, sanitizers, personal care items, groceries and other fundamental commodities were the common items sold by the online retailers. There are many other examples of how entrepreneurs saw opportunities in disasters and were able to scale up their efforts to reach a bigger population in need. During the epidemic, their inventive ideas and methods kept their entrepreneurial operations afloat, and many kept on learning and innovating in the uncertain environment and ramped up their firms more effectively during the COVID-19 and post-COVID-19 scenario.

Propositions

Based on the discussion in the above section, we came to the following conclusions, which we have framed in the form of propositions. These propositions are based on literature review and supportive case instances discussed in the previous segment the major propositions are as follows:

(i) During the pandemic, start-ups which adopted innovative practices and were creative and pragmatic in responding to the emergent challenges of pandemic situation often enhanced their chances of survival and growth.

(ii) Start-ups with adaptive and innovative strategies were evidently more effective in fulfilling the needs (both economic and social) of people.

(iii) Creative ideas and practices adopted during the pandemic have provided them avenues to come forward with exemplary initiatives.

(iv) Social networks, both conventional (physical) and virtual (online), of entrepreneurs facilitated the ease of effort of start-ups in providing innovative solutions.

(v) Adoption of technology-based tools and solutions facilitated better response to the COVID-19-induced challenges.

(vi) The emerging platforms of social media provide novel avenues for entrepreneurs to reach out to the needy people and connect them to the solution providers.

(vii) Entrepreneurs operating in areas with affective networks are able to create ecosystems with interdependent and mutually supportive constituents (connecting people, govt bodies, voluntary associations, volunteers, NGOs etc.).

(viii) The unique and innovative ways adopted by start-up entrepreneurs during COVID-19 are likely to reap rich dividends for them in the post-COVID-19 scenario with regard to their sustainability and competitive advantage.

Implications

The study provides numerous opportunities for start-ups, researchers, policymakers and other relevant stakeholders to build future strategies, conceptual frameworks and policies to take on future crisis scenarios like the COVID-19 pandemic. The propositions can be used by future scholars to carry on other related studies in the domain. The study provides enough takeaways for entrepreneurs who are expected to play significant roles in social and economic activities and take on the uncertain challenges facing society in most pragmatic ways.

The study has relevance for government bodies and other policymakers involved in framing policies and allocating resources for more equitable, sustainable development in society. Also, the various self-help groups and NGOs may incorporate some of the innovative and effective strategies discussed in this study. Government agencies, law-making authorities, policy implementers can also get ideas about the legal and administrative support entrepreneurship may require for creating a favourable ecosystem for existing and aspiring ventures. The study will encourage volunteers with scarce resources to creatively leverage their limited resources for effective outcomes. It will also encourage young bright minds to engage in entrepreneurial activities and contribute positively to economic growth.

It will provide insights on how to create a favourable ecosystem where enterprising people can come forward with innovative solutions to overcome COVID-19 pandemic-like challenges. It will also provide noble strategies to social enterprises and other voluntary associations for furthering their efforts during COVID-19-like crisis situations.

Conclusion

The innovative strategies adopted by entrepreneurs has helped start-up ventures to deal with their own business challenges and the community expectations from them in the COVID-19 pandemic crisis in effective ways. Enterprising, pragmatic and innovative leadership has been instrumental in resource mobilization and continued successful operations even in the face of unprecedented situations when many ventures went out of business and were forced to shut down. The way entrepreneurs reorient their financial, human and other resources to overcome resource constraints goes a long way in deciding their survival chances. An evolved sense of civic responsibility was evident among younger entrepreneurs during the COVID-19 times when they put their social responsibilities ahead of pure profit objectives. Entrepreneurial initiatives proved to be extremely impactful in these turbulent and uncertain times of society in providing medical and other basic amenities to the needy. While the innovation ecosystem is still not up to the desired levels in many of the developing countries, entrepreneurs across the globe are trying to over-come the deficiencies through their own enterprising initiatives and con-tinue to offer better products or services, solving ever-changing customer problems. Government and large corporates are expected to come forward and the focus needs to be concerted to encourage the innovative initiatives emerging out of the start-up community through right legal frameworks, tax-benefits, funding support, technology transfers, encouraging incuba-tors, enablers and facilitators, ensuring right mentoring, engaging them at all levels of policymaking and strategizing about economic direction of the nation.

Ample case evidences are testimony to the fact that innovative and concerted efforts implemented in well-coordinated and timely manner enabled entrepreneurs with scare resources to optimize their efforts and reach out to greater number of support-seekers. Leveraging the value-laden networks, both conventional as well as online networks went a long way in scaling up the efforts and offering help to a large populace. Social capital accessible and generated through the relevant networks of entre-preneurs added a totally new dimension to the social value creation space. It has opened new avenues and acted as a bridge between both the service providers and the people in need. It has become increasingly clear that start-up enterprises must keep looking for innovative approaches and strat-egies to ensure their long-term survival in uncertain, volatile and dynamic business environments predicted in future. Investing in R&D, technologi-cal upgradations, continuous quality improvements, networking, social media presence and continuously seeking noble and "innovative ways" to operate and connect with their stakeholders even in the post-pandemic scenario will help the startup ventures in gaining competitive advantages as well as touching the hearts of individuals and communities.

References

Al-Omoush, K. S., Ribeiro-Navarrete, S., Lassala, C., & Skare, M. (2022). Networking and knowledge creation: Social capital and collaborative inno-vation in responding to the COVID-19 crisis. *Journal of Innovation & Knowledge, 7*(2), 100181. Doi: 10.1016/j.jik.2022.100181.
Annosi, M. C., Martini, A., Brunetta, F., & Marchegiani, L. (2020). Learning in an agile setting: A multilevel research study on the evolution of organiza-tional routines. *Journal of Business Research, 110*, 554–566.

202 K. Mukul et al.

Bacq, S. & Lumpkin, G. T. (2020). Social entrepreneurship and COVID-19. *Journal of Management Studies*, *58*(1), 285–288.

Baker, T., Gedajlovic, E., & Lubatkin, M. (2000). A framework for comparing entrepreneurship processes across nations. *Journal of International Business Studies*, *36*(5), 492–504.

Baron, R. A., & Markman, G. D. (2003). Beyond Social Capital: The Role of Entrepreneurs' Social Competence in Their Financial Success. *Journal of Business Venturing*, *18*, 41–60.

Bhatt, P. & Altinay, L. (2013). How social capital is leveraged in social innovations under resource constraints? *Management Decision*, *51*(9), 1772–1792. Doi: 10.1108/MD-01-2013-0041.

Blank, S. (2010). What's a startup? First principles. (Accessed 12 March 2021). https://steveblank.com/2010/01/25/whats-a-startup-first-principles/.

Brinckmann, J. & Hoegl, M. (2011). Effects of initial team work capability and initial relational capability on the development of new technology-based firms. *Journal of Strategic Entrepreneur*, *5*, 37–57. Doi: 10.1002/sej.106.

Brush, C. G., Ceru, D. J., & Blackburn, R. (2009). Pathways to entrepreneurial growth: The influence of management, marketing, and money. *Business Horizons*, *52*(5), 481–491.

Corner, P. D. & Ho, M. (2010). How opportunities develop in social entrepreneurship. *Entrepreneurship Theory and Practice*, *34*(4), 635–659.

Cotula, L. & Schwartz, B. (2020, August 8). COVID-19 and global economic ordering: Radical shift or more of the same? https://www.iied.org/covid-19-global-economic-ordering-radical-shift-or-more-same.

Davila, A., Foster, G., & Jia, N. (2010). Building sustainable high-growth startup companies: Management systems as an accelerator. *California Management Review*, *52*(3), 79–105.

Deb, P., David, P., O'Brien, J., & Duru, A. (2019). Attainment discrepancy and investment: Effects on firm performance. *Journal of Business Research*, *99*, 186–196.

Deloitte Insights. (2018). The rise of social enterprise, 2018 Deloitte global human capital trends. [10 March 2019]. https://www2.deloitte.com/content/dam/Deloitte/at/Documents/human-capital/at-2018-deloitte-human-capital-trends.pdf.

Desa, G. (2011). Resource mobilisation in international social entrepreneurship: Bricolage as a mechanism of institutional transformation. *Entrepreneurship Theory and Practice*, 1–25. Doi: 10.1111/j.1540-6520.2010.00430.x.

Ding, W., Levine, R., Lin, C., & Xie, W. (2020). Social distancing and social capital: Why US counties respond differently to COVID-19. SSRN 3624495.

Doern, R., Williams, N., & Vorley, T. (2019). Special issue on entrepreneurship and crises: Business as usual? An introduction and review of the literature. *Entrepreneurship and Regional Development*, *31*(5-6), 400–412. Doi: 10.1080/08985626.2018.1541590.

Domenico, M. D., Haugh, H., & Tracey, P. (2010). Social bricolage: Theorizing social value creation in social enterprise. *Entrepreneurship Theory and Practice, 34*(4), 681–703.

Durkin, C. & Gunn, R. (2016). Social entrepreneurship: A skills approach.

Faccin, K. & Balestrin, A. (2018). The dynamics of collaborative practices for knowledge creation in joint R&D projects. *Journal of Engineering and Technology Management, 48*, 28–43.

Fisher, G. (2012). Effectuation, causation, and bricolage: A behavioural comparison of emerging theories in entrepreneurship research. *Entrepreneurship Theory and Practice,* 1019–1051. Doi: 10.1111/j.1540-6520.2012.00537.x.

Giritli Nygren, K. & Olofsson, A. (2020). Managing the COVID-19 pandemic through individual responsibility: The consequences of a world risk society and enhanced ethopolitics. *Journal of Risk Research.* Doi: 10.1080/13669877.2020.1756382.

Greve, A. & Salaff, J. W. (2003). Social networks and entrepreneurship. *Entrepreneurship Theory and Practice, 22*(1), 1–22.

Grimsdottir, E. & Edvardsson, I. R. (2018). Knowledge management, knowledge creation, and open innovation in Icelandic SMEs. *SAGE Open, 8*(4), 1–13.

Guillen, M. F. (2020). How businesses have successfully pivoted during the pandemic. *Harvard Business Review.* (Accessed 18 February 2021). https://hbr.org/2020/07/how-businesses-have-successfully-pivoted-during-the-pandemic.

Isenberg, D. & Schultz, E. B. (2020, June 9). Opportunities for entrepreneurs in the pandemic and beyond. Medium.com.2020. https://medium.com/@disen2/opportunities-for-entrepreneurs-in-the-pandemicandbeyond-f92f5fa1997b.

Jha, J. K. & Singh, M. (2019). Exploring the mechanisms of influence of ethical leadership on employment relations. *IIMB Management Review, 31*(4), 385–395. Doi: 10.1016/j.iimb.2019.07.010.

Kakhki, R. K., Kakhki, M. K., & Neshani A. (2020). COVID-19 target: A specific target for novel coronavirus detection. *Gene Reports, 20*, 100740.

Ketchen Jr., D. J., & Craighead, C. W. (2020). Research at the intersection of entrepreneurship, supply chain management, and strategic management: Opportunities highlighted by COVID-19. *Journal of Management, 46*(8), 1330–1341. Doi: 10.1177/ 0149206320945028.

Kirby, D. A. & Ibrahim, N. (2011). The case for (social) entrepreneurship education in Egyptian universities. *Education and Training, 53*, 403–415.

Kuchler, T., Russel, D., & Stroebel, J. (2020). The geographic spread of COVID-19 correlates with structure of social networks as measured by Facebook. *NBER Working Paper.*

Kuckertz, A., Brändle, L., Gaudig, A., Hinderer, S., Reyes, C. A. M., Prochotta, A., Steinbrink, K. M., & Berger, E. S. (2020). Startups in times of crisis–A rapid response to the COVID-19 pandemic. *Journal of Business Venturing Insights, 13*, 1–13, e00169. Doi: 10.1016/j.jbvi.2020.e00169.

Leavy, B. (2012). Collaborative innovation as the new imperative–design thinking, value co-creation and the power of "pull". *Strategy & Leadership, 40*(2), 25–34. Emerald Group Publishing Limited.

Lin, N. (2001). *Social Capital: A Theory of Social Structure and Action.* Cambridge, UK: Cambridge University Press.

Lin, W. L., Yip, N., Ho, J. A., & Sambasivan, M. (2020). The adoption of technological innovations in a B2B context and its impact on firm performance: An ethical leadership perspective. *Industrial Marketing Management, 89*(2), 61–71. Doi: 10.1016/j.indmarman.2019.12.009.

Mair, J. & Marti, I. (2006). Social entrepreneurship research: A source of explanation, prediction and delight. *Journal of World Business, 41,* 36–44.

Nafei, W. (2016). The role of organizational agility in reinforcing job engagement: A study on industrial companies in Egypt. *International Business Research, 9*(2), 153–167.

NASSCOM. (2020). Start-up Pulse Survey-Q1 2020: Reviving the Indian Tech Start-up Engine During COVID-19. https://nasscom.in/knowledge-center/ publications/nasscom-start-pulse-survey-q1-2020-reviving-indianstart-up-engine.

Nassif-Pires, L. *et al.* We need class, race, and gender sensitive policies to fight the covid-19 crisis. In *Multiplier Effect*, New York, 2 abr. 2020. https://bit. ly/2XRT1xD. (Accessed 8 January 2021).

Nazir, S., Shafi, A., Asadullah, M. A., Qun, W., & Khadim, S. (2020). How does ethical leadership boost follower's creativity? Examining mediation and moderation mechanisms. *European Journal of Innovation Management,* ahead-of-print (ahead-of-print). Doi: 10.1108/EJIM-03-2020-0107.

Nissen, V. & von Rennenkampff, A. (2017). Measuring the agility of the IT application systems landscape. In Proceedings der 13. *Internationalen Tagung Wirtschafts informatik,* St Gallen, Switzerland.

Oberoi, R., Mswaka, W., Leandro, F., Snowden, M., & Halsall, J. (2020). Reimagining social innovation and social enterprise for industrial revolution 4.0: Case study of China and UK. In P. Smith & T. Cockburn (eds.), *Global Business Leadership Development for the Fourth Industrial Revolution (Chapter 14)* (pp. 337–358). IGI Global. Doi: 10.4018/978-1-7998-4861-5. https://www.financialaccess.org/blog/2020/3/26/covid-19-how-does-microfinanceweather-the-current-storm.

Ogden, T. & Bull, G. (2020). COVID-19: How does microfinance weather the current storm. CGAP blog post 25.

Subash, S. P., Ojha, J. K., Ashok, A., & Nikam, V. (2019). Farmer producer companies in India: Trends, patterns, performance and way forward. *National Institute of Agriculture Economics and Policy Research.* Doi: 10.13140/ RG.2.2.32278.40000.

Petti, C. & Zhang, S. (2011). Factors influencing technological entrepreneurship capabilities: Towards an integrated research framework for Chinese enterprises. *Journal of Technology Management in China, 6*(1), 7–25. Doi: 10.1108/17468771111105631.

Sheehan, M., Garavan, T. N., & Morley, M. J. (2020). Transformational leadership and work unit innovation: A dyadic two-wave investigation. *Journal of Business Research, 109*(2), 399–412. Doi: 10.1016/j.jbusres.2019.10.072.

Seth, S. & Kumar, S. (2011). Social entrepreneurship: A growing trend in Indian business. *Entrepreneurship: Practice Review, 1*(4), 4–19.

Smith, M. L. (2006). Social capital and intentional change: Exploring the role of social networks on individual change efforts. *Journal of Management Development, 25*(7), 718–731.

Snowden, L. & Graaf, G. (2021). COVID-19, social determinants past, present, and future, and African Americans' health. *Journal of Racial and Ethnic Health Disparities, 8*(1), 12–20.

Son, J. Y. & Benbasat, I. (2007). Organizational buyers' adoption and use of B2B electronic marketplaces: Efficiency-and legitimacy-oriented perspectives. *Journal of Management Information Systems, 24*(1), 55–99.

Spender, J. C., Corvello, V., Grimaldi, M., & Rippa, P. (2017). Startups and open innovation: A review of the literature. *European Journal of Innovation Management, 20*(1), 4–30. Doi: 10.1108/EJIM-122015-0131.

Trapido, J. (2019). Ebola: Public trust, intermediaries, and rumour in the DR Congo. *The Lancet Infectious Diseases, 19*(5), 457–458. Doi: 10.1016/S1473-3099(19)30044-1. PMID: 30928434.

Williams, T. A., Gruber, D. A., Sutcliffe, K. M., Shepherd, D. A., & Zhao, F. Y. (2017). Organizational response to adversity: Fusing crisis management and resilence research streams. *Academy of Management Annals, 11*(2), 733–769.

Yang, M., Luu, T. T., & Qian, D. (2021). Dual-focused transformational leadership and service innovation in hospitality organisations: A multilevel investigation. *International Journal of Hospitality Management, 98*(6), 103035. Doi: 10.1016/j.ijhm.2021.103035.

Ye, Qingyan, Wang, Duanxu, & Guo, Weixiao. (2019). Inclusive leadership and team innovation: The role of team voice and performance pressure. *European Management Journal, 37*(4), 468–480.

Websites

Why Startups Fail. Lessons from 150 Founders. (Accessed 14 March 2021). https://www.wilburlabs.com/blueprints/why-startups-fail.

State of the Global Startup Economy. (Accessed 14 March 2021). https://startupgenome.com/article/state-of-the-global-startup-economy. (Accessed 31 December 2020). https://hoop.co.uk/.

https://economictimes.indiatimes.com/small-biz/hr-leadership/leadership/survival-strategies-for-businesses-during-covid-19-lockdown/articleshow/75371157.cms?from=mdr.

https://newsonair.com/2021/07/31/roaring-startup-ecosystem-as-many-as-52391-startups-recognized-by-dpiit/.

https://www.businesstoday.in/opinion/columns/story/challenges-faced-by-startups-amid-global-pandemic-316726-2021-12-24.

https://theprint.in/india/this-start-up-zone-in-bihar-is-west-champarans-answer-to-lockdown-migrant-exodus/675524/.

https://startuptalky.com/meesho-success-story-2/#Meesho_Meesho-Startup Story.

https://www.thebetterindia.com/235895/lockdown-coronavirus-job-loss-successful-home-business-how-to-start-india-gop94-2/.

https://nasscom.in/emerge50/.

https://startupgenome.com/.

https://doi.org/10.1142/9789811271786_0011

Chapter 11

Digital India and the Future of Work Enabled by COVID: Employees as Qubits Self-Managing the Work Transformation

Apoorva Goel

*Human Resource Management and Organisational Behaviour,
Indian Institute of Technology, Madras, Chennai,
India*

ms19d039@smail.iitm.ac.in

Abstract

The outbreak of COVID-19 has brought a drastic impact on the workplace and the ways of working. There is a rapid adoption of advanced technologies such as Artificial Intelligence (AI), robotics, the Internet of Things (IoT), cloud computing, and many more. This is not only limited to changes in work but also has implications for the employees who are required to have a 'digital mindset'. This chapter outlines the relevance of existing research in the form of an integrative review. It discusses how the changing work design, the requirement of new skills and competencies, leadership and changing hierarchies due to technologization have an impact on employees in the era of COVID-19. It also categorizes the influencing factors, discusses their interactions, suggests implications for practice and research.

Introduction

'The changes (from the Fourth Industrial Revolution) are so profound that, from the perspective of human history, there has never been a time of greater promise or potential peril'.

—*Klaus Schwab, The Fourth Industrial Revolution (2017)*

The impact of the COVID-19 crisis on working lives has been colossal. Due to the spread of the pandemic across the globe, there has been a fundamental change in our work and personal lives. The rapidly progressing technologies are rapidly changing the ways of working at the workplace (Cascio, 2014). The fourth industrial revolution, which includes developments in the fields of artificial intelligence and machine learning, robotics, nanotechnology, biotechnology, 3D printing, etc., is causing widespread disruption in the organizations (World Economic Forum, 2016). Disruptive technologies such as mobile computing and virtual reality are changing the existing offline and online work concepts, creating large networks of people, computers, and other related devices. Intelligent software can make complex decisions based on embedded sensors in wearable devices and machines that generate big data in terms of volume, variety, velocity and veracity, taking over previously human tasks (Cascio & Montealegre, 2016). Cognitive technology is likely to swiftly create a new class of digital labour as organizations attempt to expedite procedures and decrease operational expenses. Many roles will be restructured and rebuilt, resulting in job displacement and the need for individuals to acquire new skills (Mashelkar, 2018). It is critical to take account of Amitabh Kant's (2018) compelling argument for why India must embrace the new age of AI, blockchain and robotics while determining the future of employment in India. However, mere implementation of such technologies cannot guarantee success (Schallenmueller, 2016); they need to be adopted by the people and used as intended to reap the benefits (Venkatesh *et al.*, 2003). People are the heart of any technological transformation program in the organizations (Kohnke, 2017). Organizations need to therefore not only focus and invest in technologies but also on the skills and readiness of the users or adopters: the employees (Oxford Economics, 2017), thereby enabling 'digital dexterity,' which is the ability of the organization as a whole to move swiftly to utilize digital technologies (Soule *et al.*, 2016). They overlook the organizational implications and dynamics of digitization, such as the need for people, processes, organizational structures and culture to be aligned (Giustiniano & Bolici, 2012; Kohnke, 2016). While scholarly research has majorly focused on the macro-level of the integration of these innovative technologies and business models (Andal *et al.*, 2003; Zhu & Kraemer, 2005; Deering *et al.*, 2008; Gray *et al.*, 2013; vom Brocke *et al.*, 2016), studies have focused less on the micro-level, i.e. interdependencies and interaction between technology and people.

This chapter aims to review and structure the literature on the impact of technology adoption in the workplace on various factors such as work design, skills and competency requirements, leadership, and hierarchies in the organization, with a focus on the people component of these technologies. The chapter contributes in several ways. First, it identifies the key themes of change arising due to technological advancements in the workplace. Second, it mentions the various ways under each theme impacting the workforce. Third, it provides a model of workplace factors affecting employees' technology adoption. Fourth, it provides a comprehensive agenda for future research on this topic and offers specific research questions to guide further studies.

Problem Definition

With the increasing adoption of advanced technologies by organizations, the future of workplaces focuses on what work is done and how it is done rather than where and when it is done (Dittes *et al.*, 2019). Redundant work is likely to be overtaken by these machines, leaving time for the professionals to focus on areas where human judgement is required. The nature of work and its new ways of working make it important to understand the interrelations of human behaviour with technology, which together cover the entire organization (Mullins, 1990). Individuals are the sole arbiters of their work; their behaviour will eventually determine how technologies may (or may not) be used. The influence of technology on work environments affects not only the organizational structure but also the individual characteristics. Little is known about how the changing work and work methods are creating a change in the behaviour of employees. This chapter provides an understanding of this and offers a proposed research agenda for future studies.

Method

An integrative review of the literature is provided to address the research problem. It is a method for analyzing and synthesizing the literature on a topic to develop new perspectives on it (Torraco, 2005; Webster & Watson, 2002). This research technique is suitable when existing studies on a topic are fragmented and have not been systematically analyzed and integrated. Similar is the case with the technologization of work and its impact on employees. Research on this topic is still in its infancy stage (Cascio & Montealegre, 2016) as most of it was done during its initial stages (e.g. Kayworth & Leidner, 2001) which were mainly focused on electronic mails and enterprise application systems, now considered as basic. Moreover, the existing literature is highly fragmented and didn't aggregate their findings on a higher conceptual level. This fragmentation leads to difficulty in detecting larger patterns of change resulting from the transformation (Avolio *et al.*, 2009). In the next section, the methods for selecting and reviewing the literature on this topic are explained.

Literature Review

Relevant literature was searched in four databases (Scopus, ProQuest, Google Scholar, Web of Science). Moreover, a forward and backward search approach was used for a rigorous search process (Levy & Ellis, 2006). Forward searching employs identifying and reviewing articles that cite an original article (Webster & Watson, 2002). It pays attention to publications created after a research article is published. The forward-searching methodology is used in this review to ascertain different articles on technological transformation. The backward searching technique is identifying and reviewing references cited in an article. It is used in this review to identify more articles in the related field and topic. The following relevant keywords were used for searching articles such as: "technolog*" AND "employee*; "digital*" AND "employee*"; "future of work" AND "employee*"; "digital work" AND "employee*"; "fourth industrial revolution" AND "employee*"; "automation" AND "employee*"; "digital disruption" AND "employee*"; "workplace trans-formation" AND "employee*". The academic journal articles included in this study are peer-reviewed in the search parameters and include concep-tual articles and empirical articles. The keywords were searched for in the titles and abstracts of articles and not in the full text to reduce the number of false-positive results. A total of 91 articles were reviewed after all duplicate articles were removed. The first stage involved a staged review process (Torraco, 2005), in which the abstract's fit with the research objective was evaluated. Articles that did not fit the objective were discarded. The second stage of the review consisted of reading and analyzing all the remaining articles in depth. This integrative review includes 74 articles in total.

Effect of technological transformation on work design, skills, leadership and hierarchies: Reviewing core topics in previous research

The widespread deployment and adoption of technological advancements will have a substantial impact on the organizations in two ways: it will affect the way people work and it will accelerate the rate at which organizations evolve. As a result of both these implications, organizations must meet three fundamental requirements to be successful in their transformation efforts. These are changes in work design, requirements of new skills and competencies, and changes in leadership.

Effect on work design

Technology is changing the way we work in many ways. These technological changes affect the work design (Barley, 2015): the conditions and how employees work in the organizations (Parker *et al.*, 2001). With cloud computing and mobile devices, employees are nowadays constantly connected to their workplaces, affecting their work and private lives (Mazmanian, 2013). Many organizations today are equipping their infrastructure and employees with sensors that can enable them to monitor the organizational environment, report their status, and take appropriate actions based on the information, which is better known as the 'Internet of Things (IoT).' This enables the companies to take better control of the operations and people to mitigate risks and adversities by taking preventive measures and informed decisions. Monitoring as a step is neither good nor evil unless it is considered intrusive (Cascio, 2016). In fact, monitoring is found to increase productivity by helping people understand how effectively they can allocate time and accomplish goals (Osman, 2010). Theoretical and empirical researchers have found three aspects of monitoring systems that create the perception of fairness or invasiveness (Ambrose & Alder, 2000). These are bias-free data, consistency of data collected and accuracy of data collected. When monitoring systems are considered unfair and invasive, companies are at the risk of employees not complying with rules and regulations and engaging in deviant behaviours (Zweig & Scott, 2007). It can also lead to increased stress (Lu, 2005) and is seen as a means to control rather than aid development (Castanheira & Chambel, 2010).

Robots have been on the factory floors for decades; however, they are now being programmed to work collaboratively with humans (Davenport & Kirby, 2015). These cobots (coworker robots) are entering the workplace (Coovert & Thompson, 2014) since they are considered to increase the overall productivity and decrease labour costs (Aeppel, 2014). They are being evolved to enable them to communicate effectively and efficiently with human teammates to receive as well as transmit information (Redden *et al.*, 2014). However, their social acceptance is of concern. Since robots are meant to perform redundant tasks, freeing humans' time to focus on other important work, the allocation of work between humans and machines requires much research attention. This includes reduced situational awareness; scepticism of automation; misuse, disuse and abuse; lowered attentiveness; complacency; and negative consequences on other aspects of human performance (Redden *et al.*, 2014). Focus on selection, work analysis, training, performance management and motivation can support the successful design and integration of robots into organizations (Coovert & Thompson, 2014).

Teleconferencing or Teleworking is another aspect of the technologization impacting the working method. It allows interactive group communication through a virtual digital medium (Rogan & Simmons, 1984; Bailey & Kurland, 2002). Any organization, be it large or small, is making use of it (Farr *et al.*, 2014). It helps bring diverse talent and intellectual resources together by crossing the geographic, cultural, organizational and time boundaries (Potosky & Lomax, 2014). The antecedents of teleworking are demographic variables (Olszewski & Mokhtarian, 1994) and job characteristics (Mannering & Mokhtarian, 1995), whereas the outcomes of it which have been accessed are employees' job satisfaction and performance (Golden & Veiga, 2005; Gajendran & Harrison, 2007). Teleworking increases temporal flexibility by allowing people to be connected with their workplaces (Mazmanian *et al.*, 2005) and work even after their working hours (Mazmanian, 2013). This flexibility may increase employees' stress levels (Kelliher & Anderson, 2010), also known as Technostress (Tarafdar *et al.*, 2007).

Technology not only influences when and where employees work but also how they work. While technology simplifies work, it also reduces employees' freedom due to increased standardization of work. It becomes more transparent for the employees as well as the leaders who does what in the company, their current status, and what their contribution is.

Effect on job skills and competencies

Another strand of research has dealt with the changing requirements of skills for the employees with the technology adoption in the organizations. With the routine work being automated (Autor *et al.*, 2006), a skilled workforce is becoming more critical (Brynjolfsson & Hitt, 2000). The significant competencies required are problem-solving (Parker *et al.*, 2001), efficiently dealing with a vast amount of information (Van Knippenberg *et al.*, 2015), creative mindset (Frenkel *et al.*, 1995), quick decision-making (Perlow *et al.*, 2002), digital savvy and sharp business acumen (McAfee & Welch, 2013), knowledge and social skills (Frey & Osborne, 2017). People with obsolete skills may be at a disadvantage (Aeppel, 2015) as the existing skills may not match with those demanded by the employers (Katz, 2010). They are required to think interdisciplinarily and be abreast with the latest technological developments (Gimpel & Roglinger, 2015). Digital skills have been found to help employees operate efficiently in the developing workplace (Briggs & Makice, 2012). They help promote inclusion and well-being in the workplace (Collard *et al.*, 2017) as well as effective management of social relationships in a virtual work setting (Jones & Hafner, 2012). However, the acquisition of such skills may be affected by the 'Generation Divide'. The younger employees may be more acquainted and receptive to digital tools than their tenured colleagues (McAfee & Welch, 2013). An absence or insufficiency of such skills can reduce an organization's as well as an individual's ability to benefit from the technologically advanced workplace (Jones & Hafner, 2012). The impact of the mentioned skills on technology acceptance and continuation requires much attention (Mohammadyari & Singh, 2015).

Effect on leadership

The challenges faced by the organizations due to technological changes are demanding more leadership flexibility, speedy decision-making and risk-taking ability (Horney *et al.*, 2010). The leaders are required to support technology-enabled change processes, translate the vision into day-to-day operations and prepare their employees for action (McAfee & Welch, 2013). There seems to be a unidirectional relationship between technologization of leadership and work since the high pressure on leaders to constantly innovate and initiate change might also be felt by their employees establishing the norms of workplace behaviour. Leaders' requirement to handle the complexities and uncertainties at work will need them to attain more and more competencies to initiate and handle changes actively. They will also have to provide direction and optimal support to their employees (McCann *et al.*, 2009). Leaders play a crucial role in managing employee stress by ensuring that the flexibility of work time and space doesn't lead to perceived overload by the employees. Employees' job demands might have a reciprocal relationship with leaders' health management behaviour as they might feel that they must take care of employees' health due to increased job demands. People become emotionally and physically disturbed if they are either under- or over-challenged. Leaders will be engaging in more personal development to help employees cope with increased job demands, and the employees should reduce the felt job demands by better living up to the job requirements (Arthur *et al.*, 2003).

In the same way, the higher job demands for the leaders in terms of pressure for innovation, higher speed in decision-making might also play a role in increasing stress and pressure on the leaders. 'Leadership around the clock' is a phenomenon that is fast becoming common due to the lack of boundaries between work and private life, with private life becoming professional and professional life becoming private. The increased temporal and spatial flexibility of employees also increases the amount of time for which leaders need to be available for their employees. This demand for their increased availability negatively affects their work–life balance, leading to a cycle of mutual reinforcement. Consequently, there appears to be a reciprocal relationship between employees' changed work–life balance and leaders' job demands. Employees may feel less likely to influence leaders' technology usage, as they have less discretion to decide about it at work (Lewis *et al.*, 2003). Leaders will be required to provide autonomy and trust their employees, reinforcing employees' influence at work (Lorinkova *et al.*, 2013).

Effect on hierarchies

The technological changes are demanding a shift from the traditional decision-making procedures based on rigid hierarchies. The hierarchical structure of organizations promotes 'silo thinking', leading to slower decision-making in dealing with the rapid, technological and cross-functional nature of technologization (Bonnet & Nandan, 2011). The automation increases the transparency in the organizations (McAfee & Welch, 2013) by democratizing information, bypassing the management levels (Bonnet & Nandan, 2011).

Due to technologization, increased involvement and participation of employees in organizational decision-making is possible. This relates to more autonomy at work, i.e. they will have more leeway in decision-making and take more responsibility for the quality of work. Considering the high complexity and uncertainty of the technologized work, decisions will be made less up to down. This transformation may result in the flattening of hierarchies in the organizations. The managers/leaders may see this coming as a leadership threat by a perceived loss of control and reacting by resisting technology acceptance and adoption. Superiors will be expected to lead in a participatory way, by actively incorporating the ideas of their subordinates during decision-making. Hence, there will be more autonomy given to the employees. It will no longer be the superior's role to distribute tasks but to let the employees find their way through the goal based on their skills. This will involve investing more trust in them, who are typically more competent in their area of expertise. Reinforcement of employees' influence at work will increase due to greater trust and autonomy invested in them (Lorinkova *et al.*, 2013).

Discussion

The relationship between the factors and their impact on employees is represented in Figure 1. The factors impacting jobs are mentioned on the left side with the various reasons encouraging or discouraging the adoption of technology at work for the employees, on the top and bottom of the arrow, respectively. The reasons act as a feedback loop for the concerned

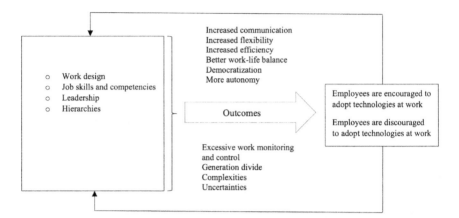

Figure 1.   A Model of Workplace Factors Affecting Employees' Technology Adoption

stakeholders, such as organizations and educational institutes, to take necessary and timely actions.

Practical and Research Implications

The emerging scholarly literature on technologization and digitization of the workplace can provide valuable insights to practitioners (Koffer, 2015). There is a scope for organizations to understand their employees' technology readiness levels and their behavioural intentions to use such technologies (Marsh, 2019). Government-backed 'Digital India' has further aided the prospects of adoption of digital tools by the organizations and take timely measures to effectively use them at work. Supporting employees in learning desired skills and expertise would help them operate more efficiently and reduce cognitive load (Kasemsap, 2018; Ng, 2012). At the present time, half of India's population is under the age of 25, and two-thirds are under the age of 35.

By 2027, India is predicted to have the world's biggest workforce of persons aged 15–64. Currently, just 18% of the country's workforce is officially skilled (Mashelkar, 2018). Skill development and employability continue to be major challenges, particularly in light of the emergence of exponential technologies (Jain *et al.*, 2021). Researchers have a significant role to play in the readiness of employees towards the work change. They are required to map skills with each new upcoming job role or modifications of the existing job roles. It is also crucial for scholars to be more knowledgeable about each role's learning pedagogies and its subsequent required skills and expertise. They need to develop models and theories of learning that will be needed to support the continually changing and dynamic work environment (Fenwick, 2016). These theories and models would account for the human and nonhuman actor interventions in these environments. To bridge the gap between researchers and practitioners, they may seek out new collaborations with technology inventors and designers, ensuring that both sides consider the impact on work and employees in the design process. Although technological change is inevitable, involving Human Resources in the initial design of emerging technologies may result in technologies that enhance and augment human capabilities rather than replacing their efforts and existence in the work process, thus limiting the negative impact of technology on humans.

Conclusion

India is one of the world's fastest-growing economies, thanks to a recent digital revolution. Digital India is the government of India's flagship initiative, which was started on July 1, 2015, with the goal of transforming India into a digitally enabled society and knowledge economy. It benefits a variety of major industries, including telecommunications, services, health, retail, media, e-commerce, agriculture and education. The path, however, creates both possibilities and threats for organizations and their members. This chapter provides a brief overview of the challenges and opportunities related to the technological transformation of work on employees in the time of the COVID-19 crisis. The crisis emphasizes the continued importance of technology adoption and the transformation of work as a viable area of study for both research and practice. The technological transformation of work and workplace by cloud computing, robotics, IoT, teleconferencing, etc. have a significant effect on how employees who are ultimately humans think, feel and do within and outside the organizations. The structural changes brought by technological advancements are changing the work design, skill requirements, leadership and hierarchies in the organizations. The realization of benefits associated with this transformation is highly reliant on managing people and organizational aspects.

The complacent employees may see no reason to bring about a change. They may even filter any information that does not support their views. These employees will ultimately fear the technological

Table 1.   Agenda for Future Research

Problem or Issue in Need of Research	Proposed Research Questions
1. The collaboration of technology and humans in the workplace has brought much uncertainty about the unstructured, virtual environments (Hagiu, 2015). Traditional full-time employment is being gradually replaced by gig, freelance and contractual work (Dokko *et al.*, 2015). This has blurred the roles and expectations of employees and employers.	1(a). How are the technology changes at work changing the work roles, employment relations and working conditions? 1(b). How are people feeling in their new job roles?
2. These technological interventions are creating a fear of job insecurity (Marvit, 2014) and social as well as professional isolation (Heller, 2017). In-depth research is required to explore the personal, social and psychological aspects of the work changes.	2(a). What are the psychological and social dimensions of working in a technologized work environment? 2(b). What are the personal, social and professional problems faced by them? 2(c). How can the Human Resource Development (HRD) address the concerns related to employee safety, health and work–life balance?
3. Work-related changes demand a newer set of skills and knowledge to adapt to the changing work or job-title (Rainie & Anderson, 2017). The employees are expected to quickly get their hands on the new skills suitable for their work. This can be very uneasy for the older (aged) employees who were immensely capable in their work but now must shift to an entirely different method of working.	3(a). What are the Knowledge, Skills and Abilities (KSAs) required to sustain and succeed in the changing work environment? 3(b). How can the KSAs for older employees be taken care of? Will the reverse-learning technique work? How to proceed?
4. The need to update quickly and continuously to the changing skills requires appropriate training. Human resource practitioners in the respective organizations play a vital role in responding to the continuous learning demands of changing work.	4(a). What role do Human Resource Development (HRD) professionals play in the development of the required skills? 4(b). How to develop training mechanisms for employees of various ages and roles?
5. The recent developments in the nature of work change the skills and expertise required as well as the means of acquiring them. HRD researchers and practitioners must support this change.	5(a). What do these work changes mean for HRD researchers and theory? 5(b). What new theories and models are required for the new learning? 5(c). What do these work changes mean for HRD professionals? How will their roles change?

transformation in the workplace. They need to feel that they are a part of this transformation vision. This vision must help them in determining how they must modify their behaviour. However, the question which remains unanswered is how to assess the technological impact on employee behaviour? If employees appreciate this change, then how to sustain this impact? But if employees are not welcoming this change, then what is stopping them? What can be done to help them better cope with this change? Since almost all companies at any scale are bound to adapt to the digital transformation in the near future, it will be the humans who will have to work with these machines to accomplish goals. The way technology is introduced and implemented in an organization will examine employees' intentions to accept (or not accept) the changes brought henceforth.

Indian organizations have enormous potential to reap the full advantages of the digital revolution. Although the Indian government has put in place the necessary policies to maximize the benefits of digitization, sustainability has emerged as the most crucial concept. Implementing it in the organizations needs a more nuanced understanding of employee behaviour.

Future Directions

Table 1 contains a detailed agenda for future research on issues and improvements in the technologically advancing workplace, as well as lists specific research questions to guide the study.

References

Aeppel, T. (2014). Robots work their way into small factories. *The Wall Street Journal*. September 18. pp. B1–2.

Aeppel, T. (2015). What clever robots mean for jobs: Experts rethink belief that tech always lifts employment as machines take on skills once thought uniquely human. *The Wall Street Journal*. http://www.wsj.com/articles/what-clever-robots-mean-for-jobs-1424835002.

Ambrose, M. L. & Alder, G. S. (2000). Designing, implementing, and utilizing computerized performance monitoring: Enhancing organisational justice. *Research in Personnel and Human Resources Management, 18*, 187–219.

Andal-Ancion, A., Cartwright, P., & George, S. Y. (2003). The digital transformation of traditional businesses. *MIT Sloan Management Review, 44*(4), 34–41.

Arthur, W., Bennett, W., Edens, P. S., & Bell, S. T. (2003). Effectiveness of training in organisations: A meta-analysis of design and evaluation features. *Journal of Applied Psychology, 88*, 234–245.

Autor, D. H., Katz, H. L., & Kearney, M. S. (2006). The polarization of the U.S. labor market. *American Economic Review, 95*, 189–194.

Avolio, B. J., Walumbwa, F. O., & Weber, T. J. (2009). Leadership: Current theories, research, and future directions. *Annual Review of Psychology, 60*, 421–449.

Bailey, D. E. & Kurland, N. B. (2002). A review of telework research: Findings, new directions and lessons for the study of modern work. *Journal of Organisational Behavior, 23*, 383–400.

Barley, S. R. (2015). Why the internet makes buying a car less loathsome: How technologies change role relations. *Academy of Management Discoveries, 1*, 5–35.

Bonnet, D. & Nandan, P. (2011). Transform to the power of digital: Digital transformation as a driver of corporate performance. Report, Capgemini Consulting.

Briggs, C. & Makice, K. (2012). *Digital Fluency: Building Success in the Digital Age*. Bloomington, IN: SociaLens.

Brynjolfsson, E. & Hitt, L. (2000). Beyond computation: Information technology, organisational transformation and business performance. *Journal of Economic Perspectives, 14*, 23–48.

Cascio, W. F. (2014). Looking back, looking forward: Technology in the workplace. In Coovert, M. D. & Foster Thompson, L. (eds.), *The Psychology of Workplace Technology*. (pp. 307–313). New York: Routledge.

Cascio, W. F. & Montealegre, R. (2016). How technology is changing work and organisations. *Annual Review of Organisational Psychology and Organisational Behavior, 3*, 349–375.

Castanheira, F. & Chambel, M. J. (2010). Reducing burnout in call centers through HR practices. *Human Resource Management, 49*, 1047–1065.

Collard, A., De Smedt, T., Dufrasne, M., Fastrez, P., Ligurgo, V., Patriarche, G., & Philippette, T. (2017). Digital media literacy in the workplace: A model combining compliance and inventivity. *Italian Journal of Sociology of Education, 9*(1), 122–154.

Coovert, M. D. & Thompson, L. F. (2014). Toward a synergistic relationship between psychology and technology. In *The Psychology of Workplace Technology*. (pp. 1–17). New York: Routledge.

Davenport, T. H. & Kirby, J. (2015). Beyond automation: Strategies for remaining gainfully employed in an era of very smart machines. *Harvard Business Review, 93*(6), 58–65.

Dittes, S., Richter, S., Richter, A., & Smolnik, S. (2019). Toward the workplace of the future: How organisations can facilitate digital work. *Business Horizons, 62*(5), 649–661.

Dokko, J., Mumford, M., & Schannzenbach, D. W. (2015). Workers and the online gig economy: A Hamilton Project framing paper. Washington, DC: Brookings. http://www.hamiltonproject.org/assets/files/workers_and_the_online_gig_economy.pdf.

Farr, J. L., Fairchild, J., & Cassidy, S. E. (2014). Technology and performance appraisal. In *The Psychology of Workplace Technology*. (pp. 77–98). New York: Routledge.

Fenwick, T. (2016). *Professional Responsibility and Professionalism: A Sociomaterial Examination*. London, England: Routledge.

Frenkel, S., Korczynski, M., Donoghue, L., & Shire, K. (1995). Re-constituting work: Trends towards knowledge work and info-normative control. *Work, Employment and Society, 9*, 773–796.

Gajendran, R. S. & Harrison, D. A. (2007). The good, the bad, and the unknown about telecommuting: Meta-analysis of psychological mediators and individual consequences. *Journal of Applied Psychology, 92*, 1524–1541.

Gimpel, H. & Roglinger, M. (2015). Digital transformation: Changes and chances — Insights based on an empirical study. Project Group Business and Information Systems Engineering (BISE) of the Fraunhofer Institute for Applied Information Technology (FIT).

Giustiniano, L. & Bolici, F. (2012). Organisational trust in a networked world: Analysis of the interplay between social factors and information and communication technology. *Journal of Information, Communication and Ethics in Society, 10*(3), 187–202.

Golden, T. D. & Veiga, J. F. (2005). The impact of extent of telecommuting on job satisfaction: Resolving inconsistent findings. *Journal of Management, 31*, 301–318.

Gray, P., El Sawy, O. A., Asper, G., & Thordarson, M. (2013). Realizing strategic value through center-edge digital transformation in consumer-centric industries. *MIS Quarterly Executive, 12*(1), 1–17.

Hagiu, A. (2015). Work 3.0: Redefining jobs and companies in the Uber age. *Forbes, 196*, 12–14. https://www.forbes.com/sites/hbsworkingknowledge/2015/09/29/work-3-0-redefining-jobs-and-companies-in-the-uber-age/#7dfc39c43aa1.

Heller, N. (2017). Is the gig economy working? *The New Yorker, 109*, 1–35. https://www.newyorker.com/magazine/2017/05/15/is-the-gig-economy-working.

Horney, N., Pasmore, B., & O'Shea, T. (2010). Leadership agility: A business imperative for a VUCA world. *Human Resource Planning, 33*(4), 34.

Jain, M., Goel, A., Sinha, S., & Dhir, S. (2021). Employability implications of artificial intelligence in healthcare ecosystem: Responding with readiness. Foresight.

Jones, R. H. & Hafner, C. A. (2012). *Understanding Digital Literacies: A Practical Introduction.* Abingdon, Oxfordshire: Routledge.

Kasemsap, K. (2018). Encouraging digital literacy and ICT competency in the information age. In M. Khosrow-Pour (ed.), *Encyclopedia of Information Science and Technology* (4th ed., pp. 2253–2263). Hershey, Pennsylvania: IGI Global. Doi: 10.4018/978-1-5225-2255- 3.ch196.

Katz, L. (2010). Long-term unemployment in the great recession. Presented to US Congress Joint Economic Comm. http://www.jec.senate.gov/public/index.cfm?a=Files.ServeandFile_id=e1cc2c23-dc6f-4871-a26a-fda9bd 32fb7e.%2520.

Kayworth, T. R. & Leidner, D. E. (2001). Leadership effectiveness in global virtual teams. *Journal of Management Information Systems, 18,* 7–40.

Kelliher, C. & Anderson, D. (2010). Doing more with less? Flexible working practices and the intensification of work. *Human Relations, 63,* 83–106.

Köffer, S. (2015). Designing the digital workplace of the future–what scholars recommend to practitioners. In *The 36th International Conference on Information Systems (ICIS)*, Fort Worth, Texas, December 13–16.

Kohnke, O. (2017). It's not just about technology: The people side of digitization. In *Shaping the Digital Enterprise*, pp. 69–91. Springer, Cham.

Levy, Y. & Ellis, T. J. (2006). A systems approach to conduct an effective literature review in support of information systems research. *Informing Science, 9,* 181–212.

Lewis, W., Agarwal, R., & Sambamurthy, V. (2003). Sources of influence on beliefs about information technology use: An empirical study of knowledge workers. *MIS Quarterly, 27,* 657–678.

Lorinkova, N. M., Pearsall, M. J., & Sims Jr., H. P. (2013). Examining the differential longitudinal performance of directive versus empowering leadership in teams. *Academy of Management Journal, 56,* 573–596.

Lu, J. L. (2005). Perceived job stress of women workers in diverse manufacturing industries. *Human Factors and Ergonomics in Manufacturing, 15,* 275–291.

Mannerin, J. S. & Mokhtarian, P. L. (1995). Modeling the choice of telecommuting frequency in California: An exploratory analysis. *Technological Forecasting and Social Change, 49,* 49–57.

Marsh, W. (2019). Digital skills are key to well-being in the digital workplace. https://www.linkedin.com/pulse/digital-skills-key-wellbeing-workplace-elizabeth-marsh.

Marvit, M. Z. (2014). How crowdworkers became the ghosts in the digital machine. The Nation. http://www.thenation.com/article/how-crowdworkers-became-ghosts-digital machine/.

Mashelkar, R. A. (2018). Exponential technology, Industry 4.0 and future of jobs in India. *Review of Market Integration, 10*(2), 138–157.

Mazmanian, M. (2013). Avoiding the trap of constant connectivity: When congruent frames allow for heterogeneous practices. *Academy of Management Journal*, *56*, 1225–1250.

Mazmanian, M., Orlikowski, W. J., & Yates, J. (2005). Crackberries: The social implications of ubiquitous wireless email devices. In C. Sorenson, K. Yoo, K. Lyytinen, & J. I. DeGross (eds.), *Designing Ubiquitous Information Environments: Socio-Technical Issues and Challenges*, (pp. 337–344). New York: Springer.

McAfee, A. & Welch, M. (2013). Being digital: Engaging the organisation to accelerate digital transformation. *Digital Transformation Revolution*, *4*, 37–47.

McCann, J., Selsky, J., & Lee, J. (2009). Building agility, resilience and performance in turbulent environments. *People and Strategy*, *32*, 44–51.

Mohammadyari, S. & Singh, H. (2015). Understanding the effect of e-learning on individual performance. *The Role of Digital Literacy Computers and Education*, *82*, 11–25. Doi: 10.1016/j.compedu.2014.10.025.

Mullins, L. J. (1990). *Management and Organisational Behaviour*. (2nd ed.) London: Pitman Publishing.

Ng, W. (2012). *Education in a Competitive and Globalizing World: Empowering Scientific Literacy through Digital Literacy and Multiliteracies*. Hauppauge: Nova Science Publishers.

Olszewski, P. & Mokhtaria, P. (1994). Telecommuting frequency and impacts for State of California employees. *Technological Forecasting and Social Change*, *45*, 275–286.

Osman, M. (2010). Controlling uncertainty: A review of human behavior in complex, dynamic environments. *Psychological Bulletin*, *136*, 65–86.

Oxford Economics. (2017). Building the digital workplace: What comes next in the mobile revolution. http://www.oxfordeconomics.com/my-oxford/projects/365465.

Parker, S. K., Wall, T. D., & Cordery, J. L. (2001). Future work design research and practice: Towards an elaborated model of work design. *Journal of Occupational and Organisational Psychology*, *74*, 413–440.

Perlow, L. A., Okhuysen, G. A., & Repenning, N. P. (2002). The speed trap: Exploring the relationship between decision making and temporal context. *Academy of Management Journal*, *45*, 931–955.

Potosky, D. & Lomax, M. W. (2014). Leadership and technology: A love-hate relationship. In *The Psychology of Workplace Technology*. (pp. 118–146). New York: Routledge.

Rainie, L. & Anderson, J. (2017). *The Future of Jobs and Jobs Training*. Washington, DC: Pew Research Center.

Redden, E. S., Elliott, L. R., & Barnes, M. J. (2014). Robots: The new teammates. In *The Psychology of Workplace Technology*. (pp. 185–208). New York: Routledge.

Rogan, R. G. & Simmons, G. A. (1984). Teleconferencing. *J Extension, 22*(5). http://www.joe.org/joe/1984september/a4.php.

Schallenmueller, S. (2016). Smart workplace technology buzz. In J. E. Lee (ed.), *The Impact of ICT on Work*, pp. 127–150. Switzerland: Springer.

Schwab, K. (2017). The Fourth Industrial Revolution, World Economic Forum, Geneva, Switzerland. https://www.weforum.org/about/the-fourth-industrial-revolution-by-klausschwab.

Soule, D. L., Puram, A. D., Westerman, G. F., & Bonnet, D. (2016). Becoming a digital organisation. *The Journey to Digital Dexterity*. https://ssrn.com/abstract=2697688.

Tarafdar, M., Tu, Q., Ragu-Nathan, B. S., & Ragu-Nathan, T. S. (2007). The impact of technostress on role stress and productivity. *Journal of Management Information Systems, 24*, 301–328.

Torraco, R. J. (2005). Writing integrative literature reviews: Guidelines and examples. *Human Resource Development Review, 4*, 356–367.

Venkatesh, V., Morris, M. G., Davis, G. B., & Davis, F. D. (2003). User acceptance of information technology: Toward a unified view. *Management Information Systems Quarterly, 27*(3), 425–478. Doi: 10.2307/30036540.

Van Knippenberg, D., Dahlander, L., Haas, M. R., & George, G. (2015). Information, attention, and decision making. *Academy of Management Journal, 58*, 649–657.

vom Brocke, J., Becker, J., & De Marco, M. (2016). The networked society. *Business and Information Systems Engineering, 58*(3), 159–160.

Webster, J. & Watson, R. T. (2002). Analyzing the past to prepare for the future: Writing a literature review. *MIS Quarterly, 26*, xiii–xxiii.

World Economic Forum. (2016). *The Future of Jobs: Employment, Skills and Workforce Strategy for the Fourth Industrial Revolution*. Geneva, Switzerland: World Economic Forum.

Zweig, D. & Scott, K. (2007). When unfairness matters most: Supervisory violations of electronic monitoring practices. *Human Resource Management Journal, 17*, 227–247.

https://doi.org/10.1142/9789811271786_0012

Chapter 12

COVID-led Adoption of Video Resumes for Deep Archival Candidate Screening in India

Apoorva Goel[*,§], Ankita Modi[†,¶] and Richa Awasthy[‡,ǁ]

Indian Institute of Technology, Chennai, India

†*LG Electronics India Pvt. Ltd., Noida, India*

‡*School of Business, Public Policy and Social Entrepreneurship, Ambedkar University, Delhi, India*

§*ms19d039@smail.iitm.ac.in*

¶*ankitamodiece2k11@gmail.com*

ǁ*richa@aud.ac.in*

Abstract

Despite the popularity of traditional paper resumes, they have been largely discredited. It has been shown they can even undercut the impact of more useful information. In this chapter, we determine the challenges faced by recruiters in job screening as well as explore job applicants' perception towards using video resumes for seeking a prospective job. Two studies were conducted utilizing interview and survey methods. Study 1 ($n = 16$) using in-depth interviews, demonstrates that major challenges faced by recruiters in candidate screening are hiring cost, hiring time and quality of hire. Building on the findings of study 1 and using a semi-structured survey design, study 2 ($n = 206$) determined the reasons for preference of job applicants' usage of video resumes. Taken together, these studies reach out to the recruiters, job applicants and researchers for suggesting effective recruitment processes. Our studies relate to the role of the community of practice in structuring e-recruitment practices through video resumes and highlight the element of the "privacy" of video resumes.

Introduction

The COVID-19 pandemic has resulted in several substantial and unexpected changes for organizations (Gunay, 2020). The entire global economy is undergoing enormous changes and challenges. Many firms have seen layoffs and downsizing (Béland *et al.*, 2020; Fana *et al.*, 2020; Mamgain, 2021). Organizations that are seeking suitable job candidates are having a difficult time finding them. Though everyone in the job market is aware of the notion of a resume, the importance of having an up-to-date resume in the current pandemic circumstances is even greater. While posing significant hurdles, COVID-19 forces us to acquire new ways of living and thriving, which includes a novel outlook to resumes that catches the recruiter's attention and helps one stand out from the crowd of job applicants. Because of the social distancing and quarantine, the technological aspect of a resume, together with the visual element, is quite significant. Video resumes can assist in the initial screening at a time when face-to-face interviews are a challenge. Regardless of how significant or beneficial video resumes are thought to be, their acceptability by job candidates is critical to their widespread adoption and this topic is quite under-researched.

Video resumes can be implemented as a new practice as they improve the performance of recruitment, there is a potential for a community of practice (Lanke & Nath, 2021; Wenger & Snyder, 2000). They offer solutions to certain issues such as (a) reducing hiring time, (b) decreasing hiring cost, (c) increasing quality of hire and (d) reducing hiring biasness.

Organizations can harness this technological solution for an effective recruitment process. The adoption of this practice can foster new approaches to recruitment where candidates can express themselves in a potent way and can emphasize their skills and experience according to job requirements. On the other hand, this practice helps recruiters understand the candidate in a better way and can shed light on their inherent qualities other than their academic achievements. Video resumes can help the recruiter know more about the surface-level qualities such as communication skills (how candidates present their portfolio), persuasion (how motivated the candidate seems to be), time management skills (the ability of a candidate to expresses in the limited time), creativity (how creatively the candidate can express themselves), and adaptability (how adaptive the candidate is to the new technique of video resume). Recent technological advancements and their massive availability have opened new avenues for research in the field of video resumes. A search of the literature on video resumes in Web of Science and Scopus reveals that there has been little research done on this topic (see Appendix A). The majority of it was conducted in the previous few years, suggesting that video resumes have gained a recent research focus. Despite the multiple advantages and cutting-edge technological infrastructure available for video resumes, past research has been unable to investigate the perspectives and perceptions of job applicants who are utilizing this new recruiting tool. In light of previous research, the goal of this study is to examine the challenges that recruiters face when searching for and screening potential candidates, as well as to determine the perceptions of MBA-enrolled jobseekers towards video resumes on various dimensions, as well as the reasons for their preference and non-preference.

The main contributions of this work are the following: First, it uses qualitative insights to address the challenges faced by recruiters in screening candidates out of the vast resume pool. Second, this study addresses the solution to the challenges faced by recruiters by examining video resumes from a job applicant's viewpoint both qualitatively and quantitatively, which will add to the paucity of research on this topic. Third, this study highlights the element of the "privacy" of video resumes, which has received little attention.

This chapter is structured as follows. In the next section, we discuss existing research on the topic. We then demonstrate study 1 and study 2 along with their analysis and findings. Consequently, we discuss the limitations, scope of future research, and theoretical and practical implications. We finally conclude in the last section.

E-recruitment: Video Resumes for Employee Recruitment

E-recruitment, according to Bartram (2000), serves as a conduit for communication between job applicants and recruiters. Traditional media, such as newspapers (Selden & Orenstein, 2011), might be cumbersome at times, therefore e-recruitment takes its place. Some companies employ e-recruiters, who are part of the e-recruitment process and help to link the IT artefacts with other aspects of the recruiting process. E-recruitment is an emerging phenomenon and seems to be the appropriate choice during the pandemic with video resumes coming into their own as one of the major milestones in the process of e-recruitment.

In most organizations, recruitment and selection is a process of matching job descriptions with the prospective candidate's resume followed by an interview. However, studies show that interviews are not strongly correlated with job performance (Campion *et al.*, 1988; Gusdorf, 2008; Judge *et al.*, 2000; Peck & Levashina, 2017); rather, cognitive abilities are strongly correlated with job performance (Schmidt, 2002). This shows how identifying skills and implementing a pre-screening method based on competencies to assess a candidate's job fit may significantly enhance an organization's selection process. Job competencies are a person's underlying behavioural capabilities that contribute to effective workplace performance (Brown *et al.*, 2018; Sanghi, 2016; Takey & de Carvalho, 2015). According to Ashkezari & Aeen (2012), competency-based recruitment is a process of hiring people based on their ability to articulate their job knowledge, skills and technical know-how. The major reason for this type of recruitment is not just to fill a vacancy but also to select the right person who is committed and can perform at a high level (Daniels *et al.*, 2011). A video resume is a brief video message in which job applicants present themselves to potential employers (Hiemstra, 2013). Video resumes, as opposed to traditional paper resumes, convey more about a person than just their educational background and professional experience (Hiemstra, 2013). They also provide the applicant the flexibility to underline their skills, knowledge, potential, personality, communication ability and why they are preferable to the competition for a certain job or company (Cole *et al.*, 2007; Hiemstra *et al.*, 2012; Waung *et al.*, 2014). The primary point of difference between a traditional paper resume and a video resume is the level of media richness, which affects the type and variety of information available to the recruiters for making selection judgements. The rich communication media (Daft & Lengel, 1984, 1986) offers multiple verbal and non-verbal cues (such as words, facial expressions, body posture and gestures), provision for immediate feedback (real-time exchange of information) and a personal focus (customization of the video based on the job). Video resumes are richer media than paper resumes due to the availability of verbal and non-verbal cues. They contain more varied information in the form of behaviours exhibited in the resume as well as biographical information presented by the applicant. On the other hand, paper resumes are low in media richness due to the fact that they can only offer biographical information regarding academic achievements and work experience. The different types of information available by the resume format determine how efficiently a recruiter can select a suitable job candidate.

Hausknecht *et al.* (2004) have highlighted the reasons for the importance of organizations to study applicant perceptions. These reasons are majorly based on Gilliland's model. Gilliland (1993) states that an applicant's perceived fairness is influenced by their procedural justice perceptions (i.e. whether they perceive selection procedure as fair in terms of job affiliation and opportunity to express) and their perceptions of distributive justice (i.e. whether they receive the hiring decisions with equity and equality). The effect of resume format, such as paper resumes only, video resumes only, or both, on applicant evaluation was investigated in a laboratory experiment, and the results revealed that video resumes may result in different assessments of applicant personality and harsher evaluations of applicant skills and abilities than paper resumes. Hence, recruiters are cautioned in the use of video resumes (Waung *et al.*, 2014).

Study 1

Screening of resumes is a ubiquitous procedure in the first selection stage of organizations. However, it has received much less research attention (Hiemstra & Derous, 2015). Our first study sought to identify what challenges organizations face in screening candidates for further rounds of selection leading to final job offers. This study responded to continued calls for more meticulous approaches to examine the first selection stage of recruitment for greater efficiency leading to better hiring decisions.

Method

Sample

Owing to the exploratory nature of the study, restricted sample size was drawn in accordance with methodological arguments that exploratory studies require a small sample size to generate in-depth insights (Vasileiou *et al.*, 2018; Yin, 2014). Data were obtained from 16 senior managers from varied industry sectors such as IT/ITeS, consulting, retail and manufacturing (Table 1). According to the non-probabilistic sample size for interviews (Guest *et al.*, 2006), theoretical saturation was attained within 16 interviews and broad themes emerged within 12 interviews.

Table 1.   Interviewee Demographic Profile

Code	Gender	Tenure (Years)	Position	Industries where Participants have Experience	Organization Size
1	Female	10+	Head, HR	Manufacturing, Service	1,500+
2	Female	13+	Division Head	Banking, IT	2,000+
3	Male	24+	DGM	FMCG, Manufacturing	2,500+
4	Female	5+	Founder	Service	100+
5	Male	17+	Head, HR	Manufacturing, FMCG	2,000+
6	Male	11+	Senior HR Manager	Banking, Consulting	1,000+
7	Male	22+	Head, HR	IT, Service	500+
8	Female	10+	Assistant Senior Manager	Manufacturing	800+
9	Female	25+	GM	IT, Consulting	3,500+
10	Female	32+	Head, HR	Service	2,000+
11	Female	18+	Head, HR	Service	25,000+
12	Female	38+	VP, HR	Banking	20,000+
13	Male	27+	GM	Manufacturing, Consulting	5,000+
14	Male	3+	Founder	IT	25+
15	Male	15+	Senior HR Manager	Consulting	110+
16	Male	20+	VP and HR	Manufacturing	2,500+

Procedure

Interviews were conducted online in India through Skype and the average duration of the interviews ranged from 40 to 50 minutes. The interview questions included: What is the usual recruitment process in your organization, what are the challenges faced in the process of screening applicants for recruitment? How do you think it can be made efficient? Probing questions like *"can you tell me more about it"*, *"how did that happen"*, *"please elaborate on the context"*, etc. were used to receive rich data on their experiences and were posed wherever required for greater clarity.

Given the exploratory nature of the study, qualitative content analysis was undertaken by employing subjective interpretation of the content through a systematic classification process of coding and identifying themes (Hsieh & Shannon, 2005).

The interviews were transcribed and read carefully to understand the content to perform open coding. The qualitative content analysis was guided by NVivo (Version 12) software. A combination of content and context helped derive the nodes. These nodes were then clubbed under a parent node (theme) to form categories. The "constant comparison" method ensured consistency in the process. The major themes were centred on the time for hiring a candidate, hiring cost and the quality of hiring.

Data analysis and results

An exploratory study gave us an opportunity to uncover the challenges that the recruiters today are facing in the initial screening round of the selection process in organizations. The following are the areas of concern for the recruiters as determined by the study participants:

Hiring time

The major problem faced by 95% of the recruiters in our study is the time-consuming activity of shortlisting the resumes of prospective candidates. It took a lot of time for them to shortlist eligible and qualified candidates out of the resume pool. The majority of their time is absorbed in matching candidate suitability with the job requirement by reading the resumes and understanding each resume in-depth to identify the candidate's qualification, ability and specialization(s). They also mentioned the concerns that due to various writing formats of the resumes, it is a herculean task for them to take a glance at a resume. This issue is explained in the following quotes by our participants:

> *"We go through around 1,000 resumes to shortlist 500 out of them for an aptitude test, 300 out of them are then called for technical interview one and subsequently, 100 are called for technical round two. After this round, further only 50 candidates are then called for an HR interview and only 10 of the total 300 interviewed candidates get selected. So, to select 10 candidates we go through 1,000 resumes (Table 2) which consumes 50% of our time in the first phase of recruitment itself." (Participant 12)*

> *"A major issue is that candidates do not want to come for the interview if they do not have surety. This increases hiring time." (Participant 6)*

Hiring cost

The second major concern faced by the recruiters is the cost of hiring a candidate. The hiring cost for any organization is considered to be a liability which becomes an asset only after the candidates join the organization and start contributing by helping the organization in achieving its objectives. The following quote by one of our participants mentions this:

> *"A lot of money has to be shelled out right from putting up job vacancies till the final joining. This cost is regained only after the selected candidates start producing outputs." (Participant 3)*

Table 2.   Recruitment Cycle Output

Phase of Recruitment	Number of Candidates at Each Phase	Time Taken (Number of Days)	Percentage of Time Taken (%)
Screening of resumes	1,000	5	50%
Aptitude test	500	2	20%
Technical interview (1)	300	1	10%
Technical interview (2)	100	1	10%
HR interview	50	1	10%
Final result	10	10	—

Recruitment is a cost for any company. It requires a considerable amount of money to be spent on hiring suitable candidates for a job. Based on how much a company is willing to spend, they accordingly arrange for their organization's sourcing, screening and selecting processes. They even go to various geographical locations in search of the best suitable candidates. This issue is explained in the following quotes by our participants:

> *"Companies spend a lot of money only in sourcing candidates. It is a cost to the company as well as to the candidates. We travel to different locations to find our best job fit as well as the candidates who are located in a specific geographical area usually only come. The availability quotient is a major contributor. It misses out on other candidates who cannot be available. It all depends on the money the company wants to spend on it." (Participant 5)*

> *"Hiring cost is a major point of concern, especially for start-ups. The company size is small, and we need to hire multitasking individuals. Due to less time and budget constraints, we often have to compromise on the quality of talent." (Participant 14)*

Participants in our study also mention how the cost of recruitment increases due to consultants who assist the companies in hiring suitable candidates. The following quote highlights this:

> *"When the screening pool is big and we have less time, then we hire some consultants which add to our cost burden. Due to dependency on these consultants, sometimes we miss on some suitable candidates as well." (Participant 5)*

Quality of hiring

Another concern faced by recruiters is the quality of hiring candidates. Managers are always concerned about the quality gap between the candidates they want and those they get for a specific position. A lot of times they have to compromise on the quality due to lack of time and other resources. The pressure on them to hire within the limited availability of resources compels them to select the most approachable candidates. This issue is explained in the following quote by one of our participants:

> *"Due to lack of time and hiring pressure, we have to compromise on the quality of candidates selected." (Participant 4)*

Recruiters are also sceptical of the candidate's fit into the organization by shortlisting them on the basis of a resume which is usually in written form. This issue is explained in the following quotes by our participants:

> *"Selecting candidates based on resumes is just like flipping a coin. It is a tough process of calling probable candidates for final interviews based on their resumes which only give details about their educational qualification and previous work experience." (Participant 7)*

> *"Judging the candidate's personality and suitability for a job role requires much more than just education and experience." (Participant 11)*

Discussion

Study 1 sought to isolate the challenges faced by recruiters in candidate screening. Results indicate that paper resumes possess a limited ability to aid in assessment of suitable candidates. They are found to be old school, boring and ineffective. They lead to higher time and cost and lower quality of candidate selection. It is hard to evaluate grit in a candidate or spot disorganization simply by reading a resume. It is also noted that the "keyword search"-based screening is not suitable for filling voluminous vacancies from a vast pool of applicant resume repositories (Maheshwari & Haque, 2020) and our recruiter participants would like it if the screening process is made quicker by easy and quick resumes. This they suggested by adding a visual element to the resumes, preferring video resumes to efficiently determine the candidates most suitable for a particular job and, hence, selecting the most appropriate candidates only for the further rounds of the selection process. Due to lengthy hiring time, the hiring cost and hiring quality are also impacted (Figure 1). The war for talent is pervasive and selecting the right candidate at the right time is the biggest challenge in recruitment.

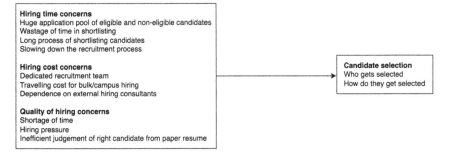

Figure 1.   Proposed Candidate Selection Model Based on the Data

Note: Arrow does not indicate causal relationship. It represents associations revealed in the study.

Study 2

From our study 1, we determined that recruiters would prefer video resumes over paper resumes for candidate selection as it will save a lot of their time in screening the candidates. However, before the video resumes-based applicant system is implemented, job applicants need to be made aware and comfortable with it. Their degree of readiness is of importance in accepting this system at this transitional period of change (Andersen, 2008). In study 2, we built on the findings of study 1 by conducting a semi-structured survey including both open and close-ended questions focusing on the perspectives of potential job seekers towards video resumes' usage in attaining a job. The closed-ended questions covered participants' perceptions about video resumes on parameters of validity, impression, preference and discrimination. Whereas the open-ended question led to the emergence of categories of format, goal, content, ease of use, fairness and privacy.

Method

Sample

MBA students enrolled in several Indian universities in the first or second year of their programme were invited to participate in this study.

Judgement sampling technique (Marshall, 1996) was used. A total of 210 people took part in the research. To eliminate skewness and assure diversification, an attempt was made to acquire a roughly equal number of responses from each university. Four responses were excluded from the participants who completed the survey due to missing information. As a result, 98.1% of people took part. Females provided 48% of the 206 viable responses, while males provided 52%. Furthermore, 32% of individuals had at least one year of work experience.

Procedure

The data were collected by sending a survey to the participants. It was in the form of a Google Form, so it could be filled out online for a greater demographic reach. The consent of participants was requested on the first sheet of the form, which also guaranteed total confidentiality of the information. First, they were asked if they were familiar with video resumes. If they were unaware, they were instructed to use a video resume platform that they could either search on the internet or pick from one of three (randomly determined) video resume platforms offered in the form. They were then directed to fill out a self-designed semi-structured questionnaire (Bryman, 2016). The survey was divided into two sections: closed and open-ended questions (Heale & Forbes, 2013). The closed-ended questions were designed to elicit information regarding video resumes from the perspectives of validity, preference, impression and discrimination (Hiemstra, 2013). *"Please mention any other opinions regarding video resumes"* was the open-ended question intended to gather any thoughts they had on video resumes. Quantitative data analysis was used to analyze data on the percentage of responses that are in-favour or against or neutral on each of the pre-decided dimensions. For the qualitative data collected from open-ended responses, content analysis was utilized to make valid inferences by interpreting and coding textual information (Hsieh & Shannon, 2005) to discover the reasons for favourability and unfavourability towards videos.

Data analysis and results

The results of our closed-ended survey questionnaire reveal the favourability and non-favourability towards video resumes, the questions to

Table 3. Descriptive Statistics of Respondents Based on Closed-ended Questionnaire

Measure	Result
Validity	Out of 206 participants, 76.7% believe video resumes are valid for job applicants and fulfil their objective, while 23.3% disagree.
Impression	72.3% of participants believe that video resumes help applicants make a favourable impression on recruiters, while 18% are unsure. 9.7% of those surveyed believe it will have no effect.
Preference	Around 54% of participants think video resumes are just as good as paper resumes, while 27.2% prefer video resumes less and 18.8% think video resumes are better.
Discrimination	According to the data gathered, the following is the order of discrimination in hiring due to video resumes: Attractiveness> Disfigurements> Personality> Disability> Gender> Age

which were based on the parameters of validity, impression, preference, and discrimination as shown in Table 3.

The term "validity" relates to the precision with which employment choices are made. When it comes to the validity of the video resume, the majority (76.7%) of participants believe it is valid for a job application and fulfils its goal, while 23.3% disagree. Video resumes provide applicants with a concise and clear platform to present themselves to recruiters. Some of them may find it handy for their needs.

The term "impression" refers to a judgement made about someone based on facts. In this dimension, the majority (72.3%) of participants believe that video resumes help applicants make a favourable impression on recruiters, while 18% disagree. Furthermore, 9.7% of participants believe it will have no effect. These impressions are more influenced by the personal characteristics of each candidate.

The term "preference" refers to a preference for one option over another. The majority (54%) of participants prefer video resumes to paper resumes, with 27.2% preferring video resumes less and 18.8% preferring video resumes more. Due to personal and unique reasons, some applicants may prefer a video resume over, equal to, or below a paper resume.

"Discrimination" is defined as the unfair treatment of diverse groups of people for various reasons. The following is the order of hiring prejudice due to video resumes based on the data collected: (">" stands for "followed by")

Table 4.   Categories Emerging from Open-ended Question

Category	Explanation	Participant Quotes in Relation to Favourable and Unfavourable Towards Video Resumes
Format	Format characteristics including the communication code (verbal *vs.* nonverbal); the administration duration; the number of actors involved; the direction of communication (one-way *vs.* two-way) the degree of surveillance	Favourable: • These are as good as paper resumes and take very less effort • These apps give the person a method to express oneself fully • These websites/apps will save a lot of time and energy Unfavourable: • Difficult to convey quantity of information • Difficulty to produce a natural and relaxed-looking video • Felt it to be informal • A well-lit and noise-free area is a mandate to shoot the video resume • A candidate needs to pay a lot of attention to what and how he or she is speaking since there is a time limit • Shooting video resumes require good speed internet connectivity
Goal and Content	Type of information that is exchanged	Favourable: • It is a very good tool in getting attention of the recruiter • Full flexibility to showcase your best talent • More control in what the recruiter will get to know • Great for someone like me who gets conscious in front of the panel while giving interviews Unfavourable: • Still believe that traditional resumes are way better than these video ones

Ease of use	Usage convenience	Favourable: • I can now carry my resume wherever I go without having to worry about a hardcopy • These are very handy and useful Unfavourable: • I feel paper resume is much more convenient • I don't find it comfortable to use
Fairness	The perception it will make on another person non-judgmentally	Favourable: No responses Unfavourable: • This is good only for those who can speak well but not for those who can't speak well but are good at working. Not fair for everyone • Can build bias easily • They may lead to biases
Privacy	Security of personal information	Favourable: Nil Unfavourable: • I am concerned about my privacy. What if my video is used wrongly and leaked? • I am not comfortable sharing my video resume online as I do not know who will see it and what will be done about it. • The thought of video tampering of my resume demotivates me to make one.

Attractiveness> Disfigurements> Personality> Disability> Gender> Age

The majority of participants believe that a person's attractiveness can have the greatest halo effect (Gerald *et al.*, 1981; Nicolau *et al.*, 2020) on the recruiter, which means that the recruiter will only notice the good qualities in a person while ignoring any flaws or disfigurements, no matter how minor they may be, and can have the greatest horn effect (Sundar *et al.*, 2014) on the recruiter, which means that the recruiter will only notice the good qualities in the applicant.

The results from our open-ended question in the questionnaire reveal further the reasons for job applicants' favourability and non-favourability towards video resumes. The quotes from the participants were categorized based on the collected data. These categories have emerged after analyzing all the quotes. These categories are format, goal and content, ease of use, fairness and privacy. These are explained in Table 4.

Discussion

Results from study 2 indicate that the majority of participants are in favour of this new recruiting tool, but they, like those who aren't, have certain similar issues that, if addressed, might lead to greater acceptance. The majority of these concerns are related to discomfort with the usage of technology, traditional mindset attached with the notion of resume, confidence in communication skills, and the issue of privacy. This study is one of its kind to explore the video resumes from job applicants' point of view on various parameters and from the participant pool which is geographically spread across to incorporate diversity. This study puts light on the issue of "privacy" of video resumes, which is much ignored in research and practice. Individuals, groups or organizations have the right to decide when, how and to what degree information about them is shared with others (Westin, 1967; Lee *et al.*, 2020). One of the reasons for the unfavourability of video resumes is the fear of the video going viral and being misused for unforeseen causes. This can be inferred from one of the respondents who say, "What if my video is misused and leaked?" The concept of dealing with privacy concerns becomes very crucial as the candidates will be willing to reveal their information only if they can trust the process. This implies that they want to have control over the breadth and depth of information that is shared with others. Goel & Awasthy (2020) in their exploratory study summarized job applicants' recommendations related to the technical aspects of video resumes and privacy issues. Those recommendations were uniformity in the background, noise cancellation feature, ability to shoot video on the platform without temporary internet connectivity, eye detection feature, development of a mobile application, and, permission to forward the video to ensure privacy issue of video resumes. Organizations should ensure the adoption of preventive cybersecurity measures to prevent privacy infringement.

Discussion: Study 1 and Study 2

Our studies relate to the role of the community of practice in structuring e-recruitment practices through video resumes. Our results, coming from job applicants as well as recruiters, point out the relevance of video resumes as a prerequisite for a streamlined recruitment process. This research work presented the video resume as a relatively new instrument that can be utilized for the early screening of job candidates. In this fast-paced online world, video resumes are a step in this direction. They play a crucial role in the selection process since the world is getting competitive and having a video resume ensures that you have your resume a click away on your mobile device at any given moment. It is becoming the need of the times, especially during the COVID-19 pandemic, and must be adopted with care by the user (candidate) as well as the provider (video resume platforms) for its effective implementation. However, they have a possibility to instigate discriminatory hiring practices, hence must be used with caution.

Our study reaffirms Gissel *et al.*'s (2013) work on video resumes' wide variety of advantages to different stakeholders in the recruitment process such as applicants (Lorenzi, 2008; Bruner, 2007) as well as recruiters (Apers & Derous, 2017). For the job applicant, it has the benefit of gaining more control over what and how the recruiter gets to know about them. It also gives them the flexibility to modify their environment and presentation to a specific job opening in creative ways that present them in the best light and demonstrate that they are suitable for the job and up to date with the technology. On the other hand, for the recruiter it gives the benefit of attracting a wider reach of potential candidates irrespective of the geographical boundaries; this saves tremendously on travel expenses as well as shortens the length of time to hire. It also offers an added advantage to the recruiter to assess the personality-fit of the candidate even before meeting them for the face-to-face interview and hence come closer to better person–job fit which may result in better employee performance with low attrition rates due to more informed hiring decisions (El-Rayes *et al.*, 2020; Mujtaba & Mahapatra, 2019). Moreover, video resumes serve as an elevator pitch for the recruiters and establish an accurate image of the candidate.

Theoretical and Practical Implications

The increase in recruitment practices through technological mediums such as video resumes provides an advantage of greater interaction and hence hiring a better fit for a particular job role. Moreover, video resumes are gaining penetration and acceptance more so with their inclusion on job portals and professional networking sites such as naukri.com, LinkedIn, etc. (Dabic *et al.*, 2019), leading to significant transformation in recruitment. This evolution has led to two competing perspectives. On the one hand, projecting your achievements and motivation for a job in the form of a video provides an edge over the other applicants by the exchange of more personalized information. On the other hand, it also exposes your appearance, voice and other phenotypic characteristics. Preventing any biased hiring decisions based on phenotypic information remains a challenge for HR professionals. Organizations could make efforts in increasing recruiter awareness of impression formation processes and biased decision-making through training in dealing with the evaluation of video resumes.

The video resumes as an innovative approach to recruitment and selection is a stepping stone for an HRM policy. Yet, addressing its shortcomings so that applicants perceive it to be a valid tool for their assessment by the recruiters in an accurate way could be considered as an overarching question of this study. This question may be equally relevant to the researchers as the practitioners. Media richness theory (Daft & Lengel, 1986) has been used often in the area of business, communication, science information and advertising (Ishii *et al.*, 2019). Findings from our study suggest that even though video resumes are more information-rich than traditional paper resumes, they may not always lead to better information transfer. The privacy issue in the Indian ethos is a crucial aspect, which underscores its attention.

Limitations and Future Study

There are a few limitations of this study which can be a scope for future research. The sample size was sufficient for this study (Hair *et al.*, 2010) as it focused on the perspectives of MBA students. However, these groups of students are not representative of the entire job-applicant pool. There is a scope for future studies to study video resumes from the perspective of women job applicants. Women are usually more cautious in sharing photos and videos on social platforms due to the reason that their content may be misused or tampered with. Video resumes could also be compared based on Gen X, Gen Y and Gen Z. Younger generations are likely to be more favourable to video resumes. In line with this, the boom in social networking sites and people's inclination to upload videos in their network (Ahmad *et al.*, 2021) is perhaps paving the way for greater acceptance of video resumes. Future studies could consider using experimental research on the factors identified to determine a better understanding of antecedents/factors of acceptance of video resumes by job applicants. More research on the use of artificial intelligence in video resume selection is the need of the hour. Last but not least, research examining the application of technology for job search and selection is needed to further innovative practices.

Conclusion

A video resume for recruiting is a revolutionary method of thinking in which innovative ideas are encoded into codification programmes in order to draw significant archival value from them. Our study of previous deliberations during the COVID-19 pandemic demonstrates the critical significance of technology interventions. However, research-led discourse will aid in adoption as well as effective implementation in a variety of management functions, such as the e-recruitment process. The recruitment process in organizations has become more competent than ever. Job description, keywords in resumes are no longer found to be efficient and effective indicators of job performance. In organizations where video-based resumes are new, recruiters are likely to have little or no experience in video resume screening and selection of candidates. Such recruiters run the risk of misinterpreting video resumes for a person's fit either in the job, organization, or both, in an ineffective way. When resumes become visual, there is a tendency of recruiters to discriminate against applicants based on physical attributes, hence resulting in perceptual bias. In line with this, future recruiters should devise a standardized criterion of selection and provide sufficient training to the recruiters for its efficient usage. It is imperative to understand the perceptions of job applicants in advance to facilitate the adoption of video-based recruitment systems. The influence of technology on employee recruitment and selection is likely to continuously grow. The goal of adopting and implementing video resumes is an innovative approach that solves the challenge of recruitment and enriches the quality of practice to deepen the archive of the organization by aligning it with the changing times. These recruiting strategies contribute to the quality of hiring in a cost-effective and creative manner, enhancing organizational resilience and lifespan via organizational renewal (*Punarjanma*).

References

Ahmad, A. R., Jameel, A. S., & Raewf, M. (2021). Impact of social networking and technology on knowledge sharing among undergraduate students. *International Business Education Journal, 14*(1), 1–16.

Andersen, L. S. (2008). Readiness for change: Can readiness be primed? Master's Theses. Paper 3517, SJSU Scholar Works, San Jose State University.

Apers, C. & Derous, E. (2017). Are they accurate? Recruiters' personality judgments in paper versus video resumes. *Computers in Human Behavior, 73*, 9–19. Doi: 10.1016/j.chb.2017.02.063.

Ashkezari, M. J. & Aeen, M. N. (2012). Using competency models to improve HRM. *Ideal Type of Management, 1*(1), 59–68.

Bartram, D. (2000). Internet recruitment and selection: Kissing frogs to find princes. *International Journal of Selection and Assessment, 8*(4), 261–274.

Béland, L.-P., Brodeur, A., & Wright, T. (2020). The short-term economic consequences of COVID-19: Exposure to disease, remote work and government response. IZA Discussion Paper Series (13159). http://ftp.iza.org/dp13159.pdf.

Bellemare, C., Goussé, M., Lacroix, G., & Marchand, S. (2020). Video resumes and job search outcomes: Evidence from a field experiment. IZA Discussion Paper No. 13656. Available at SSRN: https://ssrn.com/abstract=3687133.

Brown, L., George, B., & Mehaffey-Kultgen, C. (2018). The development of a competency model and its implementation in a power utility cooperative: An action research study. *Industrial and Commercial Training, 50*(3), 123–135.

Bruner, P. (2007). Video resumes and grooming standards as they relate to EEOC rules [Transcript of SHRM live chat with the EEOC]. http://moss07.shrm.org/communities/memberdiscussionarea/hrtalkchat.aspx.

Bryman, A. (2016). *Social Research Methods.* 5th ed. London: Oxford University Press.

Campion, M. A., Pursell, E. D., & Brown, B. K. (1988). Structured interviewing: Raising the psychometric properties of the employment interview. *Personnel Psychology*, *41*(1), 25–42.

Cole, M. S., Rubin, R. S., Field, H. S., & Giles, W. F. (2007). Recruiters' perceptions and use of applicant résumé information: Screening the recent graduate. *Applied Psychology: An International Review*, *56*, 319–343. Doi: 10.1111/j.1464-0597.2007.00288.x.

Dabic, T., Adamovic, S., Suzic, R., & Sarac, M. (2019). An integrated approach for developing showcase profiles of information technology students. *The International Journal of Engineering Education*, *35*(3), 878–888.

Daft, R. L. & Lengel, R. H. (1984). Information richness: A new approach to managerial behavior and organisational design. In L. L. Cummings & B. M. Staw (eds.), *Research in Organisational Behavior.* (Vol. 6, pp. 191–233). Homewood, IL: JAI Press.

Daft, R. L. & Lengel, R. H. (1986). Organisational information requirements, media richness and structural design. *Management Science*, *32*(5), 554–571. Doi: 10.1287//mnsc.32.5.554.

Daniels, D. R., Erickson, M. L., & Dlik, A. (2011). Here to stay — Taking competencies the next level. *Work at Work Journal*, *10*(1), 70–77.

El-Rayes, N., Fang, M., Smith, M., & Taylor, S. M. (2020). Predicting employee attrition using tree-based models. *International Journal of Organisational Analysis*, *28*(6), 1273–1291. Doi: 10.1108/IJOA-10-2019-1903.

Fana, M., Torrejón Pérez, S., & Fernández-Macías, E. (2020). Employment impact of COVID-19 crisis: From short term effects to long terms prospects. *Journal of Industrial and Business Economics*, *47*, 391–410. Doi: 10.1007/s40812-020-00168-5.

Gerald, L., William, E., & Helmreich, R. (1981). The strength of the Halo effect in physical attractiveness research. *Journal of Psychology*, *107*, 69–75.

Gilliland, S. W. (1993). The perceived fairness of selection systems — An organisational justice perspective. *Academy of Management Review*, *18*, 694–734. Doi: 10.2307/258595.

Gissel, A. L., Thompson, L. F., & Pond, S. B. (2013). A theory-driven investigation of prospective applicants' intentions to submit video résumés. *Journal of Applied Social Psychology*, *43*(12), 2449–2461. Doi: 10.1111/jasp.12191.

Goel, A. & Awasthy, R. (2020). Are video resumes preferred by job applicants? Information technology in recruitment. In Sharma, S. K., Dwivedi, Y. K., Metri, B., & Rana, N. P. (eds.), *Re-imagining Diffusion and Adoption of Information Technology and Systems: A Continuing Conversation. TDIT 2020. IFIP Advances in Information and Communication Technology.* (p. 618). Cham: Springer. Doi: 10.1007/978-3-030-64861-9_13.

Guest, G., Bunce, A., & Johnson, L. (2006). How many interviews are enough? An experiment with data saturation and variability. *Field Methods, 18*(1), 59–82.

Gunay, S. (2020). COVID-19 pandemic versus global financial crisis: Evidence from currency market. Available at SSRN: https://ssrn.com/abstract=3584249.

Gusdorf, M. L. (2008). *Recruitment and Selection: Hiring the Right Person.* Alexandria, VA, USA: Society for Human Resource Management.

Hair, J. F., Black, W. C., Babin, B. J., & Anderson, R. E. (2010). *Multivariate Data Analysis: A Global Perspective.* (7th ed.). Englewood Cliffs, NJ: Pearson Prentice Hall.

Hausknecht, J. P., Day, D. V., & Thomas, S. C. (2004). Applicant reactions to selection procedures: An updated model and meta-analysis. *Personnel Psychology, 57,* 639–683. Doi: 10.1111/j.1744-6570.2004.00003.x.

Heale, R. & Forbes, D. (2013). Understanding triangulation in research. *Evidence-Based Nursing, 16*(4), 98.

Hiemstra, A. M. F. (2013). Fairness in paper and video resume screening. Ph.D. Thesis. Netherlands: Erasmus University Rotterdam.

Hiemstra, A. M. & Derous, E. (2015). Video résumés portrayed: Findings and challenges. *Employee Recruitment, Selection, and Assessment: Contemporary Issues for Theory and Practice.* pp. 45–60.

Hiemstra, A. M. F., Derous, E., Serlie, A. W., & Born, M. Ph. (2012). Fairness perceptions of video résumés among ethnically diverse applicants. *International Journal of Selection and Assessment, 20,* 423–433.

Hsieh, H. & Shannon, S. E. (2005). Three approaches to qualitative content analysis. *Qualitative Health Research, 15*(9), 1277–1288.

Ishii, K., Lyons, M. M., & Carr, S. A. (2019). Revisiting media richness theory for today and future. *Human Behavior and Emerging Technologies, 1,* 124–131.

Judge, T. A., Higgins, C. A., & Cable, D. M. (2000). The employment interview: A review of recent research and recommendations for future research. *Human Resource Management Review, 10,* 383–406.

Lanke, P. & Nath, P. (2021). Job switching and communities of practice: Mapping facilitators and dampeners to life cycle. *VINE Journal of Information and Knowledge Management Systems.* Forthcoming. https://doi.org/10.1108/VJIKMS-09-2020-0167.

Lee, J. K., Chang, Y., Kwon, H. Y., & Kim, B. (2020). Reconciliation of privacy with preventive cybersecurity: The Bright Internet approach. *Information Systems Frontier, 22,* 45–57. Doi: 10.1007/s10796-020-09984-5.

Lorenzi, N. (2008). Video resumes: A new way to hire. *Rock Products, Psychology, 80,* 500–509.

Maheshwari, N. & Haque, M. M. (2020). A role of competency-based recruitment screening: A case study on Indian manufacturing unit. *International Journal of Indian Culture and Business Management, 20*(4), 467. Doi: 10.1504/ijicbm.2020.108919.

Mamgain, R. P. (2021). Understanding labour market disruptions and job losses amidst COVID-19. *Journal of Social and Economic Development, 23*(2), 301–319. Doi: 10.1007/s40847-020-00125-x.

Marshall, M. N. (1996). Sampling for qualitative research. *Family Practice, 13*(6), 522–526. Doi: 10.1093/fampra/13.6.522.

Mujtaba, D. F. & Mahapatra, N. R. (2019). Ethical considerations in AI-based recruitment. In *2019 IEEE International Symposium on Technology and Society (ISTAS).* (pp. 1–7). Doi: 10.1109/ISTAS48451.2019.8937920.

Nicolau, J. L., Mellinas, J. P., & Martin-Fuentas, E. (2020). The halo effect: A longitudinal approach. *Annals of Tourism Research, 83,* 1–10. Doi: 10. 1016/j.annals.2020.102938.

Nguyen, L. S. & Gatica-Perez, D. (2016). Hirability in the wild: Analysis of online conversational video resumes. *IEEE Transactions on Multimedia, 18*(7), 1422–1437. Doi: 10.1109/tmm.2016.2557058.

Peck, J. A. & Levashina, J. (2017). Impression management and interview and job performance ratings: A meta-analysis of research design with tactics in mind. *Frontiers in Psychology, 8*(201), 1–10. Doi: 10.3389/fpsyg.2017. 00201.

Sanghi, S. (2016). *The Handbook of Competency Mapping: Understanding, Designing and Implementing Competency Models in Organisations.* New Delhi: SAGE Publications.

Schmidt, F. L. (2002). The role of general cognitive ability and job performance: Why there cannot be a debate. *Human Performance, 15*(1–2), 187–210.

Selden, S. & Orenstein, J. (2011). Government e-recruiting websites: The influence of e-recruitment content and usability on recruiting and hiring outcomes in US state governments. *International Journal of Selection and Assessment, 19*(1), 31–40.

Sundar, A., Kardes, F., & Noseworthy, T. (2014). Inferences on negative labels and the horns effect association for consumer research.

Takey, S. M. & de Carvalho, M. M. (2015). Competency mapping in project management: An action research study in an engineering company. *International Journal of Project Management, 33*(4), 784–796.

Tong, D. Y. K., Tong, X. F., Balakrishnan, K., & Luo, S. (2020). Job seekers' acceptance towards producing video resumes for company's recruitment. *International Journal of Management Studies, 27*(2), 97–132.

Vasileiou, K., Barnett, J., Thorpe, S., & Young, T. (2018). Characterising and justifying sample size sufficiency in interview-based studies: Systematic analysis of qualitative health research over a 15- year period. *BMC Medical Research Methodology, 18*(1), 148.

Waung, M., Hymes, R. W., & Beatty, J. E. (2014). The effects of video and paper resumes on assessments of personality, applied social skills, mental capability, and resume outcomes. *Basic and Applied Social Psychology, 36*(3), 238–251.

Waung, M., Hymes, R., Beatty, J. E., & McAuslan, P. (2015). Self-promotion statements in video resumes: Frequency, intensity, and gender effects on job applicant evaluation. *International Journal of Selection and Assessment*, *23*(4), 345–360.

Wenger, E. C. & Snyder, W. M. (2000). Communities of practice: The organizational frontier. *Harvard Business Review*, *78*(1), 139–146.

Westin, A. F. (1967). *Privacy and Freedom*. New York: Atheneum Books.

Yin, R. K. (2014). *Case Study Research Design and Methods*. Beverly Hills, CA: Sage Publications.

Appendix A

Table 1A.   Comprehensive Literature Review on Video Resumes

S. No.	Author, Year	Title of Study	Brief Overview of the Study
1.	Bellemare *et al.* (2020)	"Video Resumes and Job Search Outcomes: Evidence from a Field Experiment"	This study tested the effectiveness of video resumes by randomly sending applications to 2021 private companies in Quebec (Canada) that were advertising job openings. They discovered that video resumes raise callback rates by more than 10%.
2.	Maheshwari & Haque (2020)	"A role of competency-based recruitment screening: a case study on Indian manufacturing unit"	The research was carried out in one of the major machine manufacturing companies in order to find methods to enhance present recruiting and selection practices. According to the data, extensive recruiting and meeting the need for adequate human resource demands of several departments is a top priority. The most difficult problem in talent acquisition is finding the appropriate candidate at the right time.
3.	Tong *et al.* (2020)	"Job seekers' acceptance towards producing video resumes for company's recruitment"	Based on the notions of perceived stress, problem-focused coping methods, self-presentation, and self-efficacy, the goal of this study was to investigate job applicants' acceptance of making video resumes for the company's video-based recruiting. There was a substantial difference in perceived stress between the experienced and non-experienced groups of applicants, according to the moderation analysis, however not in problem-focused coping strategies.
4.	Apers & Derous (2017)	"Are they accurate? Recruiters' personality judgements in paper versus video resumes"	The goal of this study was to see if recruiters can deduce personality traits more accurately from video and audio resumes than from less information-rich paper resumes, and if candidates' perceived attractiveness (physical/vocal) has an impact on accuracy judgments. Personality was not correctly rated based on paper resumes, according to the findings.

(Continued)

Table 1A. (*Continued*)

S. No.	Author, Year	Title of Study	Brief Overview of the Study
5.	Nguyen & Perez (2016)	"Hirability in the Wild: Analysis of Online Conversational Video Resumes"	The researchers used a YouTube dataset of conversational English-speaking video resumes to analyze and comprehend the population that uses video resumes to find jobs. The majority of applications were young people searching for internships and junior roles, according to the results.
6.	Waung *et al.* (2015)	"Self-promotion Statements in Video Resumes: Frequency, intensity, and gender effects on job applicant evaluation"	The purpose of the study was to see how efficient self-promotion is in the context of video resumes. High amounts of self-promotion in video resumes are ineffective for male candidates and perhaps harmful for female applicants, according to the ratings by recruiters and college students.
7.	Waung *et al.* (2014)	"The Effects of Video and Paper Resumes on Assessments of Personality, Applied Social Skills, Mental Capability, and Resume Outcomes"	The impact of resume format (paper resume or video resume or both) was investigated in this study. Video resumes may result in different assessments of applicant personality and harsher judgments of applicant skills and abilities than paper resumes, according to the findings.
8.	Gissel *et al.* (2013)	"A theory-driven investigation of prospective applicants' intentions to submit video résumés"	The purpose of this study was to determine if the theory of planned behaviour (TpB) may be utilized to better understand future job applicants' intentions and behaviours when it comes to video resume submission. TpB was backed up by the findings.

Part IV
The Strategic Development Approach

Chapter 13

Cyber Branding in India

Veeramangala Sali* and Bommagowni Anitha†

Sri Krishna Devaraya Institute of Management,
Sri Krishnadevaraya University, Anantapuramu, India

*sveeramangala@gmail.com

†anita_skim@yahoo.co.in

Abstract

Internet may play a critical role in increasing brand associations and company reputations in the new era of e-branding. It has enormous potential in comparison to traditional mass media. The ease with which consumers transition from awareness to action on the Internet is a significant distinction and a source of contention for e-marketers. In this chapter, the future outlook of ebranding in India is identified on four key elements.

Introduction

Cyber branding is a process that is connected to both offline and online marketing. It refers to the use of the Internet to supplement general branding strategies in non-e-commerce markets and the use of the Internet to attract customers and boost acceptance of new online services and goods. In either geographical or virtual markets, successful brand development is dependent on customers' recognition and support for the products and services associated with a particular organization.

Future of Digital Marketing in India

With over 560 million internet users, India is the world's second-largest online market, trailing only China. By 2023, the country is expected to have over 650 million Internet users. Despite the enormous number of internet users, the country's internet penetration rate was approximately 50% in 2020, meaning roughly half of India's 1.37 billion people had internet connections that year. Recent years had seen a steady rise in internet access, compared to just five years ago, when only 27% of people had access to the Internet.

The recent rise in popularity of the Digital India campaign infuses the future of digital marketing in India with a plethora of fresh flavours and fervors. Another factor contributing to the expansion of digital marketing opportunities in India is the growing start-up movement.

In India, there are more than 900 private television channels and more than 250 radio stations, making traditional marketing both expensive and complicated due to the system's large number of in-built vacillations. Although digital marketing is the only and most reliable marketing method in today's internet-enabled world, it is often considered the best and most preferred space for all marketing communications and related interactions.

In 2021, after a challenging year due to the pandemic, Indian businesses saw a v-shaped recovery. As a result, advertising spending in India recovered to reach INR 742 billion in 2021 and surged above INR 1 trillion in 2022. There has also been increase in the digital advertising industry's market size, from INR 246 billion in 2021 to INR 330 billion in 2022.

Trends of Digital Marketing Giving Boom to Cyber Branding in India

Digital Marketing will remain the most powerful and result-oriented way of marketing. Future outlook of four key channels in deciding the future of digital marketing in India is as follows:

1. *Mobile Marketing*: Understanding changing customer needs and characteristics enables marketers to plan more effectively. Mobile marketing plays a vital role in this, according to statistics.

- According to the India Cellular and Electronics Association's (ICEA) "Contribution of Smartphones to Digital Governance in India" report, India will have 829 million smartphone users by 2022. Additionally, data use has climbed from 2.7GB per month in 2016 to around 10.4GB per month in 2019, but costs have decreased from INR 152 per GB in 2016 to INR 10 per GB in 2019.
- In recent years, India's mobile adoption has increased exponentially. Thanks to falling data and phone prices, the usage has exploded and is no longer limited to tier 1 cities. Mobile penetration will reach 92% by 2022, giving marketers and brands many ways to reach consumers.

2. *Video Marketing*:
   - YouTube, the country's largest video platform, claims that 55% of its videos are seen on mobile devices in India. Earlier this year, YouTube released an offline option to enable viewers to watch videos offline, ensuring that even people with a sluggish connection may download and watch videos later. According to Bloomberg, Facebook is also developing an offline mode for its video.
   - The YouTube Partnership program distributes 55% of revenue to contributors, and estimates suggest that top channels earn between $50,000 and $1 million from YouTube alone. Not surprisingly, if the statistics don't line up, you should know that each of the top ten YouTube channels has over a billion views on their videos, according to a Live Mint report. Of course, entering the top ten will be challenging if you consider that the top eight out of ten channels are in the media and entertainment business and are owned by major conglomerates.
   - India is one of the world's most significant video users today, with over 5 billion monthly views. From being dominated by YouTube to a new generation of independent content creators and aggregators, the industry has come a long way and significantly pushed the art of storytelling on digital platforms for brand creation.

3. *Social Media Marketing*: Social media marketing will be a big part of digital marketing for a long time. It will be used for branding, optimization, lead generation, and conversions. Knowing future trends in social media and planning strategies will ensure success for companies. Some of the key social media trends are as follows:

- India has almost 239.65 million Facebook users, making it the most populous country on the social media platform.
- LinkedIn, a professional networking platform, has over 575 million users and over 260 million monthly active users.
- The enormous evolution of Snapchat will be one of the most interesting, powerful and creative trends in social media marketing.
- According to data from February 2021, there were 146,960,000 Instagram users in India, accounting for 10.4% of the country's total population.

4. *Search & SEO Marketing*: Search engines are continuously changing, and as a result, marketers have to rethink how they target their consumers. To be successful, you must stay abreast of the most recent developments in SEO marketing and implement search engine optimization tactics that take these changes into account. Thanks to the rise of mobile marketing and social media optimization, it is estimated that various search engines carry out 14 billion web searches per month. Some of the SEO trends that will turn out to be major hits are as follows:

- Mobile marketing will take off, and in addition to Google, other search engines will play an increasingly important part in determining how well a website performs in searches.
- Search tools like Google's Keyword Planner and Moz's Keyword Planner are the best ways to find the relevant keywords that your audience is searching for.
- Another intelligent technique that experts believe will be the most dominating digital marketing trend in the future is the use of high-quality video content in your content marketing strategy.
- Customizing SEO campaigns according to target audiences, being creative, utilizing natural connections, and moving sites to HTTPS will be the SEO trends that define the development of Internet marketing efforts.

Conclusion

The Internet presents both an opportunity and a threat to new and established brands. It is now clear that developing a cyber brand in cyberspace is more complex and critical than previously believed. The most enduring brands have endured the test of time. Throughout our history, they are the brands that have been effectively maintained, developed and communicated and have responded to socio-technological developments over time. For one hundred years, numerous well-known brands have occupied a place in consumers' minds and hearts. They have overcome numerous hardships and obstacles due to changes in technology, consumer demands and preferences and have developed excellent branding for their products.

https://doi.org/10.1142/9789811271786_0014

Chapter 14

A Typology of Digital Marketing Channels with a Special Reference to India

Uttam Kaur* and Aarti Dangwal†

University School of Business Management, Chandigarh University, Gharuan 140413, India

*uttamkaur7@gmail.com

†aarti.e9992@cumail.in

Abstract

Digital marketing is the promotion of goods or services via the use of digital technology, such as websites, cellphones, display advertisements and every other digital media. Since the 1990s and 2000s, online marketing has altered the way companies and organizations adopt new technologies for promotion. Digital marketing efforts are growing highly widespread and effective as social media platforms are more interwoven into marketing strategies and daily activities, and as individuals utilize digital gadgets rather than accessing physical locations. The study's findings indicated that digital marketing messaging may even stimulate need awareness in product categories with a high level of participation. Customers are happy about digital communication, are influenced by other customers' feedback, and share their post-purchase sentiments through digital media. However, the research found that, while customers have a positive use of digital channels across the choice process, they equally value the use of different channels.

Introduction

Virtual marketing interaction is described as a conversation between firms and customers using digital or electronic media. Digital marketing communication, in contrast to conventional marketing communication, allows for more exchanges or dialogues between the provider and the receiver. Virtual show ads, explore ads (natural and reward), interaction devices and verbal interaction via the social platform are all examples of virtual interaction.

The importance of virtual interaction over conventional communication has grown in recent years, particularly during the COVID-19 era. The pandemic's massive disturbances have highlighted the value of internet communication much further. As per a CMO Study, in a reaction to the epidemic, over 80% of consumers are now more responsive to firms' online offers and value online experiences with them more. Similarly, the COVID-19 outbreak has halted modernization, at least at the moment, creating virtual interaction challenges and exposing flaws in world commerce and personal movements. Similarly, it has opened up online advertising opportunities. The proliferation of connectivity, as well as shifting conceptions of digital experiences, internet activity, e-commerce and teleworking, may encourage greater digital cross-border contacts, allowing companies to better their virtual strategic plan. Companies are speeding their virtual conversion efforts to meet this "new normal".

A Paradigm for Coordinating Online Communications Study

Previous research has a plethora of online communication applications. Such exercises are organized through two important aspects, provider and receiver, which are represented by the *x*- and *y*-axes in Figure 1. These parameters were chosen because they correspond to the transmitter and recipient parameters in the transmitter communications paradigm.

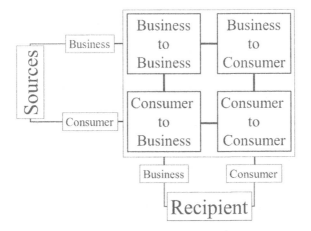

Figure 1.   Digital Communication Source–Recipient Dyads

Business-to-consumer (B2C), business-to-business (B2B), consumer-to-consumer (C2C) and consumer-to-business (C2B) are the four types of digital advertisements (C2B). These are the top regularly utilized transmitter pairs in online marketing conversations, we chose these four dyads. We describe earlier research's important results within each dyad, highlighting management insights and addressing research needs, especially in the global setting. We've compiled a list of critical research issues and initiatives based on the gaps.

We build on previous theoretical and literature reviews by giving a more thorough analysis of existing inside every dyad, doing research (which has been released in all massive advertising publications in the previous 20 years), and prioritizing the following main study issues:

a. What is the main objective of digital communication (for example, to educate or convince consumers [business or consumers])?
b. What are the best electronic information devices — networks, medium and systems being utilized, and should be employed?
c. What kind of virtual material interacted via the virtual marketing agency, communication, or posting, and how?
d. What is the response of the receiver (company or end-user) to the digital message (e.g. involvement, word-of-mouth, buying)?

The Shannon–Weaver communication model guided our choice of such marketing-related issues. Transmitter, medium, transmission, and receptor and feedback elements of the Shannon–Weaver model correspond to goals/objectives, communication vehicles, subject matter, and receiver reaction, accordingly.

Each study's keywords are thoroughly examined, and we scan it for digital, online, Internet, worldwide, and similar terms. The number of publications setting out the terms digital, globally or across time. Although the number of papers focused on digital or worldwide concerns has gradually increased over the years, the number of articles stressing both of these themes has plateaued, highlighting the necessary research that includes both digital and global challenges.

For each of the dyads in Figure 1, we extract and synthesize unique intuition and suggestions for investigators and professionals working in localized and world business settings. In particular, we suggest that businesses improve their electronic information by (1) skilfully constructing aims; (2) optimizing all over messaging services, information providers, and systems; (3) creating and implementing content; and (4) assessing the reactions to these attempts to obtain meaningful and real-time insights.

Prior study has revealed five important themes: (1) the expansion of social networks, platforms and gadgets, and (2) the development of the website and stable messaging, (3) fledgling but rapidly expanding digital media, (4) usage of insights and new technologies, and (5) rising security, transparency and regulatory roles The efficiency of websites has been the subject of research, particularly since the early 2000s. Ever since then a slew of studies have focused on social networking sites as the primary medium for C2C and C2B engagement. There has been a greater emphasis on mobile telephony since 2015. The usage of analysis has progressively increased over the last 21 years. Security, trustworthiness and online governance are becoming increasingly important as online technology becomes more individualized.

Digital contacts between businesses and consumers (B2C)

Digital information strategy for business-to-consumer (B2C) objectives of digital B2C messaging vary depending on where the consumer is in the purchasing process, but they usually involve increased understanding, involvement, satisfaction, adoption or maintenance. Advertisements can promote product awareness and believability, buy channel outputs spanning from attention to interest to buying intention. They have a greater impact on physical selling than internet selling and function well in remarketing at first. Display advertising, on the other hand, loses its efficacy fast, especially with increasing ad regularity and relevancy.

Digital connections between businesses (B2B)

Given the importance put on customer metrics in the B2B sector, digital marketing strategy is extremely important. Prior research on business-to-business virtual information has mostly concentrated on the dynamism of supplier–buyer conversations, B2B auctions and fundamental changes caused by communication intermediates or channels. The objectives of B2B are many other business-to-consumer connection scenarios, a business-to-business company must tailor its electronic information for purchasing centre persons — the many purchasers engaged in the corporate purchasing activity. Business-to-business companies utilize online communications to reach out to more clients and prospects more quickly and effectively, as well as to reduce communication costs. They make it easier for businesses (such as vendors and suppliers) to share information without being constrained by time or geography. Firms may, for example, connect with purchasing centre participants in real time, partners can define negotiating terms in advance and purchasing organizations can accomplish purchasing chores without any need for human intervention thanks to digital communication technologies.

The effectiveness of showing particular kinds of data on information assortment channels and discovering that marketers prefer mediator marketplaces with a large number of vendors because these markets are more likely to attract potential buyers. The function of online communication in B2B online information is mostly unknown. Social media usage is contagious among providers, dealers and customers.

As online selling presentations, community commerce, and selling automation along with Artificial Intelligence (AI) technologies become more prevalent, B2B digital interactions are rapidly changing. As businesses employ online experiences to escape the COVID-19 epidemic, implementation of these strategies has surged. The importance of online and social B2B selling is growing as a huge amount of customer's transition from jobs to work-from-home. Moreover, B2B organizations have begun to automate parts of the marketing and post-sale procedures (particularly lead qualifying and service and support) as a result of recent breakthroughs in AI, permitting salespeople to concentrate on the interaction components of B2B sales.

Virtual customer (C2C) connections

Customers may now become online content makers, disseminating meaningful data through multiple networks and social networking sites, thanks to recent technological advancements. Customers not just serve their knowledge with goods and services, but also make clear contrasting elements of their personalities for absorption by another customer, thanks to this data, also called user-generated content (UGC). The objective of the digital information strategy for business-to-business (B2B) is whenever customers connect electronically with each other, their primary aims are to educate, engage, buy and represent themselves. C2C interactions' aims are far broader than the business-to-customer and business-to-business interactions, which are even more concentrated on advertising. Customers' interactions with other customers can be both product characteristics and non-product-oriented (e.g. publishing customer feedback) (for example, participating in internet forums devoted to a variety of likes and interests). They impact each other both intentionally and indirectly throughout these numerous modes of C2C communication.

Digital connections between customers and businesses (C2B)

C2B internet technologies are changing due to technological advancements. The growth of collaborative consumption systems (Apartment rental, Uber) and other evaluation systems (e.g. Facebook, Wikipedia) is a crucially important modernization development, creating these middlemen as key participants of electronic communications. Demand and supply suppliers must keep a keen watch on such channels for consumer-initiated interactions, which give a wealth of data for companies to evaluate in improving consumer interactions all across the customer lifecycle. Business-to-business (B2B) digital information strategy objectives and C2B digital communication's main aims are to give recommendations to organizations and to find solutions to consumer concerns. Customer word-of-mouth (WOM) is a primary theme of C2B communication studies, reflects the increasing effort in order by companies across the distribution chain (e.g. producers, resellers and network operators) providing customers with easy ways to voice their thoughts with companies through various channels such as company websites, online review websites and social networking sites.

Approaches that Might be Used to Handle New Research Issues

Table 1 provides a review of potential research initiatives.

Conclusion

From online information in domestic and global markets, we analyzed significant studies from the B2C, B2B, C2C and C2B dyads. We generated and summarized major past studies inside every dyad, identifying important differences in the aims, platforms, information, and reactions associated with digital interaction.

"As the COVID-19 scenario continues to expand, we observed how the new reality was putting an impact on people's lives within the epidemic gloom," says Sudhanshu Nagpal, Associate Director — Marketing (Biscuits), Mondelez India. "This resulted in the #AtHomewithOreo promotion, whose goal was to connect and bind people together via fun moments, a notion that is firmly ingrained in our product OREO and which could be accomplished most successfully through user-generated content." "At Uber, we're trying to remake the way the country can start moving forward for the better," said Sanjay Gupta, Global Brand Director, Uber India SA. "By creating a proper package of measures, we've raised the bar for drivers and riders on our channel."

The capacity of UGC to become viral quickly is its most valuable feature. It also aids in the blending of local information with a global audience. Experts predict that such marketing methods will emerge at various periods to meet the individual demands of companies and customers. Consumer information will always be a fascinating part of the information multiverse since it helps information to be much more relevant, instructive and helpful without being preachy. The livestreaming platforms will

Table 1.   Potential Research Directions in Four Dyads

Element	Business-to-Consumer	Business-to-Business	Consumer-to-Consumer	Consumer-to-Business
Aims	• B2C online interaction should be standardized/localized for various aims. • The importance of brand engagement is growing, as is its place in digital media.	• Designing and implementing multimedia marketing for worldwide markets. • In the face of constantly shifting international trade, buyers and sellers use a variety of digital communication tactics.	• Examine how security considerations affect C2C engagements. • Examine the impact of cultures on the creation and spread of UGC. • Recognize the relationship between customer-to-customer interaction and brand acceptance. • Examine connectivity (externalities) in the production, diffusion, and selection of appropriate influencers for UGC.	• Examine the factors that influence the effectiveness of co-creation of value and collaboration. • Know how to control co-creation and collaboration.
Platforms, channels, and media	• A complete identification and medium impacts model for multichannel multimedia. • Utilization of funds among various digital mediums. • The efficiency of B2C interaction in developing digital platforms such as the Internet of Things.	• B2B technique and multinational technology acceptance • In developing markets, the primary and secondary expenses of implementing innovative marketing procedures (like Artificial Intelligence).	• Recognize the impact of different digital platforms or marketplace factors on UGC development. • Suggest social media strategies as a way to boost customer satisfaction. • Examine the influence of user-generated content (UGC) on multiple platforms.	• Learn about C2B interactions on various devices (such as cellular telephones and smartwatches), and also the importance of the Internet of Things. • In the creation of C2B information, assess the inter effects (earned vs. owned media). • Analyze the effect of equipment layout on lowering security issues and enhancing self-disclosure depth.
Information	• More information about actual information and digital marketing. • Examine how digital phones can help to create a connection across advertisements and marketing. • Efficacy of digital information in the event of a product recall.	• In B2B digital information, the function of online sales (quality, timeliness and efficiency). • Technology, ecology and distribution network considerations all play a part in international digital information.	• Extrapolate useful features and findings from user-generated content (e.g. enhanced emotion coding, machine learning technologies). • Examine the effects of synergy among different kinds of UGC formats (textual, picture and videos) on different scenarios.	• Create a holistic perspective of the many forms of materials created during C2B interactions. • Create successful techniques for businesses to automate C2B monitoring and response, social media such as Facebook, smartphones and the Internet of Things.

- Is it possible for quickness and personalization to mitigate the negative consequences of goods damage crises?
- In digital technology, comprehending the function of customized vs. machine learning-focused advertising.

Reactions		

- Awareness of identification and accounting techniques in different nations and cultures.

- Conceptions of digital information reactivity are backed by evidence.
- The worldwide B2B marketplace's influence on digital miscommunications.

- Recognize the importance of UGC validity, particularly in the case of influencers.
- Examine how fresh content types may affect existing C2C production effectively.
- Create user-generated content.

- Improve your understanding of the role of distinct UGC forms at different points of the production process.
- Analyze the impact of user-generated content (UGC) on a variety of firm- and customer-centric KPIs across product categories.
- Recognize the importance of cultural factors in the diffusion of UGC.
- Examine how blog posts and feedback have influenced the launch of new products.
- Recognize the sticky qualities of C2C communication throughout the world.

- Shifts in consumer behaviour as a result of the acceptance of digital devices (such as wearable technology, voice control and innovative cellphones), as well as device changes between other kinds of devices that are more relevant to the Internet, such as linked home gadgets.
- The variables that contribute to the success of co-production and collaborative effort projects, such as design methods and technologies, as well as societal, economical, and behavioural considerations.
- Know how the lifespan of a business and the development of consumer technologies may affect C2B interaction.
- C2B responses have an impact on B2C effective communication.

bring even more value to the process. Even while streaming media services have been present for several years, owing to a new generation of streaming media tools enabled by enhanced technology, now anybody can go broadcast at any time and from any location, making consumer content incredibly salient.

https://doi.org/10.1142/9789811271786_0015

Chapter 15

Role of Artificial Intelligence in Ajanta Caves & Hampi

Veenus Jain* and Pallavi Mohanan†

Amity Institute of Social Sciences, Amity University, Noida, India

*vjain@amity.edu

†pallavimohanan@yahoo.co.in

Abstract

"Artificial intelligence (AI) is a wide-ranging branch of computer science that is concerned with building smart machines that have the capability of performing tasks requiring human intelligence" (Sufyan, 2021). Due to consistent human and environmental interactions, historical sites have been subject to consistent depletion. To minimize the damage and decay of cultural heritage, newer technologies like Artificial Intelligence have become the need of the hour to conserve sites of historical prominence and to create a digital repository of sites for future generations to experience, access and understand. Therefore, use of Digital tools and technology is becoming a standard norm for collecting, preserving and accessing efforts of cultural heritage worldwide. "From 3D configuration of ancient artefacts to applying artificial intelligence to shed new light on how we perceive the lineage of humanities, cultural heritage is headed toward a digital future" (Boo, 2020).

Artificial intelligence aids in facilitating "a more rapid process of tracking a cultural heritage's lifespan and the type of measures that should be taken to guarantee its existence into the future" (Boo, 2020). Cultural Heritage is a pivotal part of our humanity and comprehensive understanding of these unique heritages aids in developing a holistic understanding of our future. "Protection of Cultural Heritage is becoming increasingly important in our contemporary world where we are facing challenges from multiple fronts to preserve them" (Antony, 2020). This study aims to elaborate on the use of Artificial Intelligence made until recent times to preserve, access and experience the historic sites of Hampi and Ajanta Caves.

Introduction

Located in Aurangabad, Maharashtra, the Ajanta Caves are "approximately 30 rock-cut Buddhist cave monuments dating from the 2nd century BCE to about 480 CE" (Madan, 1990). The art and architecture of the caves are among the finest examples of Ancient Indian Art and are categorized as marvels of Buddhist Religious Art. The site became a UNESCO World Heritage Site in 1983.

"The caves were built in two phases, the first starting around the 2nd century BCE and the second occurring from 400 to 650 CE, according to older accounts, or in a brief period of 460–480 CE according to later scholarship" (UNESCO, 2006).

The caves comprise ancient monasteries and worship halls of various Buddhist traditions. "The caves also present paintings depicting the past lives and rebirths of the Buddha, pictorial tales from Aryasura's *Jatakamala*, and rock-cut sculptures of Buddhist deities" (Cohen, 2013).

The caves served varied purposes of the people, "Textual records suggest that these caves served as a monsoon retreat for monks, as well as a resting site for merchants and pilgrims in ancient India" (Cohen, 2013).

The evidence of its existence has been mentioned in numerous records ranging from medieval era Chinese Buddhist travellers to Mughal Era officials of Akbar. Prior to its discovery, the caves were covered by dense vegetation, but they were later "accidentally "discovered" and brought to Western attention in 1819 by a colonial British officer Captain John Smith on a tiger-hunting party" (Spink, 2007).

Hampi is located in east-central Karnataka, India. "Hampi was the capital of the Vijayanagara Empire in the 14th century" (Verghese, 2002). It is a cluster of historical monuments and is recognized as a UNESCO World Heritage Site. Chronicles written by Portuguese state that "Hampi was a prosperous, wealthy and grand city near the Tungabhadra River, with numerous temples, farms and trading markets" (Verghese, 2002). It has been noted that by 1500 AD, "Hampi-Vijayanagara was the world's second-largest medieval-era city after Beijing, and probably India's richest at that time, attracting traders from Persia and Portugal" (Howard, 2011). The Empire declined after facing defeat by a coalition of Muslim Sultanates; "its capital was conquered, pillaged and destroyed by sultanate armies in 1565, after which Hampi remained in ruins" (Verghese, 2002).

The UNESCO World Heritage site hosts the ruins of the historic city which comprises "more than 1,600 surviving remains of the last great Hindu kingdom in South India that include "forts, riverside features, royal and sacred complexes, temples, shrines, pillared halls, mandapas, memorial structures, water structures and others" (UNESCO). References about the city of Hampi have been made since ancient times, "it is mentioned in the *Ramayana* and the Puranas of Hinduism as Pampaa Devi Tirtha Kshetra" (Verghese, 2002). Moreover, "Hampi continues to be an important religious centre, housing the Virupaksha Temple, an active Adi Shankara-linked monastery and various monuments belonging to the old city" (Fritz & Mitchell, 2016).

The ruins of Hampi were first surveyed in 1800 by Scottish Colonel Colin Mackenzie, Surveyor General of India. His observations suggest that "the Hampi site was abandoned and only wildlife live there" (Fritz & Mitchell, 2016). The studies which were established after Mackenzie's observations state that "the 18th-century armies of Haidar Ali and the Marathas are to be blamed for the damage to the Hampi monuments" (Fritz & Mitchell, 2016).

Up until mid-19th century, the site was largely untapped. The interest in the site gained momentum when "Alexander Greenlaw visited and photographed the site in 1856" (Fritz & Mitchell, 2016). An archive of the catalogued photographs of temples and royal structures that were standing in 1856 was made and kept in private collection in the United Kingdom and was later published in 1980. It is considered the "most valuable source of the mid-19th-century state of Hampi monuments to scholars" (Fritz & Mitchell, 2016).

The initial studies sparked interest of scholars in the study of Hampi and various works have been published in the 19th and 20th centuries on the same. "Alexander Rea, an officer of the Archaeological Survey department of the Madras Presidency, British India, published his survey of the site in 1885" (Fritz & Mitchell, 2016). "Robert Sewell published his scholarly treatise *A Forgotten Empire*, bringing Hampi to the widespread attention of scholars" (Sewell, 1900). The growing interest of scholars led to clearing and repairing of the Hampi group of monuments.

Tourism

The Ajanta Caves are a prominent site for tourists, and receive approximately "15,900 tourists annually, generating revenue of about 99 Lakhs" (Press Information Bureau).

Due to conditions created by the COVID-19 pandemic and subsequent lockdowns, the site faced a dip in tourist footfall, which consequently pushed guides and people earning a livelihood through the site to face issues.

ASI authorities state that "Earlier the workload of managing tourists used to take much of the manpower, this year the ASI used the workforce for the maintenance of these monuments" (Press Trust of India, 2021), which explains the plan of action taken by competent authorities to manage the site.

But people dependent on the site for livelihood faced vulnerability, "Some guides tried to venture into the taxi business but had to eventually sell the vehicles due to lack of funds for paying the monthly instalments of the vehicle cost" (Press Trust of India, 2021); moreover, despite the lifting of lockdowns, tourists were hesitant to visit the site; "tourists preferred going to other states in the country where there were less restrictions" (Press Trust of India, 2021).

Whereas, the temples of Hampi, its monolithic sculptures and monuments, attract tourists because of their excellent workmanship. The Hindu style of architecture found at Hampi reflects the splendour of the Vijayanagara Empire. The rugged landscape adds to the historic ambiance of this site. The major attractions of the site include Virupaksha Temple, Vittala Temple, Lotus Mahal, Elephant stables, Queen's Bath Place and Mahanavami Dibba.

"For the last 20 years, the place has been a reliable destination of choice for tourists from around the world and India" (Kadidal, 2021). The footfall of tourists has seen variances through decades. Fairly recently, two dilemmas have arisen in tourism of Hampi.

K Basappa, vice president of the Hampi Tour Guides Association, explains that "nine out of ten tourists prefer to visit the monuments on their own" (Kadidal, 2021). Moreover, the COVID-19 pandemic pushed the authorities to "shut the site down for approximately two months, which was followed by night and weekend curfews" (Buradikatti, 2021). These factors have pushed the local tourism economy to a state of vulnerability.

But the situation since the unlock phase has shifted substantially, with "Hampi witnessing more footfall of tourists" (Buradikatti, 2021); still the people dependent on tourism are still wallowing in their inability to fetch customers.

Cultural Preservation

Cultural heritage comprises tangible, intangible and natural heritage, which are vital for studying human history, as they aid with concrete basis for ideas, and can validate them. With constant human and environmental interaction, it is inevitable for a historical site to endure damage and decay Therefore, its preservation is as essential as is its discovery and analysis.

David Lowenthal in his book *The Past is a Foreign Country* observes that "preserved objects also validate memories" (Lowenthal, 2015). "While digital acquisition techniques can provide a technological solution that is able to acquire the shape and the appearance of artefacts with an unprecedented precision in human history, the actuality of the object, as opposed to a reproduction, draws people in and gives them a literal way of touching the past" (Cignoni & Scopigno, 2008).

But preservation comes with a lot of risks such as "places and things are damaged by the hands of tourists, the light required to display them, and other risks of making an object known and available, besides, all artifacts are in a constant state of chemical transformation, so that what is considered to be preserved is actually changing and doesn't remain in its original state. Similarly changing value each generation may place on the past and on the artefacts that link it to the past can alter its course of preservation" (Lowenthal, 2015).

India attributes "supreme importance to the preservation of tradition and cultural heritage. It is believed to be their moral imperative that what had been inherited should not be consumed, but should bc handed over, possibly enriched, to successive generations" (Singh *et al.*, 2001).

Various governmental and international initiatives have been undertaken to preserve the site. Based on the reports submitted to UNESCO in 1997, 2001 and 2002, various issues have been highlighted regarding the Ajanta Caves, which range from deliberate destruction of heritage, illegal activities, impacts of tourism/visitor/recreation, and invasive/alien terrestrial species, to relative humidity, fragile mural paintings, infiltration of rainwater into the caves, minor cracks on carved surfaces, flaking of the paint layer and infestation of bats and insects within the caves. (UNESCO).

Based on the reports, the organization has made the following suggestions:

1. Revising present methods for stabilizing and cleaning the wall-painting surfaces.
2. Testing of new and alternative methods on small wall-painting surfaces.
3. Undertaking continuous monitoring of the microclimate conditions in the Ajanta Caves.
4. Enhancing documentation and archival material to evaluate changing conditions of the wall-painting material.
5. Conserving further, the unique natural setting of the Ajanta and Ellora Caves, by following the concept of minimal intervention with the historically established environment and giving preference to conservation solutions which involve minimal changes.
6. Enhancing co-operation between the complementary ASI branches to enhance the long-term protection and conservation of the two sites (UNESCO).

Moreover, the committee also states that "the World Heritage Centre (is) to continue assisting the authorities of India to mobilize international technical assistance to enhance co-operation between numerous national and international conservation and development activities" (UNESCO).

Preservation of Hampi dates to 19th century, "much of that work was piece-meal, amateur and ultimately unsuccessful" (Global Heritage

Fund). Hampi was added to the UNESCO World Heritage List in 1986, which led to various researches being undertaken on the site which unearthed a plethora of archaeological remains consisting of "walled settlements, religious structures, forts, tanks, canals, fields, trade routes, civic buildings and industrial complexes" (Global Heritage Fund).

The site of Hampi faces various threats in the way of its preservation, which includes unplanned development, inadequate protection, seasonal flooding, narrowly defined protected zone being stripped for building materials to fuel the modern city's construction boom" (Global Heritage Fund). These threats pushed Hampi into the List of World Heritage in Danger in 1999.

Since then, the Government and International Organizations like Global Heritage Fund have collaborated to better preserve Hampi, under its Master Conservation Plan. Moreover, this plan focuses on structural, social and economic needs of the site.

Digital Restoration and Conservation Initiatives

Scholars are now adopting newer technology in order to adequately conserve this Ancient Indian marvel of Buddhist Religious Art and Architecture. Artificial Intelligence is now coming in aid for restoration of the fragile mural paintings that are getting damaged by varied factors ranging from vandalism to infiltration of rainwater into the caves and insect infestation.

This restorative initiative is undertaken by Mumbai-headquartered Sapio Analytics, "The digitized form of these paintings are being preserved on an island called Svalbard, in Norway, as part of a project called Arctic World Archive" (ANI, 2021).

Sapio Analytics has partnered with London-based UTIV, "to digitize, restore and preserve for eternity ancient Indian heritage associated with the culture, artworks and artefacts of India and other Asian countries" (ANI, 2021).

Besides this initiative also promotes Indian Scholars from various fields to partake in this project, therefore "Experts from the Indian Institute of Technology (IIT) Roorkee, who have been selected for this project, have developed this AI which uses a deep-learning technique to restore the damaged murals of the Ajanta Caves" (ANI, 2021).

This digital restoration and conservation are believed to be the next phase of historical preservation, and the organizations ensure that the use of Artificial Intelligence and Deep Learning would not alter the original source in any sense.

Another initiative is undertaken by Tech4Heritage hackathon for restoration and conservation of Ajanta caves. They aim to "digitally preserve and restore the murals recovered from these sites" (Chhabra & Babbar, 2020).

"The hackathon had set a specific problem statement, which demanded technical knowledge in image processing and deep learning in computer vision. Our team had been exploring practical applications in these fields and this was a big help given how complex the issue was. Once the problem statement was communicated, we had 15 days to come up with viable solutions. We decided to pilot multiple strategies and proceed with the optimum solution. Although 15 days was not enough to produce a perfect solution, it created a strong base upon which our solution could be scaled and applied across so many cases", Tech4Heritage stated (Chhabra & Babbar, 2020).

The once flourishing city of Hampi has aged today. The wonderful art and architecture of the site bears witness to the magnanimity of this city. But with time, Hampi has experienced heavy wear and tear from natural and man-made elements. "Recognizing the fact that this rich heritage site faced the risk of being lost forever from our mental and physical landscape, researchers saw this challenge as an opportunity leading to the creation of the Indian Digital Heritage (IDH) project" (Mahajan, 2020).

A public–private partnership model brought together experts from the fields of Technology, Computer Science, Architecture and the Humanities. "More than 10 prominent national academic institutions such as the Indian Institutes of Technology, Indian Statistical Institute, and National Institute of Design as well as multi-disciplinary cultural institutions such as the National Institute of Advanced Studies (NIAS) participated under the guidance of Government of India's Union Department of Science and Technology along with private partners like Microsoft for the creation of a more complete experience of the city as it was during its heyday" (Mahajan, 2020).

The aim of Digital Hampi was to apply technological and cultural perspectives to reconstruct the site digitally by applying a research-based approach. It wasn't a redundant display of art and architecture, rather it "provided a creative ground for researchers to experiment with different technology and expertise to revive the tangible and the intangible heritage that was associated with the site" (Mahajan, 2020).

The highlights of this initiative include, digital walkthroughs with a 3D view of the sculptures previously damaged, digitally restoring artefacts such as mural paintings, inscriptions and sculptures, study of murals through an interactive map, and reconstruction of damaged architectural features based on 19th century photographs by Greenlaw.

Moreover, "3D data acquisition and generation of point clouds were undertaken which could be digitally rendered. Kinect-based models or in layman's language 3D camera, 3D laser scanning and printing made it possible for a visitor to experience a certain level of 'physical interaction, with the 3D printed miniature models of structures" (Mahajan, 2020).

Conclusion

"Heritages structures are considered to be of immense value to society, culture, and country as they reflect the history and uniqueness of the place" (Bakri *et al.*, 2012). With consistent human and environment interaction, Ajanta caves have been facing gradual damage and decay. Various organizations, whether public or private, have been making various efforts to restore and conserve it for the future generations. They have devised both conventional and recently artificial intelligence methods and tools to preserve the site from further damage.

With regard to preservation of art, "AI is considered as an artist's best friend rather than making them outdated in the future. Artisans may have thought that, unlike many other markets, there would be no chance for machines to take over their lovely reins. But AI can prove them wrong. Many art fields are progressing in absorbing machine learning in their crafts" (Sufyan, 2021).

In this phase of transition from 3D to Metaverse, artificial intelligence is the need of the hour. "The transition to digitally sourced preservation efforts provides exciting new opportunities to better protect endangered cultural heritage and expand the scope of knowledge beyond what was imagined in the pre-digital era. Data-driven technology will enhance research capacities and possibly lead ways to constructing macro perspective on humanities" (Boo, 2020).

In this journey of conserving and simultaneously creating a digital repository of historical sites, organizations like IBM and Microsoft have been essential with their technology and funding initiatives. "Microsoft, a leader in the tech industry, has initiated a new extension to their

$125M *AI for Good* program. The company aims to use artificial intelligence as a way to preserve cultural heritage" (Guimapang, 2017). They have partnered with two French companies, HoloForge Interactive and Iconem, "Both specializing in 3D digital renderings to help recreate photo-realistic models of historic cultural sites, this new collaboration is exploring interactive experiences with 3D model making" (Guimapang, 2017).

Newer opportunities for cultural interaction can be established by preservation of historical sites, therefore it is essential for people to utilize newer technology to digital repositories for cultural heritage. This will lead to better access to history, for tourism, research and future generations to experience.

Alongside conventional preservation, artificial intelligence proves to be a newer and effective solution for preserving sites of historical significance. It aids in expanding the domains of accessing, preserving and experiencing a site.

Digital Hampi was an ambitious project that attempted to examine a holistic outlook of the past by working with the physical structures and incorporating public and private entities who make a heritage site a living entity. It bought together researchers and practitioners to preserve a legacy.

Indian Digital Heritage program hasn't restricted itself to one site, but has used AI to decipher and digitalize various other historical sites in India like Konark Temple and Taj Mahal. It has paved the way for various public and private players to undertake the same initiative like Mahabharata Research Foundation and Snaptrude.

Throughout the world, AI is being utilized to structurally preserve historical sites and artefacts. "The international research teams involved in the open-source Time Machine project aim to not only digitize huge amounts of information currently stored in archives and museums, but to then use AI to analyze the data to reconstruct 2000 years of European history with a Large Scale Historical Simulator" (Ibaraki, 2019). Frédéric Kaplan, Director of EPFL's Digital Humanities Laboratory analyzes "1,000 years of the city's history, trade routes, art, and impact on the history and culture of the rest of Europe" (Ibaraki, 2019).

Moreover, Intel recently teamed up with the China Foundation for Cultural Heritage Conservation "to use the latest drone technology to gather thousands of photos and then analyze the data with AI to pinpoint exact areas in the Wall that need restoration" (Ibaraki, 2019).

Initiatives like AI for Good worldwide movement by the UN ITU with participation by government, industry, academia, media and more than 30 UN Agency partners together with the ACM and XPRIZE with the aim to familiarize people with the potential of AI in preservation of the repository of historical sites and artefacts.

AI not only aids in preservation of historical sites, but also pushes newer research to be undertaken. It aids in unlocking the potentially untapped aspects of history, which helps in understanding human civilization better.

Use of AI and subsequent digitalization of historical sites and artefacts like *Digital Giza, Digital Hampi, Digital Konark and Digital Taj Mahal* can also be used as tools in the educational curriculum to enhance the teaching and learning experience. Moreover, by using AI for historical management, countries can enhance their tourism sector, and by applying audio–visual simulation to the historical experience, one can access, experience and learn all at once.

References

Ajanta Caves (India). UNESCO. https://whc.unesco.org/en/soc/3018.

Ajanta Caves: Advisory Body Evaluation. UNESCO International Council on Monuments and Sites. (1982). Accessed 27 October 2006.

Antony, A. (2020, September). Protecting the Cultural Heritage of Cochin using Artificial Intelligence. In *International Conference 'Solidarity in Culture: Heritage Protection Under Conditions of Crisis'*. National and University Library, Zagreb, Croatia.

Bakri, A. F., Yusuf, N. A., & Jaini, N. (2012). Managing heritage assets: Issues, challenges and the future of historic Bukit Jugra, Selangor. *Procedia — Social and Behavioral Sciences*.

Boo, H. (2020, April 2). A digital future for cultural heritage. Art Management and Technology Laboratory. https://amt-lab.org/blog/2020/3/a-digital-future-for-cultural-heritage.

Buradikatti, K. (2021, July 13). Hampi sees increase in footfall after restrictions are lifted. The Hindu. https://www.thehindu.com/news/national/karnataka/hampi-sees-increase-in-footfall-after-restrictions-are-lifted/article35295936.ece.

Chhabra, P. & Babbar, K. (2020, November 26). Preserving the past with tools of the future. The Hindu. https://www.thehindu.com/education/how-ai-and-machine-learning-ml-based-solutions-can-be-used-to-restore-ancient-cave-murals/article33183127.ece.

Cignoni, P. & Scopigno, R. (2008, June). Sampled 3D models for CH applications: A viable and enabling new medium or just a technological exercise? *ACM Journal on Computing and Cultural Heritage, 1*(1), 1–23.

Cohen, R. (2013). Encyclopaedia of Monasticism. Routledge, New York.

Fritz, J. M. & Mitchell, G. (2016). *Hampi Vijayanagara*. Jaico.

Group of Monuments of Hampi. UNESCO, Bellary District, Karnataka.

Guimapang, K. (2017, July). Microsoft plans to preserve cultural heritage sites through AI. Archinect News. https://archinect.com/news/article/150146443/microsoft-plans-to-preserve-cultural-heritage-sites-through-ai.

Hampi: Investing in local opportunities and pioneering public-private partnership to lift a vast metropolis off the world heritage in danger list. Global Heritage Fund. https://globalheritagefund.org/places/hampi-india/.

Howard, M. C. (2011). *Transnationalism and Society: An Introduction*. McFarland.

Ibaraki, S. (2018, March 28). Artificial Intelligence for good: Preserving our cultural heritage. Forbes Digital. https://www.forbes.com/sites/cognitiveworld/2019/03/28/artificial-intelligence-for-good-preserving-our-cultural-heritage/?sh=37c5fdbd4e96.

Kadidal, A. (2021, July 31). Hampi's new Quietude. Deccan Herald. https://www.deccanherald.com/spectrum/spectrum-top-stories/hampis-new-quietude-1014904.html.

Lowenthal, D. (2015, October 1). The Past is a Foreign Country. Cambridge University Press. London.

Madan, G. (1990). *India Through the Ages*. Ministry of Information and Broadcasting, Government of India.

Mahajan, R. (2020, May 18). Indian digital heritage: Digital Hampi project. Asia-Europe Foundation. https://culture360.asef.org/magazine/arttechnology-indian-digital-heritage-digital-hampi-project/.

Maharashtra: Footfalls Down At Ajanta, Ellora & Other Tourist Sites In 2021. (2021, December 23). Press Trust of India. https://www.business-standard.com/article/current-affairs/maha-footfalls-down-at-ajanta-ellora-other-tourist-sites-in-2021-121122300202_1.html.

Preserving World Famous Ajanta Caves Using AI. (2021, April 8). Hindustan Times. https://www.hindustantimes.com/lifestyle/art-culture/preserving-world-famous-ajanta-cave-paintings-using-ai-101617890196912.html.

Revenue Generated by Monuments. Press Information Bureau, Ministry of Culture, Government of India. https://pib.gov.in/newsite/PrintRelease.aspx?relid=108190.

Sewell, R. (1900). A Forgotten Empire. Swan Sonnenschein & Co., Ltd. London.

Singh, B. P. R., Dar, V., & Pravin, S. (2001). Rationales for including Varanasi as Heritage City in the UNESCO world heritage list. *National Geographic Journal of India, 47*, 177–200.

Spink, W. M. (2007). *Ajanta: History and Development, Volume 5: Cave by Cave.* Leiden: Brill.

Sufyan, U. (2021, May 20). Art and Artificial Intelligence: The ways Artificial Intelligence will help change art. Medium. https://medium.com/divedeepai/art-and-artificial-intelligence-bc8de5b0fd01.

Verghese, A. (2002). Hampi. Oxford University Press. New Delhi.

https://doi.org/10.1142/9789811271786_0016

Chapter 16

Digital Mission for India to Achieve SDG 9 for Building Resilient Infrastructure, Sustainable Industrialization and Fostering Innovation: A Study of Navratna Companies in India

Navita Mahajan*, Meghna Mehta† and Seema Garg‡

Amity International Business School, Amity University, Noida

navitamahajan07@gmail.com

†*mehta.meghna350@gmail.com*

‡*seemagarg1@gmail.com*

Abstract

The objective of the Sustainable Development Goals, more specifically goal number 9 in the 2030 Agenda for Sustainable Development, is to develop strong, resilient and flexible infrastructure for sustainable and steady industrialization in nations and fostering technological innovations across the members of the United Nations.

SDG 9 focuses on improving the overall lives of citizens of a country by improving present infrastructural facilities and fostering the growth and introduction of new, advanced and sustainable technologies. For this goal to be achieved, it is the responsibility of the governments all over the world to work towards making their nations technologically advanced and bold enough to foster innovative projects. Developing countries like India show a lot of potential to adapt and make use of advanced infrastructure being offered to them to become the leading producers of the world.

This concluding chapter focuses on understanding the role of Navratna companies in India, i.e. the major public sector undertakings in India, to understand their role and contribution towards achieving the Sustainable Development Goal in question. The study focuses on 10 Navratna companies based in India that come under the central public sector enterprises. The study talks about how the Digital India initiative by the Government of India mission has impacted the industries operating in India and how the incorporation of technologies has affected the overall productivity of Indian enterprise. The data were collected through secondary resources like websites, annual reports, research materials and other data available in journals. The implication of the current study is that other companies operating in India and abroad can learn about implementing the Sustainable Developmental Goal in their day-to-day practices to increase productivity and improve infrastructure, thereby fostering innovation and growth. This will help India reach its goal of becoming a major manufacturing hub and a digitally advanced nation.

Introduction

This research chapter deals with the ninth United Nations (UN) Sustainable Development Goal (SDG 9) that focuses on building and improving the infrastructure of a nation through industrial development measures that are sustainable in nature and that also contribute to the overall technological advancement of the nation. This research chapter revolves around this SDG from the perspective of Navratna Companies, i.e. the major public sector enterprises that are duly recognized by the central Government of India. This chapter aims at understanding the contribution of these

Navratna Companies towards the overall infrastructure and technological growth of India. The chapter also emphasizes the due effect of the Digital India Mission on the functioning of the companies. This study also aims to analyze how India is working towards achieving these goals by 2030, as specified by the United Nations. The chapter gives special attention to SDG 9 revolving around technological advancement, giving a special emphasis to India's Digital Mission.

The study focuses on the Navratna Companies recognized and owned by the Government of India. These companies contribute heavily, if not majorly, to the infrastructure and technology of our economy. These companies have existed and ruled over the last 50–100 years, having their name registered in the legacy of the country. These Navratna Companies not only produce heavy goods and materials for our country, but are also the major exporters of both basic and advanced devices. While a country like India is still looked at as a developing nation, the following Navratna Companies have proven their worth by becoming major brands all over their world through their mergers and acquisitions.

The chapter focuses on establishing and identifying the link between these government undertakings and the SDGs laid down by the United Nations. While the United Nations have several SDGs laid out by them to improve the overall living and earning conditions of nations across the globe, this particular chapter explores SDG 9, which focuses on industry, innovation and infrastructural development of the world. India's overall development as a nation is highly affected by the digital literacy measures taken by the government. The Digital India mission launched in 2015 significantly improved online infrastructure and even increased the accessibility of Internet among citizens. Since the Navratna Companies are giant industries, which hold a competitive advantage in terms of both resources and manpower in India, this chapter will highlight how significant technologies have been introduced and are being implemented by the Navratna Companies that have a grip over the manufacturing sector of the Indian economy.

Literature Review — Role of Navratnas in SDG 9 and Adoption of Digital India Mission

The members of the United Nations, which consists of over 93 nations, got together and recognized a need and urgency for taking the right action as quickly as possible to reverse what all is needed to sustain a happy, healthy and sustainable life for people living now and for generations to come. The United Nations Sustainable Development Summit held in the year 2015 came up with global goals for the betterment of nations across the globe. These global goals established primarily focused on three aspects of sustainability, namely environment, economics and the general well-being of the members of society. A total of 17 Sustainable Development Goals were laid down in order to tackle the problems our Earth and mankind face, and due to the successful measures by the members of the United Nations, a lot of nations are on their way to achieving the goals and eradicate their problems forever.

Though subsequent progress has been made over the years, nations are still not close to eradicating their problems completely. Fifteen years may not be sufficient enough to reverse years of damage done to the Earth and environment by taking some steps, but not doing anything might prove to be even more troublesome for the world at large. In this effort taken by the United Nations body to improve and empower the lives of humans, a major responsibility lies on the shoulders of the governments of the nations to make sure proper and necessary steps are taken in the right direction and on a regular basis.

While it is important to take imperative action towards transforming the human and environmental conditions for good, it is also necessary to recognize the fact that growing economies like India need a proper plan of action to grow in terms of infrastructure, technology and business. Just like China, India has a huge population and thus a large labour pool. Countries with large labour pools have a potential of becoming manufacturers of goods which are both complex and diverse in nature.

The targets for SDG 9 have eight dimensions, which include enhancing research and upgrading industrial technologies, sustainable upgradation of industries and infrastructure, easier and increased access of financial services and markets, promoting sustainable and inclusive industrialization, developing sustainable, resilient and inclusive infrastructure, enabling infrastructure development that is sustainable in nature for countries that are working towards becoming independent and developed, helping in technology development on the domestic front and diversification of industries, along with universal access to information and communications technology.

The Digital India mission has a significant role to play since it is a core component of the mission of SDG 9. Despite increased use of new-age technologies and the IT industry, India had a big divide in terms of people who have access to this digital knowledge and those who don't, and that created economic inequities between those who can and cannot afford technology, harming the country's overall digital growth. To address this gap, the government launched the "Digital India" effort, which includes a variety of programmes such as e-governance, mobile e-health services, and digital banking for digital inclusion. The "Digital India" effort is helping all parts of the country, especially small towns and rural areas, to improve in terms of digital infrastructure through initiatives such as Aadhaar card, which offers a unique identity proof to each citizen, and public Wi-Fi hotspots which increase overall accessibility. According to a McKinsey report, Uttar Pradesh (with over 36 million internet customers), Madhya Pradesh and Jharkhand were among the five fastest-growing states in terms of internet penetration between 2014 and 2018.

The Navratna Companies of India, as the name suggests, was the title given to the nine companies by the Government of India in the year 1997 as the Government recognized these companies to have a greater comparative advantage and offered them their full support. The number of Public Sector Enterprises holding the Navratna status is now 16 companies.

Infrastructure and technology have always been key determinants of the economic status of a nation. One can say that the availability of technology and its access to the residents of that nation determines the overall status of the nation. A rapid yet steady growth in technology and infrastructural facilities can change the overall standing of a nation. Countries that are still developing, like India, need to focus on these factors as they still need to establish their position and standing as a nation. Therefore, whenever there are talks about infrastructural development, innovation and growth, the basic focus is still on providing every person with good education and access to basic digital devices. However, countries that are well settled in the sense of availability of technology and innovation need to think out of the box to sustain in the global market. So, for developed countries like Germany, innovation is their friend as such countries are beyond the point of focusing on "Technology and Infrastructure for all" and instead focus on how to become the innovators and superpowers.

According to a survey by Futurescape (2020), 60% of India's top 100 companies have included SDGs in their long-term business strategies, and all of the top ten companies align their organizational goals with Global Goals.

Therefore, we explore how the highly recognized Navratna companies have been contributing to the growth and development of India and how they are helping India achieve SDG 9. We also discuss how the Digital India mission has been a game changer not only for these companies but also for the overall nation.

India's roadmap for SDG 9 in collaboration with Digital India mission

For any business to flourish, it is necessary to have an environment that is technologically sound and financially stable. Business depends on resources, labour and services from all over the world and its ability to access it. It is very important for businesses to be aware of what is happening around the world, and one way for this is to be connected digitally. However, even in the 21st century, there are certain economies around the world that remain stagnant and constant as they don't have access to suitable technologies. By sticking to industrialization that is sustainable and promoting innovative measures across all the industries, businesses can contribute to development of the regions in and around them. It is, therefore, possible by upgrading local infrastructure, investing in information and communication technology and by making these technologies accessible to all the people.

The SDG 9 consists of eight targets in order to create action to build infrastructure that is resilient, promote inclusive and sustainable industrialization in all areas of the economy and foster innovation. Digital India mission by the Government of India is a major component of India's overall mission to be better in terms of Infrastructure and Technology. The Government of India launched various schemes under the Digital India mission, which made lives of the citizens a lot easier when it came to keeping a track of the things they need to be aware of. Initiatives like Aadhaar Card, Digi Locker, My Government application, Bharat Net internet services and digitization of government banking systems have brought significant improvement to the way businesses were conducted earlier.

During the pandemic when the world moved to an online mode of working and education, there was a significant worry as to how people with less or no access to technologies like smartphones and internet would cope with the change. However, thanks to the previously taken measures by the Government of India, children in both rural and urban areas were able to incorporate the online mode of education into their lives. This was possible because of a number of initiatives, one of them being the Pradhan Mantri Gramin Digital Saksharta Abhiyaan, a scheme that aimed to help over 6 crore rural citizens by March 2020 be digitally literate by targeting at least one member from each eligible household.

According to the Annual Report released by the Government of India for the year 2021–2022, the Government of Madhya Pradesh launched "Hamara Ghar Hamara Vidyayala" 2.0, with the aim of making online education during the pandemic accessible. Teachers and students were both taught to use WhatsApp to connect with each other for teaching and learning purposes. In Odisha, live YouTube telecasts were made available for all classes so that students could continue studying from home.

In May 2020, the Hon'ble Prime Minister charged NITI Aayog with collaborating with the corporate sector to produce cutting-edge technology goods that will allow India to leapfrog in the post-COVID-19 era. Several private sector companies (Tata, Reliance, Mahindra, Khan Academy, IBM, PhonePe, Amul, BigBasket, Amazon Web Services, Apollo Hospitals and others) and government agencies (National Industrial Corridor Development Corporation [NICDC], Ministry of Civil Aviation, Ministry of Road Transport and Highways, Ministry of Finance, Quality Control of India, Bank of Baroda, SBI and others) collaborated to develop products which offered rapid and agile growth in the technology sector.

The Indian Government has worked significantly over the past few years to improve the condition of the infrastructure and has even worked on the proper allocation of resources. Installed power generation capacity has been steadily increasing during the last five years. Installed capacity in non-fossil-fuel industries has increased by 51.3%, while renewable energy capacity has more than doubled (solar, wind, bio- and small hydro power). Furthermore, under its "Make in India" initiative, India is attempting to become an information technology and manufacturing centre. These efforts have significantly increased FDI inflows and helped the economy maintain an average annual growth rate of 7.5% over the fiscal years 2014–2015 and 2016–2017. Small-scale business owners were given cheap credit, which helped to develop employment-intensive industrial areas. Furthermore, the "Start-up India" initiative encourages entrepreneurship and labour-intensive economic growth (Voluntary National Review Report on the implementation of sustainable development goals, 2017).

Sdgs and related targets, along with several outcome Indicators, have been set out by NITI Aayog for Central Ministries, Centrally Sponsored/ Central Sector Schemes, and other government initiatives. Several states have structured their departments and strategies in a similar way. There are nodal ministries at the federal level and nodal departments in several states. SDG Cells or Centres of Excellence have been created in several states to coordinate SDG implementation. For a periodical evaluation of SDG implementation throughout the country, NITI Aayog has established a Task Force with participation from Central Ministries and States.

As per a presentation given by the NITI Aayog to the states in the year 2019, there are six key indicators in India which indicate the status of SDG 9. These are: percentage of rural population living within 2 km of all-season roads, share of manufacturing sector employment in total employment, carbon dioxide emission per unit of value added, research and development expenditure as percentage of GDP, number of patents and intellectual property rights filed and, lastly, access to mobile phones. ("Niti Aayog Presentation")

Research gap

Past research on SDGs has largely focused on their long-term implications for business stakeholders and their significance for future generations (Mio *et al.*, 2020); however, there has been little research on the role of MNCs from developed countries in emerging economies such as India in achieving Global Goals. Furthermore, previous study looks into training and development as an important instrument for achieving strategic success for enterprises (Gusdorf, 2009), however the concept of using this tool to achieve SDGs in an organization has not been extensively studied. The current study focuses on Navratnas, and how they focus on technology and infrastructural development for the betterment and general progress of the communities they serve.

The research done so far on SDG 9 and its implementation in India has talked about the lack of infrastructural development being the major cause of concern. As per an article released by The Borgen Project in October 2020, the trade industry is critical to a healthy economy that includes job development, strong partnerships and a larger range of product availability. The standard of commerce and transportation infrastructure has not improved. It has maintained a consistent ranking of 2.91 out of five. Manufacturing has remained stagnant and has shown no signs of expansion. This industry has the potential to contribute to economic success as well. These determinants may be seen in India's industrial growth rate, which has declined by 0.8% between 2016 and 2019. India's industries generate a lot of hazardous waste and water waste, which contradicts the concept of sustainability.

The report further mentions how the lack of appropriate funds for research and development contribute to the slow pace of the industrial development and innovative inventions in India. Furthermore, SDG 9 research done so far has not been very inclusive of the Digital India mission launched by the Government of India. Probable reason for this could be the lack of awareness about technologies and the inability of Navratna companies to implement them. The Navratna companies, though contributing massively and steadily to the Indian economy, have not been able to adopt new age technologies completely and effectively for their daily operations as they still prefer to perform most of their activities in the traditional way.

Data Analysis — Industrial and Infrastructural Growth of the Navratnas

Navaratna Companies (Navaratnas) are Central Public Sector Enterprises (CPSE) that meet certain operational and financial criteria, including net profit, total cost of production, earnings per share and inter-sectoral performance. In 1997, nine public sector firms were granted Navratna status for the first time. There are 13 Navratnas in India as of January 2022.

Navratnas are given Financial Independence, i.e. they can invest up to INR 1,000 crore, or 15% of their net worth, on a single project, or 30% of their net worth for the entire year (not exceeding INR 1,000 crores) without seeking approval from the federal government. It enhances operational and financial autonomy, thus increasing the power to make financial decisions. It enables the PSUs to make equity investments and undertake various financial joint ventures (JV) and wholly owned subsidiaries. This status and its benefits have enabled mergers and acquisitions (M&A) in India as well as abroad. The company boards implement and modify schemes pertaining to personnel as well as human resource management and training. Companies can choose to float fresh equity, transfer assets, divest shareholding in subsidiaries, however, subject to the condition that the delegation will only be in respect of subsidiaries set up by the holding company. The missions taken on by the Government of India have significantly improved the conditions of companies operating in and out of India. While the Make in India mission brought in significant foreign direct investments, the Digital India mission made basic technology accessible for all. Digitalization has been one of the most significant changes in India in recent years. It is the second-fastest digital adopter among the 17 major digital economies. This rapid expansion propels India to the forefront of digital and technological innovation, utilizing the energy of the country's young people in particular. Since the inception of the "Digital India" programme in 2015, there have been numerous substantial improvements in digital infrastructure, digital delivery of public services and financial assistance to individuals, as well as digital consciousness and literacy. The United Nations initiative to lead the nations to implement the sustainable development goals has also contributed majorly to the betterment of the living conditions of the people in India. Not only have the goals led to significant improvement in quality of life, but they have also brought major improvement to innovation and infrastructure.

In this section, we will discuss how the major Navratna Companies have contributed and been a part of the implementation of SDG 9 through their activities and actions.

Bharat Electronics Limited (BEL)

Founded in Bengaluru, Karnataka, in the year 1954, BEL started with manufacturing equipment for communication in the year 1956, followed by germanium semiconductors, valves and radio transmitters. This government-owned entity currently produces advanced electronic devices for aerospace and on-ground applications. With over 9,000 employees and revenue of over 1.9 million dollars, BEL develops and manufactures a vast range of products like fire control systems, missiles, radars and electronic voting machines, to name a few.

Nearly 66% of the company is owned by the Central Government, 14% is owned by Mutual Funds and UTI, 6% is owned by foreign institutional investors, 5% is owned by individual investors and the remaining 4% is owned by insurance companies. The company has two joint ventures, namely BEL Thales Limited and GE-BE Pvt Limited.

Technological developments

BEL has been a strong advocate for the government's Make in India programme. It is concentrating on core industries and research and development, while all non-core areas, including MSMEs, are being outsourced to private Indian companies. A long-term Outsourcing and Indigenization Policy has been released by the government. Nodal officers for outsourcing and vendor development have been appointed. Every year, about 800 new indigenous merchants are added. In line with the "Make in India" concept, BEL will continue its indigenization initiatives. Radars, missile systems, communication and network-centric systems, tank electronics, gun improvements, electro-optic systems, and electronic warfare and avionics systems will all contribute to BEL's growth. Solar energy, homeland security, smart cards, and telecommunications are all areas where the company is looking for new business. To fight competition, maintain a technological edge and sustain leadership in strategic electronics, strategies and action plans have been put in place.

Container Corporation of India Ltd

CONCOR (Container Corporation of India Ltd.) was established in March 1988 under the Companies Act and began operations in November 1989, taking over the Indian Railways' existing network of 7 ICDs.

CONCOR has grown from a small venture to become India's indisputable market leader, with the largest network of 61 ICDs/CFSs (59 terminals and 2 strategic tie-ups). Its services have extended to include port management, air cargo complexes and cold-chain establishment, in addition to providing interior rail transportation for containers. Because of its sophisticated rail wagon fleet, customer-friendly commercial procedures and extensive use of information technology, it has played and will continue to play a key role in encouraging containerization in India. For India's international and domestic trade, the company created multimodal logistics support.

Technological developments

CONCOR has actively participated in the Digital India mission launched by the Government of India. The company launched the "Know your location system" that gives users the location of their containers. There is now a system which enables automation of contractor billing and enables automatic system of invoice savings in Document Management System. CONCOR has taken steps towards paperless offices by replacing physical files with digital ones. It has recently introduced a Chat-based Application System for Employee Grievance Management System (EGMS) and Customer Grievance Management System (CGMS) to improve employee performance and help valued EXIM/domestic customers settle their complaints. Through its association with the Government of India, CONCOR successfully took measures towards sustainable infrastructural development by taking several green initiatives and constructing classrooms and toilets for children.

Engineers India Limited (EIL)

Engineers India Ltd (EIL) is a renowned engineering consultancy and EPC firm based in India. EIL was founded in 1965 and specializes in technical consulting and EPC services for the oil and gas and petrochemical industries. To take advantage of its strong technological competencies and track record, the company has expanded into industries such as infrastructure, water and waste management, solar and nuclear power, and fertilisers. EIL is currently a "Total Solutions" engineering consultancy organization that provides "Concept to Commissioning" design, engineering, sourcing, building and unified project management services with the highest standards of safety. As of March 31, 2021, EIL's technological superiority is fuelled by over 2400 engineers and professionals working in a skilled workforce of over 2800 people. EIL's design offices have around 4.5 million man-hours of technical resources available per year, plus 1.5 million man-hours of construction management services.

Technological developments

EIL, which, among other things, builds petroleum refineries and pipelines, had successfully ventured into urban and transportation infrastructure, as well as activities relating to special economic zones. It has created over 35 process technologies, with a portfolio that encompasses petroleum refining, oil and gas processing, and aromatics. For the first time in India, the DHDT technology developed by EIL and IOCL-R&D has been applied at IOCL's Bongaigaon Refinery in Assam. EIL has 36 active patents and 31 pending patent applications covering a variety of process innovations. The company's most recent revolutionary product was a start-up effort called EngSUI, which has already passed a major milestone with the installation of a 2000 LPD prototype to capture water from the atmosphere at the EIL Gurugram Office Complex ("Technologies | Engineers India Ltd").

Hindustan Aeronautics Limited (HAL)

HAL (Hindustan Aeronautics Limited) is a state-owned aerospace and defence enterprise based in Bengaluru, India. HAL is one of the world's oldest and largest aerospace and defence companies, having been founded on December 23, 1940. The President of India, through the Ministry of Defence, appoints a Board of Directors to run HAL. HAL is now working on fighter planes, helicopters, jet engines and marine gas turbine engines, as well as avionics, software development, spare parts and refurbishing and upgrading Indian military aircraft. HAL is one of Asia's major aerospace businesses, with an annual revenue of more than US$2 billion. International contracts to manufacture aircraft engines, spare parts and other aircraft materials account for more than 40% of HAL's revenue. HAL has over 20,000 employees with a healthy revenue and consistent performance.

Technological developments

HAL specializes in the production of aircrafts, helicopters, power plants and aerospace machines among other things. The International Aerospace Community has benefited from HAL's cost-effective and extensive skills. HAL has demonstrated skills and offers collaborative arrangements in the fields of machine component production, sheet metal fabrication, assembly, sub-assembly fabrication, and design and development (structural analysis, 3D modelling and testing). HAL's effectiveness is enhanced by refined and updated IT infrastructure consisting of high-end workstations, high performance/high reliability scalable servers, high speed gigabit LANs and high speed Internet/ISDN facilities. On November 9, 2021, HAL and Zero Avia committed to work on the development of a hydrogen-electric powertrain capable of flying a Dornier 228 aircraft's

19 passengers up to 500 nautical miles. The Aeronautical Development Establishment, DRDO, has placed an order with HAL to manufacture, assemble, integrate, test and provide the ABHYAS High-Speed Expendable Aerial Target (HEAT) System. HAL and Elbit Systems have agreed to work together to improve their technological basis and obtain high-end technology for the Digital Overhead HUD System, which is largely utilized in transport aircraft around the world. With contemporary optics, the Digital Overhead HUD provides sharp brightness, a broader field of view and a larger head motion box.

Mahanagar Telephone Nigam Limited (MTNL)

Mahanagar Telephone Nigam Limited is a government-owned telecommunications company that operates in India's metro cities of Mumbai and New Delhi, as well as the African island nation of Mauritius. Until 1992, when the telecom market was opened to other service providers, the business enjoyed a monopoly in Mumbai and New Delhi. The corporation is currently owned entirely by the Indian Government. Though it only has presence in two circles, MTNL is the largest internet service provider in Mumbai and Delhi (in terms of market share) and the third largest internet service provider in India. Dialup and DSL are used by MTNL to provide TriBand Internet services. Through TriBand, it offers gaming on demand, video on demand and IPTV services in India. TriBand is aimed towards private residences and small companies.

Technological developments

MTNL has been at the forefront of technological advancements, having converted 100% of its telephone exchange network into a cutting-edge digital mode. Over the last 19 years, MTNL has grown fast by modernizing the network and adding cutting-edge technologies and a customer-centric approach. Telephone, telex, wireless data communication, telematic and other similar modes of communication are among the services provided by the company (Internet). MTNL launched its fibre-to-the-home (FTTH) triple play (voice, video and data) high-speed broadband service in Delhi. FTTH was launched in Mumbai, with a core network speed of up to 1 Gbit/s. IPTV, HDTV, 3DTV, video on demand, bandwidth on demand, rapid video conferencing, interactive gaming and a variety of additional value-added services are all available through MTNL FTTH Broadband. Due to massive corruption in the Indian telecom business, MTNL has been losing revenue and market share in recent years.

National Aluminium Company (NALCO)

NALCO is a Schedule "A" Navratna CPSE that was founded on January 7, 1981 and is headquartered in Bhubaneswar. It is the country's largest integrated Bauxite-Alumina-Aluminium-Power Complex. At the moment, the Government of India owns 51.28% of the paid-up equity capital. The company owns and operates Asia's largest integrated aluminium complex, which includes bauxite mining, alumina refining, aluminium smelting and casting, power generation, rail and port operations. Nalco, which was established in 1985–1987, has emerged as a standout performer in alumina and aluminium production, export, and, more importantly, self-sustained growth.

Technological development

NALCO has established a world-class research centre in its pursuit of organizational growth through sustained development in process, product and technology through research, development and innovation activity. QEMSCAN (SEM-EDX), ICP-MS, Sedigraph, Laser Particle Size Analyzer, UTM, ICP-OES, BET Analyzer, Potentiometer, OES, CHNS Analyzer, Metallurgical Microscope, Whiteness Index metre and other advanced equipment are available at the NALCO Research Centre. The testing activities at NRTC began on a regular basis in 2019. On May 29, 2020, the R&D wing of NALCO Research and Technology Centre was recognized by the DSIR, Government of India. The company is committed to R&D and has already filed 36 patents, 17 of which have been granted and five of which have been commercialized as of December 2018. The company is attempting to salvage iron concentrate from red mud and gallium from spent liquor as part of its effort to convert waste to wealth. The company has also successfully commissioned a first-of-its-kind de-fluoridation process based on nano-technology to de-contaminate the Smelter's effluent water, thereby addressing the area's long-standing fluoride contamination problem.

National Buildings Construction Corporation (*NBCC*)

NBCC (India) Limited is a publicly traded blue-chip Government of India Navratna enterprise and a Central Public Sector undertaking. The current areas of operation of the company are divided into three major segments, namely Project Management Consultancy, EPC Contracting and Real Estate Development. Designated as a Navratna enterprise by the Ministry of Housing and Urban Affairs, the company is certified with ISO 9001:2015 from the Bureau of Indian Standards for its Project Management and Consultancy.

Since 2012, the company has been listed on both stock exchanges. With a consolidated revenue of INR 7,096 crore (FY2018), NBCC has grown at a consistent 20% CAGR over the last five years. With over INR 80,000 crore in the order book, the company's unique business model distinguishes it as a leader in its own right in the construction sector.

Technological development

The areas of operation of NBCC include three primary segments: (1) Project Management Consultancy (PMC), which includes the execution of landmark projects in a variety of sectors, as well as Redevelopment Projects for the Government, (2) Engineering Procurement and Construction (EPC), i.e. working in a niche market and constructing Chimneys, Cooling Towers for the Power Sector, and (3) Real Estate Development, i.e. developing residential and commercial inventories for governments and the general public. Some of the notable constructions by the NBCC include construction of the 200 Bedded Indira Gandhi Memorial Hospital, Male, Republic of Maldives; New Supreme court building at Maldives and Meer Housing project in Turkey. Recently, NBCC has worked significantly to improve the condition of India, particularly Delhi and NCR, by redeveloping several colonies of Central Delhi.

NBCC has implemented a policy to incorporate environmentally friendly features into its projects. Zero waste, dual piping, rainwater harvesting, solar energy, smart electricity metering, and LED/energy efficient fixtures are among the features. The company's projects adhere to Green Building standards. Steel structures, modular construction, pre-cast, prefab components, and light weight concrete slabs are among the environmentally friendly techniques and materials used by the company. In order to contribute to a safer environment, the company also ensures strict adherence to guidelines to reduce air and water pollution at its project sites.

National Mineral Development Corporation (NMDC)

NMDC Limited, formerly known as National Mineral Development Corporation, is a state-owned mineral producer in India. The Government of India owns 72.43% of the company, which is administered by the Ministry of Steel. Its activities include the exploration of iron ore, copper, rock phosphate, limestone, dolomite, gypsum, bentonite, magnesite, diamond, tin, tungsten, graphite and other minerals. It is India's largest iron ore producer and exporter, with three fully mechanized mines in Chhattisgarh and Karnataka producing more than 35 million tonnes of iron ore. It also runs the country's only mechanized diamond mine in Panna, Madhya Pradesh.

Technological developments

NMDC's main aim is to emerge as a global environment-friendly mining organization that produces quality steel products. They aim to reach their goals by growing the existing number of mines and by operating mines that are in joint ventures with other companies. Recently, the state-owned miner NMDC announced on Saturday that it has reached a record iron ore production of 40 million tonnes (MT) so far this fiscal year. The company produced 35 MT of iron ore in the previous fiscal year. In January 2022, Indraprastha Gas Limited, an Indian natural gas distribution company, signed a Memorandum of Understanding with NDMC to establish a waste-to-energy plant and an integrated fuelling station in North Delhi to convert Solid Waste into CBG.

NLC India Limited (NLCIL)

NLC, formerly known as Neyveli Lignite Corporation Limited, is a Central Public Sector Enterprise with Navratna status that reports to the Ministry of Coal. NLC was formed in 1956 under the Companies Act of 1956 with the goal of meeting the electricity demand of India's southern states by excavating lignite for power generation. This is a major company in India's fossil fuel mining sector, focusing on thermal power generation. It produces approximately 30 million tonnes of lignite per year from opencast mines in the southern Indian state of Tamil Nadu and Barsingsar in the Rajasthan district of Bikaner. Its joint venture owns a 1000 MW coal-fired thermal power station. It has recently diversified into renewable energy production, installing a 141 MW solar power plant to generate electricity from photovoltaic (PV) cells and a 51 MW windmill power plant.

Technological developments

As per a report released in April 2021, NLCIL increased its mining capacity by 66% and it's green power generation capacity by 39% in the 2020–2021 fiscal year when compared to the financial year 2019–2020. The company has also added 515.5 MW capacity — a 500 MW lignite based thermal power plant and a 17.5 MW solar power plant with a battery energy storage system in the fiscal year 2019–2020. With this, the total installed capacity of the company increased to 6061.06 MW. The company ventured into the coal mining business launching its activities at its Talabira Mines in Odisha. At the highest levels, NLC India Limited has consistently aligned its business goals with social goals and has made CSR an integral part of its operations. The various units/departments of NLC India Limited are working in concert to achieve the best Triple Bottom Line performance. The Production, Maintenance, and Service Units are responsible for economic performance through production and productivity, as well as environmental safety, pollution/groundwater control and energy conservation through direct action. The Projects and Planning Units, Specialized Engineering Units and Technical Branches/Sections are responsible for overall Econometric performance.

Oil India Limited (OIL)

Oil India Limited, headquartered in Duliajan, Assam, is India's second largest hydrocarbon exploration and production (E&P) firm. With corporate headquarters in Noida, New Delhi-NCR, the firm is a state-owned Navratna under the administrative jurisdiction of India's Ministry of Petroleum and Natural Gas. OIL has greatly increased its exploration and production efforts in Northeast India in recent years. The Northeast Frontier (NEF) project was formed by OIL to expand its exploration activities in the Northeast's frontier areas, which are logistically challenging and geologically complicated.

Technological developments

In the areas of Upper Assam and Arunachal Pradesh, OIL has a long history of hydrocarbon exploration and production. In this regard, the company has continued to adopt new methods and technologies in order to advance its goal of accurate mapping and imaging of the fold-complicated belt's geology. In this sense, a high-density, long-offset seismic survey for enhanced illumination of complex geology is a recent innovation. To meet the upcoming challenges of inaccessibility and extreme logistics for the exploration of these frontier areas, OIL will be the first E&P company in India to deploy cable-less seismic data-collecting technology. OIL's in-house field workers are involved in the most efficient acquisition of 2D, 3D and 4D seismic data using current technology and cutting-edge equipment to satisfy a wide range of exploration and development difficulties. OIL has broadened its exploration efforts to include frontier locations with challenging logistics and geological conditions.

Discussion and Conclusion

According to the Voluntary National Review Report on the implementation of the sustainable development goals released by the Government of India in 2017, all modes of transportation have grown significantly since the SDGs were introduced. All villages will have access to roads and power. India intends to connect all village councils in the country to high-speed broadband. The installed capacity of power generation has been steadily increasing. Installed capacity in non-fossil-fuel industries has increased by 51.3%, while renewable energy capacity has more than doubled (solar, wind, bio- and small hydro power). Furthermore, with its "Make in India" initiative, India is attempting to establish itself as an information technology and manufacturing powerhouse. Foreign Direct Investment (FDI) inflows have been considerably expedited as a result of these efforts. Employment-intensive industrial segments are being strengthened by making small-scale business entrepreneurs eligible for easy borrowing. Furthermore, the "Start-up India" programme encourages entrepreneurship and labour-intensive economic growth.

The infrastructure, industry and innovation pillars of Sustainable Development Goal 9 (SDG 9) are interrelated. The goal of all of these pillars is to achieve socially inclusive and environmentally sustainable economic development. In order to build resilient infrastructure, promote sustainable industrialization and foster innovation, achieving SDG 9 by 2030 will necessitate overcoming resource constraints, building and strengthening developing countries' capacities and exploring innovative ways to solve development challenges. SDG 9 comprises roughly 20 targets and indicators relating to its three pillars and is strongly linked to other SDGs related to job creation, sustainable livelihoods, improved health, technology and skill development, gender equality, food security, green technologies and climate change.

Increasing investment in digital infrastructure appears to be critical. It is anticipated that India will require US\$35 billion in upfront investment every year to be among the top five global digital economies, with such massive investments in digital infrastructure yielding faster growth and long-term economic advantages. To make this happen, we will need an active finance model as well as a robust execution model. Investing in digital infrastructure might follow the model of India's road and bridge building projects, which have considerably contributed to the country's GDP.

SDG 9 is linked to numerous other goals, including industry-related targets such as job creation, sustainable livelihoods and food security, to name a few. Furthermore, innovation is necessary for the delivery, distribution and consumption of energy, food, water and housing, while access to ICT is crucial for meeting SDG 4 (quality education), SDG 8 (reduced inequalities) and SDG 10 (reduced inequalities), among others.

The Navratna Companies, through their activities and initiatives, have created an impact on the economy of India. The Public Sector undertakings, be it in the field of mining, construction or telecommunication services, have made significant progress in terms of the growth and reach of their businesses. The overall impact generated can be seen by their global presence and reach, the number of people they employ, and most importantly how sustainable their initiatives are. Digitization of Government and its undertakings is also an indicator of the overall progression of the companies. While the Navratnas have adopted certain digital ventures which have increased their overall reach, they still need to use the technologies to their maximum potential in terms of improving their overall productivity and delivery.

Limitations and Scope of Future Studies

The current study only deals with Navratnas, which are government-owned companies. This study does not take into consideration private entities and multinational companies that have access to the best technology and have adopted the digital world with ease. While the focus of Navratna companies is to increase their accessibility and to reach out to larger Indian audiences by focusing on improving their infrastructure, private enterprises that do have the best of infrastructure are focussing more on the innovation part of this SDG. If Navratnas are able to meet and fulfil their infrastructural needs in a quick and sustainable way, they will be able to foster resilient innovation.

The study also finds out that there is still a lot of work to be done to make the internet a necessary service accessible to over a billion people in India with the correct gadgets, as well as to support an entirely new generation of entrepreneurs. The internet backbone is the digital economy's new roads-and-bridges infrastructure, and the future rate of growth is determined by how well and quickly we build digital infrastructure. The success of India in the 21st century is dependent on how the government and business sector work together to enhance this crucial infrastructure.

Implications of the Study

The study will help growing businesses understand the importance of building and innovating themselves in ways that are sustainable in nature, grow infrastructure, develop their companies and the communities they serve and help Indian companies reach their best potential. The study also gives insights on how it is important for Navratna Companies to produce in ways that not only benefit them, but also positively impact the Indian citizens and the economy. SDG 9 implementation is progressing in many sectors; nonetheless, more resources and capacity are required in developing nations such as India to meet the United Nations' goals. Furthermore, government funding and support are required so that significant corporations such as Navratnas can take the necessary steps to enhance the country's overall situation. In addition to this, traditional PSUs need to change with the times to adopt the new digital technologies to their benefit in order to progress with the growing times.

Through this study, it is found that the Digital India mission is a significant part of the SDG 9, for incorporation of digital enhancement goals is necessary for making a strong foundation for a developed India.

Reference

Futurescape (2020). India's top companies and the SDGs. (Accessed October 2020). https://www.futurescape.in/responsible-business-rankings/indias-top-companies-and-the-sdgs/.

Websites

Bharat Electronics Limited (BEL). Profile, Latest News, Press Release, MOU, CSR. *PSU Connect*. (Accessed 22 March 2022). https://www.psuconnect.in/company/bharat-electronics-limited/5.
CONCOR/THE COMPANY. *Container Corporation of India Ltd.* (Accessed 22 March 2022). https://concorindia.co.in/upload/investor/concor-presentation.pdf.
HAL's Achievements upto Q3 Financial Year 2021–2022. *PSU Connect.* 9 March 2022. (Accessed 22 March 2022). https://www.psuconnect.in/news/hal-achievements-upto-q3-financial-year-2021-22/31641.
https://www.fortuneindia.com/opinion/how-digital-india-can-become-a-success-story/105599.
https://www.ibef.org/government-schemes/digital-india.
https://www.psuconnect.in/news/nmdc-creates-history-with-40-million-tonnes--iron-ore-production/31771.
Infrastructure and Industrialization — United Nations Sustainable Development. *The United Nations.* (Accessed 22 March 2022). https://www.un.org/sustainabledevelopment/infrastructure-industrialization/.
Niti Ayog Presentation. | *NITI Aayog.* (Accessed 22 March 2022). https://www.niti.gov.in/sites/default/files/2019-01/NITI-Aayog-SDG-Presentation-to-States.pdf.
Technologies | Engineers India Ltd. *Engineers India Limited.* (Accessed 22 March 2022). https://engineersindia.com/service/technologies/.
Updates on SDG Goal 9 in India. *The Borgen Project.* 23 October 2020. (Accessed 24 March 2022). https://borgenproject.org/sdg-goal-9-in-india/.

Index